# Crafting EU
# Security Policy

# Crafting EU Security Policy

## IN PURSUIT OF A EUROPEAN IDENTITY

Stephanie B. Anderson

LYNNE
RIENNER
PUBLISHERS

BOULDER
LONDON

Published in the United States of America in 2008 by
Lynne Rienner Publishers, Inc.
1800 30th Street, Boulder, Colorado 80301
www.rienner.com

and in the United Kingdom by
Lynne Rienner Publishers, Inc.
3 Henrietta Street, Covent Garden, London WC2E 8LU

**Library of Congress Cataloging-in-Publication Data**
Anderson, Stephanie B., 1967–
    Crafting EU security policy : in pursuit of a European identity / by
Stephanie B. Anderson.
        p. cm.
    Includes bibliographical references and index.
    ISBN 978-1-58826-582-1 (hardcover : alk. paper)
    1. European Security and Defense Policy. 2. Europe—Defenses.
3. European Union countries—Foreign relations. 4. Europe—Foreign
relations—United States. 5. United States—Foreign relations—Europe.
6. National security—Europe. I. Title.
    UA646.3.A752 2008
    355'.03354—dc22

                                                        2007040339

**British Cataloguing in Publication Data**
A Cataloguing in Publication record for this book
is available from the British Library.

Printed and bound in the United States of America

 The paper used in this publication meets the requirements
of the American National Standard for Permanence of
Paper for Printed Library Materials Z39.48-1992.

    5   4   3   2   1

*For Tom*

# Contents

# Acknowledgments

There are a great number of institutions and people who made this book possible. First of all, I thank the University of Wyoming's Political Science Department, International Programs, International Studies Department (especially Garth Massey), and the Arts and Sciences Dean's Office for their academic and financial support. I also thank the German-American Fulbright Commission and the German Institute for International and Security Studies in Berlin for their institutional and financial support during my field research in 2005. The European Commission, the General Secretariat of the EU Council of Ministers, the North Atlantic Treaty Organization, the Western European Union, the US State Department and Defense Department, and the Member State Permanent Missions allowed me to interview various officials and diplomats on the CFSP/ESDP. The people I interviewed spoke candidly, gave me their time, and allowed me follow-up interviews and e-mail correspondence. Most of them spoke to me on the condition that I cite them anonymously or use their interviews as background only. Though I can only recognize them collectively, and not by name, I want to acknowledge their kindness, generosity, and professionalism. Having met them, I have faith in the future of US-European relations.

Many other individuals also encouraged me significantly in this book project. My mentors have been unwavering in their support: Steve Ropp, of the University of Wyoming, who read an early draft of the book; Geoffrey Edwards of Cambridge University; Andy Williams of the University of St. Andrews; and Doug Stuart of Dickinson College. My wonderful colleagues in the Political Science Department at the University of Wyoming are a pleasure to work with and have been extremely helpful to my research. Thanks also to Jo Marie Paintin, Jamie LeJambre, Sam Kerr, and my research assistants, Jason Mower,

Hanneke Derksen, and Eric Snider. Adrian Bantjes has given me his constant support (as well as helpful comments on Chapter 1). I also thank the women's 2005 summer study group at the University of Wyoming, organized by Gail Leedy; from the US Army War College, Steve and Tami Biddle, Charles Krupnick, and Ray Millen; and from SWP in Berlin, Christoph Bertram, Heinz Kramer, Peter Schmidt, Benjamin Schreer, Anneli Ute Gabanyi, Volker Heise, Franz Kupferschmidt, Hannes Adomeit, Stephanie Hofmann, Walter Gruhn, and Olga Ott. My very dear friend Astrid Stroh made my time in Berlin both incredibly enjoyable and productive. I am grateful to Jarrod Wiener, of the Brussels School of International Studies, and to Steve Courtney, who has always found time to answer my questions on the military. I want to thank my publisher, Lynne Rienner; Colette Mazzucelli; and two anonymous reviewers for their comments. Jason Owens, Etienne Mangin, and Olaf Handloegten, who initially introduced me to Europe, deserve thanks, as do Pat Garrett and Oliver Woshinsky, who have been so wonderful and supportive in every way. I also appreciate the efforts and understanding of Tim and Linda Woolley, Mary Henning, and David and Karen Phillips, who arranged for me to have time to work on the book.

Last, but certainly not least, I thank my family. My children, Madeleine and Chloë, have been wonderfully supportive and incredibly patient. Most of all, my heartfelt thanks go to my husband, Tom Seitz. He never tired of discussing these concepts or of reading drafts. With great love, I dedicate this book to him.

—*Stephanie B. Anderson*

# Crafting EU
# Security Policy

# 1

# The Paradox of the European Security and Defense Policy

---

The ESDP is a thorn in the flesh. ■ BERNARD JENKIN, UK CONSERVATIVE SHADOW DEFENSE SECRETARY[1]

In 2004, the European Union (EU),[2] through its Institute for Security Studies (ISS), commemorated the five-year anniversary of the EU's Security and Defense Policy (ESDP) with a comprehensive study of the policy's roots and development.[3] In this study, Javier Solana, the EU's high representative for foreign and security policy, introduced discussion of the ESDP with the following statement: "I would like to start with a paradox: of all the prerogatives of states, security and defence policy is probably the one which least lends itself to a collective European approach; however, after the single currency, it is in this dimension that the Union has made the most rapid and spectacular progress of the last five years."[4] Solana is correct on both counts. The EU's security and defense policy has grown by leaps and bounds. In 1999, Solana faced a vast "desert"; even procuring office space, furniture, and computers was difficult.[5] By 2007, his office had overseen nearly twenty separate missions, including military, monitoring and training, humanitarian, and rule of law missions. Moreover, considering that the EU is made up of twenty-seven different countries with an equal number of security cultures and national security concerns, and that states usually jealously guard their sovereignty in this area, such rapid expansion is noteworthy.

Nicole Gnesotto, head of the ISS, also found the development of the ESDP surprising, for another reason: "Why, after 50 years without any military role, are the European member states now collectively engaged in constructing a Union defence policy?"[6] The EU faces no outside military threats. Heretofore, the EU took pride in being a civilian power. Why develop a defense identity now?

Solana and Gnesotto have just scratched the surface; the motivation behind the ESDP is not obvious. For a myriad of reasons, the ESDP is paradoxical. First, as Solana said, states are not supposed to integrate in national security areas. Realists argue that while states might integrate in areas of low politics—for example, trade—they do not in areas of high politics, such as security, because a collective approach could jeopardize their very survival. As a result, through realists' eyes, the ESDP seems unwise for several reasons. First, it compromises a cheap, effective, and proven defense alliance—the North Atlantic Treaty Organization (NATO). Second, it may well push the United States out of Europe, thus promoting US isolationism at a time of a unified Germany. In addition, the division created by the ESDP weakens the perception of unity among the Europeans (integrationists versus Atlanticists versus neutrals) and between the United States and Europe—a division which Russia has sought to exploit.[7] In short, the ESDP could negate Lord Ismay's dictum of keeping the Americans in, the Russians out, and the Germans down.

Twenty-one of the twenty-seven EU member states are members of the Atlantic Alliance.[8] Why change the EU into another security organization? Europe faces no external threats. The EU's Security Strategy (2003) opens with the statement, "Europe has never been so prosperous, so secure, nor so free." Why, then, does the EU need a security dimension? In any case, the EU's influence as a security actor has been minimal because of its relative ineffectiveness at using force, as demonstrated in the Gulf War, Yugoslavia, Bosnia, and Kosovo. The EU's failure in these cases seemingly reinforces theoretical perceptions that only states matter, and that the EU is really a civilian power that is irrelevant when the use of force is required.

To further complicate matters, six non-NATO EU member states identify themselves as neutral, yet they support the ESDP.[9] Why does participation in the ESDP not compromise their neutrality? Additionally, the EU member states vary significantly in size (ranging from Germany to Malta), military power, and inclination to get involved in world crises. With such disparate abilities and interests, why would they seek to work collectively in the security arena? Considering how strapped European governments are for cash to keep their generous pension schemes afloat for their aging citizenry, why channel money toward an EU security dimension?

If these analyses are correct, then the EU should not waste its energies and its money on creating a security or defense identity that would duplicate national armed forces or the work of NATO. Nevertheless, starting with the Maastricht Treaty in 1993, the EU has actively pursued a security policy. To show the seriousness of this endeavor, the EU has taken measures to consolidate its defense industry, stopped reductions in member states' spending on defense, and made firm commitments to a multinational rapid reaction force. Even Ireland has promised to contribute, saying that its participation will not dilute its neutrality.[10] Why?

Finally, what does the EU's incursion into security mean for Europe, its relationship with the United States, and even the world? Does the inclusion of a common security policy mean its transformation into a superpower? As early as 1981, Johan Galtung argued that one purpose of European integration was to create a "superpower"; specifically, a Eurocentric world and a unicentric Europe.[11] UK prime minister Tony Blair envisioned "an EU whose vision of peace is matched by its vision of prosperity; a civilised continent united in defeating brutality and violence; a continent joined in its belief in social justice. A superpower, but not a superstate."[12] As such, both T. R. Reid, in his book *The United States of Europe: The New Superpower and the End of American Supremacy,* and Mark Leonard, in his work *Why Europe Will Run the 21st Century,* argue that the European model is superior to the US model, and will become the world's new benign hegemon.

Or, is talk of a superpower just another example of the hyperbole that surrounds the European Union? Many academics and journalists have noted that EU rhetoric, especially with regard to the ESDP, far outstrips the reality. Gareth Harding is especially skeptical of EU superpower ambitions: "The cruel truth is that without America, Europe lacks the capability to project force on the world stage. Railing against the United States or creating new layers of bureaucracy will not change this, only increased defense spending and more efficient pooling of resources will."[13]

This paradox, this "thorn in the flesh," has had a profound impact on US-European relations. Especially in light of the Iraq War, the future of NATO, one of the cornerstones of transatlantic relations, has seemed uncertain. The threat to NATO was made explicit by the defection of France, Germany, and Belgium when Turkey invoked Article IV of the North Atlantic Treaty in February 2003. The subsequent French-German proposal, in April 2003, for a separate EU defense command made US secretary of state Colin Powell "a little nervous."[14] Euro-skeptic Lord Pearson argued in the House of Lords that the EU's pursuit of a military planning center separate from NATO was "inspired by France's deep psychotic need to bite the hand that freed her in two world wars."[15] In Washington, a common view is that fifty years of living in security beneath the NATO umbrella has turned Europe into a continent of "lotus eaters" unappreciative of US sacrifices or leadership in dealing with world crises. As Congressman Henry Hyde (R-IL) put it, peace, prosperity, and NATO have "created a beneficent, but artificial, environment so secure that its beneficiaries believe it to be self-sustaining." Hyde went so far as to argue that the Europeans' lack of support of US security policy is due to their living in a "cocoon."[16]

However, those with long memories will date these problems to the Kosovo crisis, which led to the Saint-Mâlo declaration in December 1998. Bronislaw Komorowski, chairman of the Parliamentary Defense Committee and former deputy defense minister of Poland, and Jan Zahradil, opposition spokesman on foreign affairs and chairman of the Foreign Affairs and European Integration Committees of the Czech Republic, said in a joint statement, "The current plans to set up a European military capability outside and apart from Nato will put great pressure on the US, and lead to a split."[17] In his famous article, "Power and Weakness," written before the Iraq crisis, Robert Kagan argued that the very foundation of the Atlantic Alliance was in question. The United States could no longer count on European support, as they lived on different planets. "[O]n major strategic and international questions today, Americans are from Mars and Europeans are from Venus. . . . When it comes to setting national priorities, determining threats, defining challenges, and fashioning and implementing foreign and defense policies, the United States and Europe have parted ways."[18]

Those with even longer memories will recollect that at the end of the Cold War many believed NATO's future was also in jeopardy. With the Warsaw Pact dissolved, the question was whether NATO would dissolve as well. Sir James Eberle, a retired admiral and former NATO field commander, stated publicly, "NATO should remain in being only as long as necessary to create the conditions that would allow it to be dissolved."[19] The European allies seemed to hasten that end with discussion of a common foreign and security policy less than a month after the formal end of the Cold War.[20]

Those with even longer memories or good students of history will know that NATO has sailed in the rocky waters of US-European relations for decades, dating from the Suez crisis in 1954. As early as the Kennedy administration, Washington tried to restructure and rebalance the NATO alliance to keep it intact. Henry Kissinger's book *The Troubled Partnership*, published in 1966, argued that the alliance's problems stemmed from an inherent inequality in the founding relationship. He made the case that the solution to saving the alliance lay not in burden sharing "but [in] the establishing of a psychological balance between us and Europe."[21]

In other words, as paradoxical as the advent of the ESDP may be, its roots go back a long way, as far back as the formation of NATO and the beginnings of European integration. Therefore, an explanation of the paradox must include sixty years of rocky relations. The account must also include an analysis of European integration; European security policy must have antecedents in the European Economic Community (EEC). In addition, an analysis of the Common Foreign and Security Policy (CFSP), and subsequent ESDP, must explain the timing: Why did the Europeans choose to create an independent foreign and security policy in what was once a common market, just when the Soviet Union dissolved? The answer also needs to explain the hyperbole surrounding the CFSP/ESDP. Does its existence truly herald the advent of a superpower?

Using a constructivist approach, this volume uncovers the motivation behind the ESDP and explains the paradox. As well as answering the above questions, the volume demystifies European actions in past years, ranging from French, German, and Belgian defections from NATO during the Iraq crisis to European desires to create an EU military headquarters in a suburb of Brussels in symbolic opposition to NATO. This book argues that rather than attempting to duplicate or supplant NATO, the EU is seeking a security and defense policy not for deterrence or defense, but to promote a pan-European political identity.

## Identity and Narrative as a Motivating Force

One key objective consistently overlooked in analyses of ESDP is its importance to the European Union's nation- or identity-building project that is so essential to further integration. According to Javier Solana, understanding the CFSP/ESDP requires going beyond traditional concepts either of states defending their material or security interests or of changes in the structure of the international system: "These 'realist' and 'structuralist' accounts miss out on one crucial factor. And that is the impact of identity on foreign policy. For what you do on the international stage is surely also a function of your identity—of how you define yourself and the values you seek to promote abroad."[22] In order for "Europe to be European,"[23] the EU needs a foreign and security policy to differentiate itself from US foreign and security policy, with which it is so intertwined. The formation of such a policy and its execution are vital to the success of the EU. To quote French president Jacques Chirac, "There is no Europe if it does not have the capacity to defend itself."[24] ESDP actions can build prestige for the European idea.

The use of narrative to create a European identity has been long in the making—since 1952. The story is the same: from the ashes of World War II was born an "ever closer union" of European peoples with the goal of creating prosperity out of the rubble and dousing the embers of war forever. This narrative has had limited success capturing the heart of the average European citizen because he or she has, more often than not, associated "Europe" with economics and bureaucracy rather than with the business of war and peace. Moreover, this European identity needs be grafted on top of a national (and sometimes fragile) identity, creating domestic tensions.

Although a defense dimension was originally included in the 1950s, the European Defense Community (EDC) did not succeed. Defense was too sensitive a subject. Subsequent politicians broached the subject, but with little success. Security and defense policy was left to the individual member states and to NATO for two reasons. First, the Soviet threat was so serious that the EU member states dared not experiment with their security and defense policy; the Cold War precluded it. Second, the Europeans took solace in their new identity as a "civilian power." Not only did it distinguish them from the more warlike Americans, it worked well with the narrative that, having learned their lessons from World War II, the European Community (EC) eschewed military power and sought to exert its influence through civilized, civilian methods.

However, the European elites, who supported the integration process, constantly found themselves out of touch with the common man and woman, who associated European integration not with peace and progress but with bureaucracy and regulations. To regain support, the member states worked to create a common identity based on common values with which the citizenry could connect. Each time the Europeans disagreed with US policy, this identity solidified. The member states' leaders would pledge to increase their cooperation in the security field whenever they had a break with the United States. These moves proved popular with the public, but little could be done substantively since European defense hinged on NATO to counter the Soviet threat.

The end of the Cold War meant that the Europeans could finally experiment with their security and defense policy because almost all traditional security threats to their safety vanished along with the Iron Curtain. As a result, paradoxically, the European Union's security policy was born when threats to Europe were removed. The ESDP exists not for defense, but to foster a European identity among EU citizens—in other words, for nation building.

## Outline of the Book

Chapter 2 explains the shortcomings of various contending theories with regard to the ESDP conundrum. Traditional security analysis falls short of providing an explanation for all the paradoxes. Recognizing the change from a bipolar to unipolar system does little to explain the slow emergence of a European security identity. Moreover, as the only concrete military outgrowth has been the formation of 1,500-soldier battle groups, the ESDP, by definition, must have little to do with defense or balance-of-power concerns.

Other explanations, such as its potential usefulness or that it is a sign of the "coming of age," also fall short. Although an EU force could be useful, why not channel European troops through the UN or NATO? What explains the need for an EU force per se? As to the coming-of-age argument, there is no reason to equate the coming of age with the acquisition of a security policy. The EU decision to create a military dimension for itself was a clear break from its previously cultivated, civilian identity.

Chapter 3 uses nation-building theory to explain the paradox. The ESDP is not to defend Europem, but rather, to unite the citizens of Europe. Economic prosperity has not been enough to cement support for the integration project. Closer European integration has been accompanied by a rise in the extreme right and in popular rejections of the EU treaties in referenda in four countries. The CFSP/ESDP is an active policy to create "Europeans."

Chapter 4 explains the role of the United States in the European integration process. Europeans have been most unified when they have opposed unpopular US foreign policy, whether it be the Vietnam War, Pershing missiles, or the war in Iraq. Using the United States as the "other," Europeans are able to gloss over their differences and see themselves as the same. This chapter traces the ebb and flow of US-European relations, and how the in-group/out-group phenomenon has led to issues of theology within NATO.

Chapter 5 demonstrates that EU politicians are and have been consciously using security policy as a nation-building tool since the early 1970s. This chapter explains the paradox of why nation-states are integrating in this area, and why the Europeans chose to create an independent security policy at a time of no threat. The CFSP was established not because it magically "came of age," but because the end of the Cold War and the absence of a security threat made it possible, for the first time, for the EC member states to experiment with their security policies. Since Maastricht, the EU institutions and the member states have all been on the same page, working as hard as possible to increase the visibility of the European Union as an international actor to excite some enthusiasm among EU citizens.

Chapter 6 reveals that the odd and cumbersome security architecture of the European Union directly reflects popular opinion. In doing so, this chapter explains the gap between rhetoric and reality, also called the "expectations-capability gap." Rather than designed for defense, the EU security architecture aims to increase visibility at low financial and political cost: form follows function. As a result, European crisis management must perform while in a straitjacket of domestic political considerations.

The final chapter assesses the impact of EU security policy on both the international reputation of the EU and on Europeans domestically. While causalities are impossible to prove, statistics show a small, but significant, increase in favorable reputation since the first ESDP mission. Therefore, one can conclude that the policy is, at least, somewhat successful. At the same time, the author warns that the increase in expectations—and the imposition of an ideal from the label of the European Union as a "peace-power"—could lead to a crumbling of the pedestal on which Europe sits if EU policy or soldiers cannot live up to its reputation.

Nevertheless, the book concludes that the ESDP is a necessary nation-building tool that EU politicians must continue to use for the integration process to continue successfully. Just as the United States has been able to ride out its own foreign policy disasters, the EU should be able to do so as well. With Europe the site of two world wars, European integration is vital to world peace. As Stephen Larrabee warned, the United States should not overreact to the ESDP.[25] The very act of understanding the reasons behind the paradox could, in and of itself, facilitate US-EU relations. The greatest threat is failure of European integration. As several scholars have pointed out, the ESDP is a thorn in the flesh because it is divisive. Were Washington not to overreact and were it to be wholly supportive, the United States could cement this policy by making Atlanticist countries feel that they did not have to make the fatal choice: NATO or the EU.

## Notes

1. As quoted in "Nato 'Needs Reforms' to Survive," *BBC News*, 31 July 2002.

2. The term "European Union" represents a sui generis organization, with both supranational and intergovernmental traits, composed of twenty-seven member states. The EU traces its roots to the European Coal and Steel Community (ECSC), established in 1952. The same founding six member states signed the Treaty of Rome in 1957, establishing the European Economic Community (EEC). In 1967, the Merger Treaty combined the organizational structures of the ECSC, the EEC, and Euratom to create the European Communities, also referred to as the European Community (EC). The term "European Union" or "EU" came into force with the ratification of the Treaty on European Union in 1993 (also known as the Maastricht Treaty). Throughout the text, I use the term appropriate to its time in history.

3. In 1992, the Maastricht Treaty introduced the Common Foreign and Security Policy (CFSP). The CFSP provided the basis for the discussion of security affairs within the EU. Subsequently, in 1994, under the auspices of the NATO Council, the member states recognized the need to define a European identity vis-à-vis security and defense. This agreement led to the development of the European Security and Defense Identity (ESDI) to allow the EU to borrow NATO capabilities to carry out such narrowly defined military operations as peacekeeping and humanitarian tasks, also called the Petersberg tasks. Unhappy with their ability to influence affairs during the Kosovo crisis, and following a meeting of the minds between UK prime minister Tony Blair and French president Jacques Chirac at Saint-Mâlo, the EU member states agreed to a full-fledged defense policy (the European Security and Defense Policy, or ESDP) at the Helsinki Council in 1999. The ESDP was an important advance as it led to the formation of committees and other institutional structures such as the Political and Security Committee (PSC), the EU Military Committee (EUMC), and the EU Military Staff (EUMS), which paved the way for an autonomous EU defense. The ESDP is also referred to as the Common European Security and Defense Policy (CESDP) and, during the constitutional convention, as the Common Security and Defense Policy (CSDP). Most academics and even Solana's website refer to it as the ESDP.

4. Solana, preface to *EU Security and Defence Policy,* ed. Gnesotto, 5.

5. Member state diplomat who worked in Solana's office from 1999 to 2006, interview by author, Brussels, Belgium, 7 December 2005.

6. Nicole Gnesotto, "ESDP: Results and Prospects," introduction to *EU Security and Defence Policy,* ed. Gnesotto, 12.

7. Gower, "Russia and the European Union," 88. See also Vladimir Semonov, "Opinion and Analysis: Russia Would Like Europe to Have a Constitution," Novosti (Russian News and Information Agency), 30 May 2005, at http://en.rian.ru/20050530/-40439787.

8. Of the twenty-seven European Union member states, twenty-one are members of the Atlantic Alliance: Belgium, Bulgaria, the Czech Republic, Denmark, Estonia, France, Germany, Greece, Hungary, Italy, Latvia, Lithuania, Luxembourg, the Netherlands, Poland, Portugal, Romania, Slovakia, Slovenia, Spain, and the United Kingdom.

9. The six EU countries that are not members of NATO are Austria, Cyprus, Finland, Ireland, Malta, and Sweden.

10. Mark Brennock, "Irish Troops to Serve Under EU Flag," *Irish Times*, 4 March 2000.

11. Galtung, *The European Community*, 12.

12. Tony Blair, "The Warsaw Speech: A Superpower, but Not a Superstate," *Guardian Unlimited*, 7 October 2000, at http://www.guardian.co.uk/tonyblair/story/0,,378818,00.html#article_-continue.

13. Gareth Harding, "Commentary: A Paper HQ for a Paper EU Army," United Press International, 27 October 2003.

14. "Powell Looking for Answers on Europe's Defence Plans," Deutsche-Presse Agentur, 30 May 2003.

15. Lord Pearson, debate over European Union (Implications of Withdrawal) Bill [HL], House of Lords 692, No. 98, col. 1414, 8 June 2007; at www.publications.parliament.uk/pa/-ld200607/ldhansrd/text/70608-0008.htm.

16. Henry Hyde, "Pathology of Success," opening remarks of U.S. Representative Henry Hyde (R-IL) during a House International Relations Committee hearing featuring testimony from Secretary of State Colin Powell, 11 February 2003, at http://wwwa.house.gov/international relations/108/news0212.htm.

17. Bronislaw Komorowski and Jan Zahradil, "Europe Will Take the Fight out of Nato," *Sunday Times* (London), 12 December 1999.

18. Kagan, "Power and Weakness," 5–23.

19. As quoted in Craig R. Whitney, "Amid Gulf Crisis and Cold War End, Questions on US and NATO Roles," *New York Times,* 26 December 1990, A10.

20. The end of the Cold War was formally announced in the Charter of Paris on 21 November 1990 at the CSCE Paris Summit, *Financial Times*, 22 November 1990. The European Community formally opened the Maastricht Intergovernmental Conference negotiations on 15 December 1990. See Clyde Haberman, "West Europeans Formally Initiate Closer Federation," *New York Times*, 16 December 1990, 1.

21. Kissinger, *The Troubled Partnership*, 234.

22. Javier Solana, "Identity and Foreign Policy," *ESDP Newsletter,* vol. 3, January 2007, 9.

23. Delors, "European Integration and Security," 100. Delors argued, "Europe must want to be European" if it wants its political ambitions to come to fruition.

24. As quoted in John Tagliabue, "Blair Reassures U.S. on European Defense," *International Herald Tribune*, 18 October 2003, 3.

25. F. Stephen Larrabee, prepared statement, "The European Security and Defense Identity (ESDI) and American Interests Before the Senate Committee on Foreign Relations, Subcommittee on European Affairs," Federal News Service, 9 March 2000. At the time, he worked at the Rand Corporation.

# 2

# Why the EU Needs the ESDP: Contending Explanations

———————————■———————————

The actions of federalist politicians and technocrats playing at arm-chair generals, building a fictitious paper army, will only serve to weaken even further our national capabilities to the detriment of our own security and world stability. They should beware: paper tigers burn. ■ ELEVEN FRENCH AND BRITISH RETIRED GENERALS AND ADMIRALS TO EU LEADERS, 2001[1]

After the end of the Cold War, many academics ignored the European Community's incursion into security affairs altogether. For example, in a 640-page National Defense University book titled *European Security Policy After the Revolutions of 1989,* no chapter or section even addressed the European Community. Others found the EC's experimentation with a security policy dangerous and pointless; very simply, the EC could not defend itself without NATO. Martin Farnsdale, former commander of the North Atlantic Group, wrote:

> NATO has from the start been built up around the forces of its members, including the USA. To remove the forces of any one country would court disaster. If that country were to be the USA, NATO would quite simply collapse. Europe can probably build a new and different defence structure in the long term, but this would demand much more expenditure, the mobilisation of more manpower and a high degree of integration of national armed forces. To attempt this with the WTO [Warsaw Treaty Organization] countries in a state of turmoil and instability would be folly of the highest order.[2]

Charles Glaser conceded that a European defense identity through the Western European Union (WEU) could provide "flexibility for Western Europe to act militarily on its own," but concluded, nevertheless, that "a

11

Western European alliance would be an ineffective substitute for NATO."[3] Moreover, as Josef Joffe noted, "[I]f NATO has lost its rationale along with its rival, why should the EC/WEU do better?"[4]

More than ten years later, academics are still asking the same questions. Sten Rynning characterized the development of the ESDP as puzzling for three reasons. First, NATO continues to have tremendous military advantages over the EU. Second, a European pillar could have been developed within NATO; there was no need for it to be developed within the EU per se; and, "finally, because the usual suspects, the French, simply cannot have masterminded the EU development single-handedly."[5] All the member states must have some reason to support the creation of a foreign, security, and defense policy for the EU: what is that reason? Academics and politicians alike suggest several different hypotheses, which fall into three theoretical categories.

## Three Hypotheses Outlining Why the EU Needs the ESDP

### Hypothesis 1: The EU Needs the ESDP for Defense Purposes

The first line of reasoning falls into traditional security or realist analysis. Realism lends itself well to strategic and security studies because of its focus on military power. In this vein, realists argue that the United States has been less committed to European defense since the end of the Cold War, to the point of becoming dangerously isolationist. Considering the newly emerging threats to Europe, the EU has no choice but to find ways to defend itself. Moreover, US isolationist tendencies, coupled with the United States' domination of a unipolar world, mean that Europe has no choice but to attempt to balance the United States militarily.

### Hypothesis 2: The EU Needs the ESDP to Help Police the World

The second line of reasoning falls into an international institutionalist perspective. Academics and politicians take the tack that the ESDP will be both efficacious and useful to many: the ESDP will aid the European Union, NATO, and the United Nations in crisis and conflict management. As the United States continues to act as a "reluctant sheriff," the ESDP will allow the Europeans to pick up the slack. Considering that the EU is both so large and so prosperous, Europe needs to become more involved in world affairs and take on its fair share of policing.

*Hypothesis 3: The ESDP Is the Natural*
*Next Stage of European Integration*

Finally, the ESDP is justified from an integrationist argument. The ESDP is not a product of revolution, but rather evolution. The EU has been integrating consistently in this area for years; the ESDP is the fruit of these long labors. In addition, the ESDP is a symbol of the coming of age of the European Union; after years of integrating, it is finally maturing. As a mature institution, the time has come for the EU to "assert its voice" on the world stage. That voice requires a common defense policy.

\* \* \*

This chapter develops these hypotheses and then examines their logical inconsistencies. The first section deals with traditional security analysis as a justification for the CFSP/ESDP. It concludes that there is no need for an EU security and defense policy per se because, very simply, there are no military threats to Europe. Significantly, despite the rhetoric, more than fifteen years after the launch of the CFSP, the EU has no defense capabilities. The argument of soft balancing against the United States also falls short, both because of the question of timing and because of internal inconsistencies. Regarding the responsibility argument, the second section explains that, although noble, this motivation is completely unconvincing due to the financial burdens involved and the lack of follow-through. Finally, with regard to the question of a mature European Union, rather than seeing the ESDP as part of a teleological evolution of integration, the third section explains how security is a divergence from previous conceptions of the European Union and discusses how the inclusion of security and defense in the EU was a conscious choice.

## Does the EU Need the ESDP for Security Reasons?

From a traditional security analysis, three reasons are most often given as to why the European Union needs its own security policy. The first is the myriad new threats facing Europe today; the European Union needs to have independent capabilities to protect itself from them. The second, often given as a corollary to the first, is that the United States is going to withdraw from Europe, eviscerating NATO. In other words, the United States is not dependable as an ally due to economic and other concerns.

The third is that the balance of power has shifted to a unipolar structure. The United States has become both too dominant and potent, requiring other countries (e.g., those in Europe) to band together to redress the balance of power.

Despite the above claims, these justifications are unsubstantiated. First, the ESDP could undermine the Atlantic Alliance by dividing it, thereby producing the Oedipal effect of pushing the United States out. Most of the threats facing Europe today are not military and are therefore not best dealt with by military means. If the balance of power has changed, why would the European allies choose to balance against the United States rather than continue to "bandwagon" with the dominant power, that is, ally with the United States as they had under NATO? In addition, the power projection envisioned by the ESDP, if achieved, will in no way redress the balance of power. Finally, the above analysis does not consider the costs involved in creating an ESDP or the lack of political will among European governments.

### Hypothesis 1a: The EU Faces Many Different Threats and Needs an ESDP for Defense

The Royal United Services Institute for Defence and Security Studies (RUSI) fellow Irina Isakova explained: "What some critics might consider to be a 'mission creep' within the ESDP framework, for the majority of Europeans is a logical development of European defence and security capabilities in a time of emerging new security threats as a response to US policies and with the evolution of the EU itself."[6] The end of the Cold War[7] and the dissolution of the Soviet Union[8] brought an end to the bipolar international system. During the Cold War, countries arranged their security policies accordingly making alliances to safeguard their survival. The uniting of Germany[9] coupled with a reduction in US troops and the loss of a common threat created uncertainty. In many cases, communism and the Cold War suppressed certain territorial and ethnic conflicts; the change in international structure allowed such problems to resurface. These conflicts could "pose severe challenges to the Western European states in the form of 'ethnic cleansing' and associated population movements or the disruption of international transportation and communications links."[10] Wars, such as in the former Yugoslavia, could spill over into Western Europe. The Stockholm International Peace Research Institute (SIPRI) noted that there had been more outbreaks of violence on the European continent than on the Asian continent in 1993 and that the number of outbreaks of violence in Europe had risen significantly compared to 1992.[11] As John Mearsheimer posited in his article, "Back to the Future," the post–Cold War world was not necessarily a safer place.[12]

The following quotations provide an indication as to the concerns among some of the member states before they entered the CFSP negotiations. Danish defense minister Knud Enggaard, in 1991, after the end of the Cold War, but before the dissolution of the Soviet Union, warned that despite the end of the Cold War, there were still worries: "The fact that there is increased pressure from the Kola Peninsula on our Norwegian friends also has an effect on us. The Norwegians consider that not very pleasant. We are experiencing pressure on NATO's flanks—including Turkey, for many reasons. They do not recognize the picture of détente that the optimists paint. After all, no one knows where all this will end."[13]

Portuguese minister of foreign affairs João de Deus Pinheiro agreed: "Our defense is sacrosanct, and we must guarantee it. . . . How could we have imagined, for example, that there would be these problems in the Gulf? Others may arise."[14]

Douglas Hurd, the British foreign secretary, expressed similar views:

> We must learn from history. There will always be hotbeds of dangers. . . . It is certainly possible that one powerful and even hostile power may develop in one of the former Soviet republics. In the Middle East and in southern Europe, too, new hot beds of dangers might form quickly—though not on the scale of Stalin's or Brezhnev's army, but dangerous.[15]

The Mediterranean countries, such as Italy, Spain, and Portugal, were particularly concerned about the threat from Islamic fundamentalism and from North Africa. These countries were concerned that Eastern Europe would divert attention from what they saw as an important area.[16]

### Hypothesis 1b: The Americans Are Undependable Allies and Will Withdraw from Europe

At this time of uncertainty, the United States pledged to reduce the number of US troops on European territory by two-thirds. Many in the French government were convinced that the United States would withdraw altogether.[17] James Dobbins, ambassador to the European Community under the George H. W. Bush administration as well as at the beginning of the (first) Clinton administration, said in an address to the Centre for European Policy Studies in Brussels, "Europe must develop an independent army to tackle security treats on the continent rather than rely on the

US to come to the rescue. . . . The American people, in my judgment, are unlikely to support a long-term US troop commitment to Europe if they see its purpose as protecting rich, prosperous Europeans against two-bit outlaws like Serbia."[18] By October 1994, the United States had either ended, reduced, or placed on standby status a total of 871 military installations.[19] To quote Trevor Salmon and Alistair Shepard, "Given that the United States now contributes less than 100,000 personnel to Europe, the new question is whether reduced expenditure and reduced physical commitment leads to a reduction in U.S. leadership and interest."[20] Adrian Hyde-Price argued that the unipolar system had made the United States a capricious and unreliable ally.[21] Even with a minimal US presence, the Europeans would need some sort of arrangement to deal with peripheral security problems of little interest to the United States.

For decades, US isolationists have wanted to reduce their country's troop commitments in Europe in order to reduce US defense expenditures.[22] Periodically, Congress will pass a resolution to bring the troops home;[23] the end of the Cold War seemed to hasten that day. In February 1992, Vice President Dan Quayle implied that if the Europeans failed to make concessions at the General Agreement on Tariffs and Trade (GATT) negotiations, the United States would withdraw its forces from Europe.[24] The United States did pledge in 1994 to maintain 100,000 US soldiers in Europe; nevertheless, US general George Joulwan believed the Europeans needed to contribute many more to keep the same level of protection: "My plea to you [Europeans] today is to help me with your member nations to continue to support adequate defence forces for Europe. . . . After all, NATO and the WEU share the same aims—the security and stability in Europe."[25]

As a result, one could argue that the European Union would need some sort of security organization to defend itself. According to Italian foreign minister Gianni DeMichelis, whether one

> call[s] it an alliance or a union . . . [this collective security system will defend the Europeans] against possible risks from the outside . . . [or] against internal risks. A security agreement is an instrument that makes it possible to defend oneself against all kinds of risks that can occur in any country. Nobody knows—a dictator might assume power in Poland tomorrow. Well, these structures reduce such a risk.[26]

Dr. Fraser Cameron, of the European Commission, put it bluntly in 1993,

> The idea was to create the WEU as a defense arm because of the sharp decline in the number of US troops in Europe, and they will continue

to decline. US policy is dictated by economic interest, and therefore the US will pull as many troops out of Europe as possible for financial reasons. . . . The WEU will be able to defend the [European] Community alone. It will not need NATO. Two nuclear powers are enough for deterrence. They will remain under national control, but there is talk of them coming under EC control in the future.[27]

More than ten years later, the EU's military chief agreed with Cameron's assessment. At a defense conference in Sälen, Sweden, Gustav Hägglund argued that Europe should bear its own defense burden because it was uncertain whether the United States would continue to have either the resources or the political will to defend Europe: "The American and the European pillar will become responsible for their respective territorial defence and co-operate in crises situations outside their own territories. My prediction is that this will happen within the next ten years. . . . There are no threats against Europe now that the EU cannot handle on its own."[28]

Even in Great Britain, the US commitment to Europe is suspect. In December 2006, Prime Minister Tony Blair of the UK argued for the need to buy a new generation of nuclear weaponry because Britain could not rely on the United States to protect it. "Our co-operation with America is very close. But close as it is, the independent nature of the British deterrent is an additional insurance against circumstances where we are threatened but America is not. . . . These circumstances are also highly unlikely but I am unwilling to say they are non-existent."[29]

In short, the end of the Cold War did not leave Europe necessarily any safer. However, it did reduce the number of US troops protecting Europe. At the behest of the Bush and Clinton administrations, as well as by common sense, the EU member states sought to create a European Security and Defense Policy to fill the void.

### Counterargument to Hypothesis 1b:
### Is the United States Leaving or Being Pushed Out?
### How the ESDP Could Undermine European Defense

Based on the evidence above, one would predict the following behavior from the European allies. First, the Europeans would increase defense spending to offset the loss of the US contingent from NATO. Second, considering how vital the United States is to the functioning of NATO, one could imagine furious lobbying on the European side in Washington to keep US troops in Europe. Finally, if, for whatever reason, the Europeans chose not to work within the NATO framework, they would pursue the formation of a functional European security pillar or organization as fast as possible to minimize vulnerability.

None of the above has happened. In the years immediately following the end of the Cold War, from 1990 to 1994, all the EU countries that were also members of NATO, with the exception of Luxembourg and Portugal, reduced their defense spending by the following amounts: Belgium, 7.3 percent; Denmark, 0.5 percent; France, 0.7 percent; Germany, 6.3 percent; Greece, 1.1 percent; Italy, 0.5 percent, the Netherlands, 2.9 percent; Spain, 3.4 percent; and the United Kingdom, 4.2 percent.[30] These figures demonstrate that if the European allies feared for their security, they did not act on that fear. This general downward spiral has continued throughout the first decade of 2000.

Moreover, if the Europeans were concerned with military security on the continent, they have chosen to focus their energies on creating a separate European identity rather than on strengthening NATO, although it was the organization credited with winning the Cold War in the first place. Rather, it was the United States who was lobbying in Brussels to keep NATO intact.

Despite US pressure over the decades for the Europeans to do more with regard to burden sharing in NATO, Washington has not welcomed the EU foray into security affairs. The United States has feared the Europeans' drive toward a common defense policy might undermine NATO. Politically, a defense initiative might mean the possible marginalization of the United States in European affairs. Strategically, the United States has felt that the new states to the east were not necessarily so benign, and that, in any case, it was better to bank on the Atlantic Alliance rather than on their goodwill. February 1991 saw a US démarche, with the United States strongly lobbying EC countries not to subvert NATO. In an official statement, William H. Taft, permanent representative to NATO, said,

> We support a European pillar [of security], but [one] which does not fulfill the same task as the [Atlantic] Alliance, which acts within the Alliance to carry out the tasks which fall upon it and only outside the Alliance where it wishes to take on new missions. . . . American public opinion would not understand any proposal aimed at replacing NATO by a different mechanism which would take on the fundamental role of dissuasion and defence. . . . Neither would it understand if NATO were to be transformed into an organization mainly charged with solving divergences between Europe and America . . . rather than acting collectively against common risks and threats.[31]

In June of 1991, James Baker, US secretary of state, supported the move toward a European defense identity, but Washington was afraid that if such a policy seemed to replace NATO, the isolationist movement in the United States might gain strength. Washington was also concerned that a unified WEU position would have the majority in NATO (nine out of sixteen members) and set its agenda. Therefore, if the WEU were to become NATO's European pillar, Baker argued, not only would its policy have to be open to the arguments of other members of the larger organization (i.e., the United States and Canada), but it would also have to incorporate, in some way, the other European states that were part of NATO but not part of the WEU (i.e., Iceland, Norway, Denmark, Turkey, and, at the time, Greece).[32]

The NATO summit in Rome in November 1991 was the venue for the members to iron out these issues. Overall, the summit was very successful. It changed the Atlantic Alliance's strategy, reinforced relations with the EC, took initiatives to augment the Conference on Security and Cooperation in Europe (CSCE), took a new approach to arms control, outlined the principles on the relations between NATO and the European security identity (so that the bolstering of the European Union corresponded to a reinforcement of the Atlantic Alliance), and published a statement on the USSR and Yugoslavia. According to Manfred Wörner, secretary general of NATO, NATO had thus "met the challenges and was preparing for the future." NATO's new mission was to maintain the strategic balance in Europe, to prevent the renationalization of defense, and to contribute to a stable and lasting peace. By explicitly recognizing the roles of other institutions like the EC, the WEU, and the CSCE, NATO strategy remained flexible. Most people were satisfied with the results. The United States was invited to stay in Europe and it did so.[33]

Nevertheless, many in Washington continue, to this day, to fear the EU's pursuit of its own security policy will pull NATO asunder. European insistence that the breakup of Yugoslavia heralded "the hour of Europe, not of the Americans"[34] seemed to herald the end of NATO instead. The Saint-Mâlo declaration specified an autonomous capacity for the European Union. In 2003, several member states supported the creation of an alternative EU military headquarters in a Brussels suburb, in an apparent face-off to the NATO headquarters in another suburb of Brussels.

Indeed, many see Europe's pursuit of an ESDP as a self-fulfilling prophecy: by building an autonomous capability, Europe will undermine NATO, as well as create ill will with the United States, thereby encouraging the latter's isolationist tendencies. Although an extreme example, one academic titled his article "Saving NATO from Europe."[35] Many "fear that French-German military and political cooperation and planning for a European army could accelerate U.S. withdrawal from Europe."[36] Julian Lindley-French argues that seeing the formation of security institutions as security ends in and of themselves is both dangerous and naïve, and could undermine NATO, the "serious" defense organization.[37] Addressing these fears, Secretary of State Madeleine Albright, in her "three *D*s speech," warned that there should be "no diminution of NATO, no discrimination and no duplication."[38] As Stephen Larrabee explained,

> [M]any of the forces and assets that will be required for ESDI [European Security and Defense Identity] already have NATO commitments. If these forces are restructured for ESDI-related tasks, and especially if EU planning for these missions is not done in close cooperation with NATO's defense planning process, ESDI could weaken rather than strengthen NATO.[39]

In other words, if the Europeans were truly worried about a US withdrawal from Europe leaving the Europeans vulnerable to a variety of security threats, the logical, easier, and cheaper option would not be the creation of an EU-based security and defense policy, but the lobbying of Washington to keep more US troops in Europe and a general strengthening of support for NATO.

The characterization of the United States as an unreliable NATO ally is unsupported. The United States, as a founding NATO member and home of the original Washington Treaty, has stood by the European allies for over fifty years. The US Department of Defense's Office for International Security Affairs has an online publication titled "United States Security Strategy for Europe and NATO," whose first chapter is "America's Enduring Interest in Europe."[40] Since the end of the Cold War, the United States has reduced its troop presence in Europe from a high of 320,000 during the Cold War to current levels of about 110,000. Clinton promised to keep a floor of 100,000 in Europe. George W. Bush has suggested that the United States reduce troop numbers even further, or perhaps move the current troops to less expensive and more welcoming countries such as Poland. Nevertheless, there is almost no talk in Washington of scrapping or pulling out of NATO. It would be political suicide. NATO is easily the best-known and most popular international organization in the United States.[41] Reflecting this opinion, the great majority of books, articles, and speeches from the United States worrying about the effect of the ESDP on the Atlantic Alliance argue to reform NATO and keep it as a bridge to Europe, rather than to eliminate it.[42]

*Counterargument to Hypothesis 1a: What Threats*
*Are Facing Europe? Would an ESDP Help Defend Europe?*

The end of the Cold War was a period of great uncertainty; no one was sure whether it heralded a period of peace and stability or of war and instability. During this time, in 1993, the Common Foreign and Security Policy (CFSP) was born. Even if one subscribed to Charles Glaser's view that "NATO is best,"[43] the CFSP might have been a reaction to the question of whether NATO would survive or not. However, the ESDP was born six years later, at a time when NATO had not only successfully expanded, but when most defense experts agreed that there were no more military threats facing Europe. The UK Ministry of Defence stated categorically in 2001 that it sees no emerging threats and in fact will stop producing tanks.[44] The German Defense Ministry has briefed its officials that Russia cannot attack Europe even if it wants to.[45] The European Security Strategy (ESS) begins with the sentence, "Europe has never been so prosperous, so secure nor so free." It identifies terrorism, the proliferation of weapons of mass destruction, regional conflicts, state failure, and organized crime as the key threats to Europe.[46] With the possible exception of "regional conflicts," the ESS lists no traditional security threats.

In any case, how useful would a European rapid reaction force (ERRF) be in dealing with these threats? Salmon and Shepherd argued that although there is little threat of all-out war within or involving EU states, instability across the globe as well as terrorist attacks could be combated if the EU had force projection capabilities: "Many of the force projection capabilities necessary for ESDP will also be useful for some operations aimed at *preventing* the most recent danger—large-scale terrorist attacks."[47] No detail is given on how EU force projection could be used to prevent a large-scale terrorist attack. The US military colossus has not helped defend the United States against large or small terrorist attacks, whether against the USS *Cole*, a naval ship with tremendous firepower, or against the World Trade Center and the Pentagon. US success stories with regard to preventing attacks—for example, the bombing of US airliners crossing the Pacific—have come from intelligence operations. With the exception of regional conflicts, a European military response is likely to have little impact on these threats. Mark Leonard and Richard Gowan agreed:

> [I]t is difficult to think of any imminent examples where Europe is constrained from achieving its political or security objectives by a lack of military power. None of the problems on the immediate horizon—proliferation of weapons of mass destruction in North Korea,

> Iran, Syria, Pakistan and the former Soviet Union; the dangers of autocracy and instability in Central Asia and the Middle East—demand military solutions.[48]

Why is the EU seeking a military identity to address nonmilitary threats?

Ironically, Europeans often criticize the United States for addressing nonmilitary problems with military solutions. The participants of the 2005 Club de Madrid conference, which brought together world leaders (including UN secretary-general Kofi Annan, Afghan president Hamid Karzai, and various heads of government or state) as well as about 180 experts from 50 countries, agreed that military power had limited usefulness. The consensus was that "a 'soft' power approach based on prevention—not like the United States has in mind, but [rather] with engagement with North African Muslim nations, economic development, assimilating and integrating immigrants into host nations" was best.[49] These views inform EU foreign and security policy. Many prominent Europeans have been critical of the US "military first" approach toward terrorism, missile defense, and general disregard for multilateral, cooperative solutions. Hubert Védrine, the French foreign minister, criticized military solutions: "Should we reduce all the world's problems solely to the battle against terrorism? Must this be waged solely by military means, ignoring the deep-seated causes and roots? That is what would be too simplistic, dangerous and ineffectual."[50] EU commissioner for external affairs Chris Patten echoed these sentiments.

> Walls are not the answer to global woes. But engagement is—with more help for the poor, more access for them to our markets and more commitment on their part to improve their standards of government in return for our more generous help. Liberal mush? Actually, no—just a more comprehensive and effective way of beating the current generation of bin Ladens and preventing the development of new ones.[51]

Jack Straw, British foreign secretary, argued,

> Promoting human rights, fighting poverty, exclusion and injustice, and preventing and resolving conflicts are not merely right and just: they can act as a first line of defence against future crises. By engaging with the world, and driving back the boundaries of chaos, we are helping to prevent instability and insecurity, in order to stop conflict, tyranny and terrorism.[52]

Why then would the EU spend so much time, money, and energy on a military solution to emerging threats when they are arguably better dealt with through development strategies and diplomacy?

In any case, why have the Europeans chosen to create a new security organization? Sten Rynning asked, "Why not NATO?" Is NATO no longer suitable as an organization to deal with Europe's new security agenda focusing on nontraditional threats such as environmental concerns, political instability, and terrorism? Not necessarily. NATO was and is a political organization with the original intent of creating a security community in Europe. Article II of the North Atlantic Treaty of 1949 states clearly the importance of economic cooperation in this regard:

> The Parties will contribute toward the further development of peaceful and friendly international relations by strengthening their free institutions, by bringing about a better understanding of the principles upon which these institutions are founded, and by promoting conditions of stability and well-being. They will seek to eliminate conflict in their international economic policies and will encourage economic collaboration between any or all of them.[53]

Moreover, NATO, since the end of the Cold War, has transformed itself from a collective defense organization to a multipurpose, collective, general security organization with the addition of the Euro-Atlantic Partnership Council (EAPC) and Partnership for Peace (PfP). The Atlantic Alliance's Strategic Concept of 1999, which set out NATO's goals and strategies, clearly recognized the broad set of threats that face the Euro-Atlantic area, including organized crime and terrorism, and "is committed to a broad approach to security, which recognises the importance of political, economic, social and environmental factors in addition to the indispensable defence dimension."[54] With new members and a more flexible and responsive force, NATO has gone into the Balkans, arrested ethnic cleansing in Kosovo, and even assisted in disaster relief (for example, in Pakistan in 2005, after a major earthquake).[55] Considering the rifts between the Atlanticist, Europeanist, and neutral member states, keeping security in NATO's hands would have been easier and cheaper than creating an ESDP.

Moreover, many in the military establishment have found this experimentation with security and defense policy dangerous, as it compromises European security and, in their eyes, even "world stability." In a public letter to Prime Minister Tony Blair warning him and other EU leaders that the ESDP was being set up for failure, eleven British and French former generals and admirals wrote,

> As former Servicemen, we wish to voice our concerns at the manner in which the ability of our nations to protect our vital interests is being whittled away.

First, by penny-pinching, cutbacks in procurement and in force strength. Second, by overstretch, by committing reduced forces to increased global peacekeeping commitments, with disastrous effects on retention and morale. Third, and most important, *by forging a common pseudo-identity in EU defence and foreign policy.*

Our two countries have differing views on the future role and shape of Nato. But we can build on our distinctiveness if our armed forces remain under national flags. A common Euro army is incompatible with both of our approaches to this issue.

The actions of federalist politicians and technocrats playing at armchair generals, building a fictitious paper army, will only serve to weaken even further our national capabilities to the detriment of our own security and world stability. They should beware: paper tigers burn.

For the sake of our two countries and for Europe as a whole, we would counsel throwing the scheme into the dustbin of history before the fires begin.[56]

Perhaps most ironically, and most damning to the "threat" argument, after more than fifteen years since the end of the Cold War and a change in the balance of power, the European Union has not been able to achieve any independent defense capabilities. The Headline Goals of 2003 have not been reached. No European Rapid Reaction Force of 60,000 yet exists. In 2007, European battle groups of 1,500 became operational, but, in any case, both sets of forces are designed for crisis management rather than to defend against external threats. While quick and mobile, they have limited power projection. Why argue for an EU security and defense policy to defend against threats, and then not follow through? Tomas Valasek, director of the Brussels office of the Center for Defense Information, argued, "The push toward an EU military identity has, in spite of high expectations, failed to generate significant new capabilities. The project is more a search for a unique identity separate from the U.S. and NATO than a response to any real threats."[57]

### Hypothesis 1c: Is the United States a Threat to Europe? Is the ESDP Needed to Defend Europe from the United States?

Jolyon Howorth argued that US policies constitute a threat to Europe. In his book *Defending Europe: The EU, NATO, and the Quest for European Autonomy*, Howorth explained the double meaning of the title: Europe must now defend its interests from an "increasingly hegemonic United States." He cited Timothy Garton Ash, who used the underlying assumptions of the US Constitution to explain that "no single locus of power, however benign, should predominate; for even the best could be led into temptation."[58] Seth Jones agreed that the shift from bipolarity to unipolarity meant that "European states . . . became increasingly concerned about American power and, with a growing divergence in security interests, wanted to increase their ability to project power abroad and decrease US influence."[59] In this way, Howorth, Ash, and Jones underscored the French view of the United States, dubbed by French foreign minister Védrine in 1999 as a "hyperpower" that must be balanced.[60]

The European public has consistently regarded the United States as one of the biggest threats to world stability over the past five years. In 2003, Europeans rated Israel first (59 percent); the United States was second (53 percent), tied with North Korea and Iran.[61] In 2007, the United States was rated as first, with Iran as third.[62] In addition, 68 percent of EU citizens believed the United States–led invasion of Iraq was unjustified.[63] Seeing the United States as a serious threat to the autonomy of Europe, could the ESDP redress the balance of power and make the United States less of a hegemon? Salmon and Shepherd said yes. When explaining the motivations for the ESDP, they placed as number one that the ESDP "may reduce the perception of a unipolar international relations system dominated by a single superpower."[64]

Nevertheless, the answer is no. From a balance-of-power standpoint, even if operational, a 60,000-person rapid reaction force could not counterbalance the military might of the United States. Stephan Brooks and William Wohlforth argued that the subsequent battle groups of 1,500 troops would also have a minimum impact on the balance of power.[65] First of all, both the battle groups and the rapid reaction force, when operational, are designed for crisis management. The battle groups are intended as a "short notice, small-scale response."[66] They are to be ready to deploy five to ten days after a decision has been made in the EU (which is to take a maximum of five days in and of itself). The goal is to be able to send two battle groups simultaneously to crises within a radius of 6,000 kilometers from Brussels, to remain deployed for 30 days and possibly extended for another 120, depending on troop rotation and reserves. Of the 1,500 soldiers in the battle groups, approximately 350 are combat ready; the rest are for support. In contrast, the United States' 82nd Airborne Division's mission is to be able to do forcible entry anywhere in the world within 18 hours of notification.

Robert Art believed Brooks and Wohlforth missed the boat with regard to the ESDP. The goal of the ESDP is soft balancing against the power and influence of the United States. The following quotation is instructive.

> Instead, they are balancing through external alignment: they are working steadily and deliberately to pool and integrate their resources and to fashion a more effective Europe-wide military force. They have created a military staff at the EU and have earmarked national military headquarters to conduct independent operations; they are developing indigenous European airlift, satellite reconnaissance and navigation systems, and precision-guided munitions capabilities; they have created a European defense agency to rationalize military procurement; and since the end of the Cold War and the advent of unipolarity, they have made the most dramatic strides in a generation to build what Seth Jones terms "an increasingly integrated and technologically-advanced defense industry" on a Europe-wide basis.

He continued, arguing that if the European Rapid Reaction Force (ERRF) does come into play and meets its goal of 100,000 troops, it will rival the United States. Most importantly, through coordination and integration, the EU countries can set the agenda in NATO, thus balancing the power of the United States.[67]

Although Art called it "soft balancing," he referred almost exclusively to the EU's potential *military* power. Robert Pape and Joseph Nye defined "soft balancing" differently. Pape defined it as measures "that do not directly challenge US military preponderance but that use non-military tools to delay, frustrate and undermine aggressive unilateral US military policies [. . . for example,] international institutions, economic statecraft, and diplomatic arrangements."[68] Joseph Nye, in his book *Soft Power: The Means to Success in World Politics*, defined "soft power" as the power of a state's values and not military might: "A country may obtain the outcomes it wants in world politics because other countries admiring its values, emulating its example, aspiring to its level of prosperity and openness want to follow it."[69] Emad El-Din Aysha agreed, stating, "Soft power . . . refers to the policies adopted by a state to promote its image abroad" using public diplomacy and cultural diplomacy.[70] If, indeed, the EU has created a CFSP and ESDP for soft balancing, why have they placed so much emphasis on a rhetorical military aspect?

The timing of the CFSP/ESDP is also problematic. Can the initiation of the Common Foreign and Security Policy in the Maastricht Treaty be considered the beginning of balancing the power of the United States, because the balance of power changed with the end of the Cold War? The answer is no. Although the CFSP was first negotiated in December 1990, almost no political progress (let alone military progress) was made in this area until 1999. If indeed the CFSP and subsequent ESDP was a reaction to the change in balance of power, why did the EU wait until 1999—nine years later—to react?

The impetus for the Saint-Mâlo Declaration, signed in December 1998, which got the ESDP rolling, was US-European relations during the Kosovo crisis. President Clinton refused to send ground troops, although the United States did provide the great majority of air strikes. In contrast, the French and the British provided ground troops, but were nevertheless at the mercy of the United States, which provided 80 percent of the aircraft and 90 percent of the equipment. According to NATO secretary-general Lord Robertson, "Even if the Europeans constituted the bulk of the troops that were mobilized, they were not more than 20 percent among the forces effectively engaged in the air attack operations. Isn't this a dramatic avowal of weakness?"[71] The French, especially, were disturbed by their lack of capability and their dependence on the United States. As André Dumoulin put it, "In any case, Europe cannot identify with American world interests which are engaged on a case-by-case basis, in a reactive and unpredictable manner, and according to the fluctuations of the Congress and voters of the Middle West. Were not the interventions in Bosnia and Kosovo [approved] by a very small majority? Is not Europe at the mercy of internal American divergences?"[72] As a result, both the Saint-Mâlo Declaration and the subsequent Cologne European Council conclude that the European Union needed the capability

> to take decisions on the full range of conflict prevention and crisis management tasks defined in the Treaty on European Union, the "Petersberg tasks." To this end, the Union must have the capacity for autonomous action, backed up by credible military forces, the means to decide to use them, and a readiness to do so, in order to respond to international crises without prejudice to actions by NATO. The EU will thereby increase its ability to contribute to international peace and security in accordance with the principles of the UN Charter.[73]

According to this reasoning, the goal of autonomy was not to soft balance the United States as much as it was to transform the European Union into a credible world actor.

In any case, the EU has made minimal progress in improving its capabilities. In an attempt to catalog its shortcomings and to track progress toward the EU's headline goals, the Council of Ministers created a capability improvement chart. Between 2002 and 2005, of the sixty-three capabilities mentioned, fifty-three had not improved at all.[74]

One lord in the UK House of Lords was so disgusted he asked whether the 2010 headline goal could even be achieved in the next fifty years.[75]

Most discussion of soft balancing against the United States came during and after the invasion of Iraq in 2003. Unhappy with the United States' "coalition of the willing" and flagrant unilateralism, many politicians, historians, and commentators wrote about the need or the desire of the Europeans to fight for multilateralism, and to temper US dominance as the sole superpower. However, even in this case, the soft-balancing analysis falters. The European Union was not unified in its reaction to United States policy in Iraq; many of the EU countries participated in the United States' coalition of the willing. Additionally, the soft-balancing analysis does not explain the "charm offensive" that occurred on both sides of the Atlantic after the crisis and Bush's reelection.[76] According to *The Economist*, "By autumn 2005, things seemed so smooth that senior American officials visiting Paris would marvel at how pleasant it is to hold talks about what the two countries could do together."[77] Indeed, by summer 2006, the French and the United States were collaborating on a UN resolution to bring an end to hostilities in Israel and Lebanon. Had soft balancing been the goal, France would have worked with its EU partners and left the United States out. Finally, Brooks and Wohlforth, in their article "Hard Times for Soft Balancing," are persuasive in arguing that European behavior during the Iraq crisis is better explained by economic interests, domestic electoral pressures, regional security concerns, and jockeying for bargaining positions rather than a collective European effort to foil US policy.[78]

From a traditional security analysis standpoint, the ESDP makes almost no sense. NATO is still alive and well and the most important organization in the defense of the European continent. Rather than being a reaction to the United States' turning its back on NATO, the ESDP may well be weakening the Atlantic Alliance and encouraging isolationist tendencies in the United States. Moreover, military solutions seem less useful than ever against the nontraditional security threats facing Europe today. In fact, prominent Europeans themselves criticize the United States for its short-sighted military approach to these problems. Both the battle groups and the European Rapid Reaction Force, even when operational, will have almost no impact whatsoever on the balance of power or be able to lessen the dominance of the United States. Finally, soft balancing falls short as an explanation for the ESDP; it could not have been a reaction to a change in the balance of power because of timing, and the pursuit of the military aspect is out of place in this context.

## International Institutionalist Perspective on the ESDP

*Hypothesis 2: The EU Needs the ESDP to Help Police the World*

Rather than seeing the ESDP as vital to the defense of Europe, international institutionalists stress the responsibility the Europeans have both to the world and to international organizations, and how the ESDP could be useful in furthering the aims of peace. According to Javier Solana, "Now that it's growing bigger and will soon have 450 million inhabitants, Europe must live up better to its global responsibility."[79] The European Security Strategy states explicitly that the size of the European Union in terms of gross national product, population, and number of members is the main reason why the EU should pursue an ESDP and share its "responsibility for global security and in building a better world."[80] Seeing the United States as a "reluctant sheriff,"[81] the Europeans could step in and share the burden of policing the world. Charles Kupchan agreed, arguing that Europe needs a security identity for when the United States does not want to get involved.[82] In doing so, the EU could support both NATO and the United Nations as well as be an active player in conflict management.[83] Brooks and Wohlforth asserted that the EU needs an ESDP to deal with regional security concerns: "Indeed, the forces that the Europeans are actually seeking to create complement, rather than compete with, U.S. capabilities because they provide additional units for dealing with Balkans-style contingencies or peacekeeping missions abroad."[84] Salmon and Shepherd argued that "given its enhanced crisis management capabilities, ESDP may reduce the burden on the United States to maintain peace and stability in and around Europe."[85]

*Counterargument to Hypothesis 2:*
*The Costs of the ESDP Are So High That Politicians Are*
*Unwilling to Pay for Them, Thereby Making the ESDP Ineffective*

Why is the EU concerned with reducing the burden on the United States in maintaining peace and stability? Why is the EU ready to create an ESDP in order to be "deputy" to the United States' "reluctant sheriff"? Rather than focusing on the usefulness to the EU, the above arguments focus on the usefulness of the ESDP to the US, NATO, and the United Nations. In this context, developing the ESDP represents a *desire,* as opposed to a *necessity.* There is no *need* for the ESDP per se. Rather, without any direct threats to the EU, no imperative for an ESDP, on a collective basis, exists. Do the benefits of an ESDP to the EU outweigh the costs?

Practically speaking, a European security and defense policy is difficult and costly. The European Union member states have generous social-welfare nets and national pension schemes facing ever-increasing demands from aging populations. With healthcare costs and the number of elderly rising, governments have come and will continue to come under financial pressure to provide for their people.[86] To make matters worse, the sluggishness of the European economies from 2000 to 2005 make finding the money to pay for a military force politically difficult. Enlargement is also problematic; much of EU funding is now directed toward the twelve new Eastern member states, especially in the form of Common Agricultural Policy (CAP) subsidies.

Furthermore, most European armies are shrinking as states abandon universal conscription—i.e., a cheap form of military labor—for more expensive volunteer forces. Since Portugal changed to a professional army, 70 percent of its defense budget now goes to salaries.[87] As a result, "The general degree of militarization in Western European populations has thus sunk and is still sinking."[88] European military capabilities are decreasing.[89] Considering that most European Union member states' governments do not perceive any direct military threats, defense spending in EU countries has been steadily decreasing as well. As stated earlier, almost all countries that have been both EU and NATO members since 1986 have significantly reduced their defense spending since the end of the Cold War.[90] To address this issue, NATO governments agreed informally to keep defense expenditures at a minimum of 2 percent of GDP. At a NATO defense ministers meeting in June 2005, General James Jones, the United States' most senior soldier in Europe, expressed his disapproval. "Sadly for the alliance most nations are slipping behind the so-called gentleman's agreement at [NATO's 2002 summit in] Prague. . . . The 2 percent floor is becoming a ceiling."[91]

Moreover, the defense spending figures show neither the fragmentation of the defense spending nor how much the Europeans get in return. Although the twenty-five EU member states spend a total of 160 billion euros on defense, France, Germany, Italy, Spain, Sweden (not a NATO member), and the UK account for over 80 percent of total EU defense spending and about 98 percent of military research and development expenditure.[92] In its 2004–2005 report, the Select Committee on European Union of the UK House of Lords laments,

European defence spending trails far behind that of the United States. . . . In 2004, the US spent more than twice as much on defence as the 25 EU Member States combined. Moreover, due to the fragmented EU defence markets and disparate procurement policies, the EU as a whole receives much less value in exchange for its military spending than the US.[93]

Considering the EU budget row of 2005 over the British rebate and CAP reform,[94] the ESDP remains problematic economically. "The insistence by powerful national capitals on slashing the budget and shifting more EU spending to domestic economic programs carries sober implications for the union's external security and foreign development policy ambitions."[95]

In the end, the usefulness of an ESDP may be more symbolic than anything else. According to Simon Duke, the ESS seems "to dwell upon what could arise if the Union does not assume its responsibilities for global security."[96] He argued that

> the Union's main contribution to a "better world" appears to be primarily that of exemplar where "relations between our states, and the lives of our citizens" have been transformed. [The EU] sees its main global role as "contributing to better governance through assistance programmes, conditionality and targeted trade measures."[97]

If Duke's analysis is correct, then the lack of follow-through is understandable. By the same token, if true, then the EU will play a limited role in world policing.

Ultimately, the ESDP could be useful to both NATO and the UN, but cannot be justified because of the cost involved. Perhaps more importantly, EU politicians are not following through with the money necessary to make the EU an effective actor in crisis management. Many politicians speak of the responsibility Europe has to play its role in the world; yet why is this feeling of responsibility so pressing after the end of the Cold War? Why does the EU specifically have to play this role, as opposed to channeling it through NATO with a European pillar? Most puzzling, if indeed the EU member states are determined to live up to their responsibility, why has so little been achieved in this regard? Why have they not followed through with increased military spending?

## The Integrationist Perspective

### Hypothesis 3: The ESDP Is the Natural, Next Stage of European Integration

Finally, the ESDP is justified in terms of European integration. Rather than seeing the ESDP as revolution, it should be seen as evolution. Discussion of the ESDP should be seen as part and parcel of years of security cooperation among the EU member states. The ESDP is a sign of the coming of age or maturity of the European Union. The creation of the CFSP, along with the ESDP, will allow the EU to assert its rightful voice in the international arena.

The ESDP can trace its roots to the 1950s. Before the formation of the European Community, after the Korean War broke out in 1950, the United States pushed the Europeans to integrate their national armies under one European command. Although this European Defense Community (EDC) ultimately failed, the member states continued to discuss ways to coordinate their foreign and security policies, from the Fouchet Report of 1961 to the formation of European Political Cooperation (EPC) in 1973. The Single European Act of 1987 added to European cooperation in this area. Admiral Rafael de Morales, director of the WEU Planning Cell, called the ESDI "one of the final steps of this evolution."[98] Even the US Department of Defense is convinced: "[T]he development of a foreign and security policy . . . is a natural, even an inevitable, part of the development of broader European integration."[99]

Frédéric Bozo saw the ESDP as a sign of the EU's vitality. "[T]he devolution of the defense role to the Union is part of a dual dynamic of legitimacy and efficacy. The legitimacy dynamic stems from the fact that if European defense has been revitalized by its wholehearted assignment to the EU, it benefits fully—without the damper of the WEU—from the political vitality intrinsic to the Union."[100] As Tomas Valasek, director of the Center for Defense Information (CDI) in Brussels, a defense think tank, argued, EU defense plans have "little" to do with the United States. Rather, it is a sign of an "EU coming of age" and deeper European integration.[101] One EU-based journalist argued, "[T]he doctrine marks the coming of age of a more assertive and self-confident Europe, determined to forge what EU leaders meeting in Greece last week insisted would be a relationship based on 'equal footing' with Washington."[102]

Many academics and politicians alike use this term, "coming of age," when discussing the EU's defense capability.[103] Joschka Fischer, German foreign minister, stated that, although the United States may not understand the integration process, where the ESDP is concerned, the EU is "coming of age."[104] François Bujon de l'Estang, French ambassador to the United States, explained,

[T]he "Franco-German defense concept" is not in contradiction with Transatlantic commitments, quite to the contrary. If you read it carefully, it is full of references to the Transatlantic partnership and to NATO as well as to European defense. But it is an expression of the fact that Europe is coming of age, and that coming of age in the international arena entails taking over defense responsibilities.[105]

This "coming of age" is a metaphor for asserting a stronger voice on the international stage.

Despite years of discussion about the role of the European Union in foreign, security, and defense affairs, there is no reason to see the ESDP as a natural end. For decades, the European integration project has been seen as a peaceful one that exerts its influence as a civilian power rather than as a military one. This civilian identity has distinguished it from the more militaristic United States. Moreover, there is little reason to see the ESDP as part of a natural evolution of the EU, considering how divided the member states are about it. The strong divisions among the integrationists, the Atlanticists, and the neutrals have stymied the ESDP's progress. Finally, why is a common defense policy necessary for the EU "to assert its identity on the international scene"?

*Counterargument to Hypothesis 3: Rather Than "Evolution,"*
*Adding a Military Dimension Was a Conscious Decision*
*to Break with Past Images of the EU as a Civilian Power*

There is no reason to see the addition of the military aspect of the European Union as part of its natural progression. Rather, having a common security and defense policy complicates matters, as the European Union has traditionally defined itself as a civilian power.

In the 1970s, François Duchêne, a key advisor to Jean Monnet, made the argument that the EC had successfully replaced military power relationships in Europe (for example, as between France and Germany) with civilian economic ties.

> Europe would be the first major area of the Old World where the age-old process of war and indirect violence could be translated into something more in tune with the twentieth-century citizen's notion of civilized politics. In such a context, Western Europe could in a sense be the first of the world's civilian centres of power.[106]

Having rendered traditional power relationships obsolete, military competition among EC partners would become impossible. Moreover, the EC, as a civilian power, would have little to fear from external aggression because of the strength of the European Community's economic power.[107]

Therefore, the European Community has long been described and defined as a civilian power. When describing the foreign relations policy and power of the EC, Christopher Hill concluded that the most accurate description is that of "civilian power"; in other words, one where all external political influence comes from economic and not military power.[108] Such a characterization is not a bad thing, in Hill's eyes; he believed that a "civilian-power Europe" is better than a "superpower Europe," because the latter would go against the EU's intrinsic nature.[109]

For other academics, including Roy Ginsberg, the EC was living proof of realism's shortcomings as an international relations theory. Rather than pursue power in the traditional sense, the EC was a peaceful, civilian, economic community with no military ambitions.

> Set against an international backdrop that is anarchic and power hungry under neorealist rubrics, the EC is an example of interstate cooperation even when the costs are high to its constituent members. Not a military body, the EC does not seek to increase military power, but rather concentrates on achieving economic goals such as growth and development.[110]

More recently, Ginsberg wrote, "[R]egardless of the fate of the CFSP, the foreign political, economic and diplomatic influence of the EU will still be largely defined by the traditional Rome Treaty–based civilian actions still found in Pillar One."[111] Others, including Lily Gardner Feldman, David Long, and Michael E. Smith, have argued that the EU's impact on the world is unique precisely *because* it is not a military superpower.[112] David Allen and Michael Smith argued that the EU has been so impotent militarily that it can only be considered a civilian power.[113] Finally, Christopher Piening maintained that the EU is a global power, but as its strength does not come from military power, it is simply in a "class of its own."[114]

Many German and Nordic writers have taken great pride in the civilian nature of European integration. Dieter Senghaas,[115] Bjorn Hettne,[116] and Pekka Sivonen have all posited that military power would have limited utility in the future. Sivonen argued that, instead, European peace should be secured through the creation of "a network of institutionalized rules for internal and international state behavior."[117] In a later work, Hill agreed; the EU's status as a civilian power "made it perfectly suited to take the lead in an environment where military force now suddenly seemed irrelevant."[118] Why, then, did the EC decide to create a security and defense identity at the end of the Cold War, when Eastern and Western Europe were to be reconciled, and when so many believed that military power was becoming irrelevant? Considering this long history of a cultivated, civilian identity, there is no reason to believe that a common defense or military force is a natural part of the evolution of European integration.

Peter van Ham has named the person who changed the EU's identity:

> The EU often takes pride in its "soft power," the ability to influence events by diplomatic rather than coercive means. But influenced by the British diplomat Robert Cooper—the most prominent strategic thinker within the European Council—the EU Strategy now aims to go beyond mere "soft power" and "get real." Cooper argues that Europe needs to understand that the world beyond the cozy confines of today's post-modern EU is still characterized by hard-nosed *Realpolitik* where military power remains an essential policy instrument to avert threats and get things done. Cooper believes that Europe can no longer wait and hope that the rest of the world will soon recognize and emulate the bliss of its own oft-heralded model of Kantian peace and prosperity. Instead, the EU has to become an active and, if necessary, forceful global player prepared to fight for its own interests. Obviously, Cooper's ideas have provoked heated debates within the EU, ruffling feathers of all kinds, especially those of member states who cling to the obsolete *Zivilmacht* model.[119]

In other words, rather than being a natural part of the EU's evolution, the decision to add a military aspect to the EU was done consciously and not without controversy. Nevertheless, the controversy regarding the role and image of the EU began with the debate over the CFSP during the Maastricht negotiations in 1991.

Interestingly, just as academics were praising the EC for its civilian nature and how the EC would become a beacon of peace and civility for the world, the member states decided to abandon the identity of soft power and replace it with a security and defense identity. Despite general agreement on the idea, the member states are very divided on how to proceed, so much so that Mette Eilstrup-Sangiovanni has argued that the ESDP is "bad" for Europe, as it wastes resources and is divisive.[120] Since the first discussions of the Common Foreign and Security Policy under the aegis of the Maastricht negotiations, member states have been divided, more or less, into three camps: the Atlanticists (the United Kingdom, Denmark, Portugal, and, to a lesser extent, the Netherlands), the integrationists (France, Germany, Italy, Belgium, Luxembourg, Greece, and Spain), and the neutrals (Ireland, later joined by Sweden, Austria, and Finland).

The controversy and divisions among the member states have stymied the development of the ESDP. After its people rejected the Maastricht Treaty in 1992, the Danish government secured an opt-out from participating "in the so-called defence policy dimension."[121] The neutral countries have tried to change the focus from the military to the humanitarian Petersberg tasks. After fifteen years of deliberation, the member states still cannot agree on whether the ESDP should lead to a common defense or how decisions should be made. Compromises such as "enhanced cooperation" (where only coalitions of the willing would act) coupled with Denmark's opt-out mean that in the area of ESDP, there exists a two-speed Europe.

Considering the endurance of these divisions and the long history of the EU as a civilian power, why would the member states in the Maastricht Treaty equate "assert[ing] its voice" with the need to develop a common defense policy possibly leading to a common defense? Certainly, EU leaders would not want to suggest that "coming of age" means hitting puberty and being able to "let off shots," or that a mature political entity must have military power.

In any event, Charlotte Bretherton and John Vogler "see little prospect of the EU assuming a role in collective defense, nor of gaining direct access to military instruments."[122] Rather, "the insecurities affecting Europe are increasingly non-military, and the notion of societal security captures the growing significance of the EU's civilian, 'soft security' instruments."[123] Austrian foreign minister Alois Mock argued that the EU can assert its voice on the world stage without military power:

> Particularly with regard to the non-military security threats of today's Europe . . . the Union alone has the cohesion, the know-how and the resources to tackle these problems with any chance of success. It alone has the capacity to approach risks to stability in a comprehensive manner, taking into account their political, economic and social dimensions.[124]

The US National Intelligence Council's 2020 Project, "Mapping the Global Future," agreed, arguing: "While its military forces have little capacity for power projection, Europe's strength may be in providing, through its commitment to multilateralism, a model of global and regional governance to the rising powers, particularly if they are searching for a 'Western' alternative to strong reliance on the United States."[125]

## Conclusion

From the above analysis, one can conclude that there is no *need* for the European Union to pursue a common defense policy. NATO is still the guarantor of European security. The ESDP is expensive, with weak political support that underlines divisions rather than unifies. It is more likely to compromise NATO, the powerful defense alliance that offers undisputed and proven military protection, rather than strengthen it. Moreover, there have been no—and there are no—emerging threats that require it. Rather, the lack of threat has afforded the Europeans the opportunity to experiment with their security. In other words, were there a serious threat, there would be no ESDP at all.

The need for a separate military organization is dubious. Although support among the public is high for an ESDP—71 percent of EU citizens favor it[126]—the same public does not perceive significant military threats. Rather, in 2001, the three perceived top threats were organized crime, an accident in a nuclear power station, and, third, terrorism.[127] In a 2004 BBC poll, respondents ranked globalization and the United States as the top threat, followed by corruption.[128] In 2006, terrorism was rated first, followed by Iran and global warming.[129] Moreover, in Javier Solana's European Security Strategy, the military is only one arrow in the quiver. His definition of "security threat" is wide and encompassing, including terrorism, nuclear proliferation, and failed states. His prescription is multilateralism, international organizations, economic aid and humanitarian assistance, increased intelligence, and police and judicial cooperation, as well as military cooperation. As John Van Oudenaren explained, "The emphasis in the report is on crisis prevention—taking political and economic steps to ensure that the need for military action will not arise."[130] A defense policy is not necessarily part of a natural process of integration, and the EU can very easily assert its voice on the international stage without such a dimension.

Therefore, the ESDP must be strongly desired to warrant such justifications. Why else would the EU leaders over a period of fifteen years, despite changes in political parties in power, prohibitive expense in a time of budget cuts and military reductions, and awkward divisions among the member states, risk undermining NATO, its security guarantor, and irritating relations with the United States for an underfunded ESDP and not-yet-operational European Rapid Reaction Force whose delays and accompanying rhetoric are often embarrassing? What could be the cause of such very strong desire?

## Notes

1. "Weakness of a Rapid Reaction Force," *Daily Telegraph* (London), 12 June 2001, 23.

2. Martin Farnsdale, former commander, North Atlantic Group (NATO Central Europe), in Sharp, ed., *Europe After an American Withdrawal,* 454.

3. Glaser, "Why NATO Is Still Best," 48.

4. Joffe, "Collective Security," 47.

5. Rynning, "Why Not NATO?" 53–54.

6. Isokova, "ESDP After the EU Constitution," *RUSI Journal* (February 2005): 33.

7. As formally announced in the Charter of Paris on 21 November 1990 at the CSCE Paris summit, *Financial Times* (London), 22 November 1990.

8. As decided by the Soviet republics in the Alma Alta Declaration of 21–22 December 1991, *Financial Times* (London), 23 December 1991.

9. Germany was unified on 3 October 1990.

10. Heisbourg, "The European-US Alliance," 667.

11. Haydon, "War on the Rise in Europe, Down in Asia," *Reuters*, 16 June 1994.

12. Mearsheimer, "Back to the Future," 5–56.

13. "Defense Minister Rules Out Peace Dividend," Foreign Broadcast Information Service, FBIS-WEU-91-085, 2 May 1991.

14. "Deus Pinheiro Interviewed on EC, Other Issues," Foreign Broadcast Information Service, FBIS-WEU-91-186, 25 September 1991.

15. "Hurd on EC, NATO Controversies, US Links," Foreign Broadcast Information Service, FBIS-WEU-91-209, 29 October 1991.

16. In May 1990, Spanish minister Fernández Ordóñez initiated the Conference on Security and Cooperation in the Mediterranean (CSCM) to focus more attention on the region. In a poll in 1991, 98 percent of Spanish leaders responded that stability in the Maghreb region was vital to Spanish security. Esther Barbé, "Spanish Responses to the Security Institutions of the New Europe," in *Reorganizing Eastern Europe*, ed. Andrew J. Williams, 67. In 1994, Italian defense minister Cesare Previti called Islamic fundamentalism in Algeria and other Arab countries in the Mediterranean a "powder keg that could explode from one moment to the next, and explode not only beyond our frontiers but here in our own home." "Islamic Fundamentalism Threatens Italy—Minister," *Reuters*, 20 July 1994 (online wire service).

17. Interview with Yves Mollard La Bruyère, consultant for the Secretariat General (Directorate F) of the European Commission and former political administrator for France in the Political Affairs Department of NATO, Brussels, 5 May 1993.

18. As quoted in Lionel Barber, "End Reliance on US, Says Envoy," *Financial Times* (London), 25 May 1993.

19. "US Military Making More Overseas Cuts," *Reuters*, 27 October 1994.

20. Salmon and Shepard, *Toward a European Army*, 211. The number 100,000 is disputed. Salmon and Shepherd say under 100,000, but the figure 120,000 was reported by Peter Spiegel, "Senator Condemns Pentagon Move to Cut the Number of US Troops Based in Europe," *Financial Times* (London), 5 March 2004, 6; while the Heritage Foundation says 110,000 at http://heritage .org/Research/NationalSecurity/cda04-11.cfm and at http://www.heritage.org/ Research/NationalSecurity/troopMarch2005.xls.

21. Hyde-Price, "'Normative' Power Europe: A Realist Critique," *Journal of European Public Policy* 13 (2006): 229.

22. Even Eisenhower, who was extremely pro-European and anticommunist, did not want US troops to stay in Europe, because of the expense. He said, "A foreign soldier is cheaper than an American soldier." Once in a conversation with General Andrew J. Goodpaster, at the time special secretary liaison to the Department of Defense, Eisenhower said that it was US policy to get US troops

out of Europe as soon as possible. Goodpaster responded, "But Mr. President, there is a qualification to this: that the Europeans must first build up their own defense capabilities." The president then said, "I'm going to get Foster Dulles in here and he'll straighten you out on this." Dulles came into the room and reiterated Goodpaster's point. The president could only sigh and say "I've lost my only friend." As told to the author in an interview with General Andrew J. Goodpaster on 21 July 1993 in Washington, D.C.

23. See, for example, the Mansfield Resolution, 31 August 1966, cited in Sherwood, *Allies in Crisis*, 126.

24. As reported in Quentin Peel, "Quayle Warns EU on GATT Talks; Failure to Liberalise Trade Could Encourage US to Pull Troops out of NATO," *Financial Times* (London), 10 February 1992, 1.

25. As quoted in François Raitberger, "WEU Told of Danger from North Africa, Troop Cuts," *Reuters,* 15 June 1994.

26. As quoted in "De Michelis on EC Common Defense Policy," FBIS-WEU-91-152, 7 August 1991, 25–26. In the interview, De Michelis approved of the use of the term "collective security system" to define the EC security project.

27. Dr. Fraser Cameron, interview by author, Brussels, Belgium, 22 March 1993. Dr. Cameron was a consultant for the Secretariat General (Directorate F) of the European Commission.

28. As quoted in Lisbeth Kirk, "Europe Must Defend Itself, Says Military Chief," *euobserver.com*, 19 January 2004.

29. As quoted in Andrew Grice and Colin Brown, "Britain Needs Trident as It Cannot Rely on US, Says Blair," *Independent* (UK), 5 December 2006.

30. NATO-Russia Compendium of Financial and Economic Data Relating to Defence, Defence Expenditures of NRC Countries (1980–2004), 9–10 June 2005, at http://www.nato.int/docu/pr/2005/p050609e.htm.

31. As quoted in *Europe Daily Bulletin* 5429, 11/12 February 1991, 4.

32. "What to Do with the WEU," *The Economist*, 2 February 1991, 30.

33. *Europe Daily Bulletin* 5606, 9 November 1991, 4.

34. David Gardner, "Crisis in Yugoslavia; EC Dashes into Its Own Backyard—Ministers Making Fresh Trip in Attempt to Salvage Peace Package," *Financial Times*, 1 July 1991, 2.

35. Cimbalo, "Saving NATO from Europe," 83.

36. William Pfaff, "Denmark, for One, Hopes to Keep American Troops in Europe," *International Herald Tribune*, 20 February 1992, 6.

37. Lindley-French, "In the Shade of Locarno? Why European Defence Is Failing," 789–811.

38. US secretary of state Madeleine Albright, press conference, NATO HQ, Brussels, Belgium, 8 December 1998; at http://www.nato.int/docu/speech/1998/s981208x.htm. Other sources cite her as saying "no decoupling, no discrimination, and no duplication" later on. However, in the press conference on December 8, four days after the declaration, she used the words "no diminution" rather than "no decoupling."

39. F. Stephen Larrabee, prepared statement, "The European Security and Defense Identity (ESDI) and American Interests Before the Senate Committee on Foreign Relations," Subcommittee on European Affairs, Federal News Service, 9 March 2000, 4. At the time, he worked for the RAND Corporation.

40. Office for International Security Affairs, US Department of Defense,

"United States Security Strategy for Europe and NATO," at http://www.defense link.mil/pubs/europe/-#toc.

41. NBC News/*Wall Street Journal* poll conducted by the polling organizations of Peter Hart (D) and Robert Teeter (R), 17–19 April 1999; and Pew Research Center poll conducted by Princeton Survey Research Associates, 24–30 March 1999, at http://www.pollingreport.com/defense.htm#NATO. See also German Marshall Fund, Transatlantic Trends 2006.

42. See Sloan, *NATO, the European Union, and the Atlantic Community;* Holmes, *The United States and Europe After the Cold War;* and Hunter, *The European Security and Defense Policy.*

43. Glaser, "Why NATO Is Still Best," 5–50.

44. Ministry of Defence, *The Future Strategic Context for Defence* (London: Ministry of Defence, 2001), assumes at para. 64: "'No conventional military threats to the UK are likely to emerge over the period to 2030.' The UK has recently indicated that the present generation of main battle tank will be its last." In Alexander and Garden, "The Arithmetic of Defence Policy," 509, fn. 1.

45. Representative II of the Permanent Representation of Germany to the European Union, interview by author, Brussels, Belgium, 7 December 2005.

46. European Security Strategy, "A Secure Europe in a Better World," Brussels, Belgium, 12 December 2003.

47. Salmon and Shepherd, *Toward a European Army,* 5. Emphasis added.

48. Mark Leonard and Richard Gowan, *Global Europe: Implementing the European Security Strategy* (Brussels: The British Council, 2004), at http://fpc.org.uk/fsblob/-187.pdf.

49. As reported in Ed McCullough, "Summit May Favor Tackling Causes of Terrorism over Military Response," Associated Press, 7 March 2005.

50. Reply by Hubert Védrine, minister of foreign affairs, to a question in the National Assembly, 2 June 2002, at http://www.un.int/france/documents _anglais/020206_mae_vedrine_amerique_2.htm, and found in Ian Davis, "A Long Way from Consensus: Threat Perceptions in European NATO and the Future of Missile Defense," presented to the Conference on Transatlantic Missile Defence sponsored by the George C. Marshall European Center for Security Studies in cooperation with the Office of the Secretary of Defense for International Security Policy, Garmisch-Partenkirchen, Germany, 5–7 April 2004, at http://www.basicint.org/nuclear/NMD/marshall.htm.

51. Chris Patten, "Engagement Is Not Liberal Mush," *New Perspectives Quarterly* 19 (2002): 36–38; and ibid.

52. Jack Straw, British foreign secretary, remarks to the Brookings Institution, Washington, D.C., 8 May 2002; and ibid.

53. The North Atlantic Treaty, Article III, at www.nato.int/docu/basictxt/ treaty.htm.

54. Atlantic Alliance Strategic Concept, approved by the heads of state and government at a meeting of the North Atlantic Council in Washington, D.C., 23 and 24 April 1999, at http://www.nato.int/docu/pr/1999/p99-065e.htm.

55. At NATO Topics, "Pakistan Earthquake Relief Operation," at http://www.nato.int/issues/pakistan_earthquake/index.html.

56. "Weakness of a Rapid Reaction Force," *Daily Telegraph* (London), 12 June 2001, 23. Emphasis added.

57. Tomas Valasek, "No Will, No Way on European Defense," *Wall Street Journal*, 2 October 2003, A11.

58. As quoted in Jolyon Howorth, "The EU, NATO and the Quest for European Autonomy," in *Defending Europe*, ed. Howorth and Keeler, 3–4.

59. Jones, *The Rise of European Security Cooperation*, 9.

60. "To Paris, U.S. Looks Like a 'Hyperpower,'" *International Herald Tribune*, 5 February 1999, 5.

61. "EU Poll: Israel Is Top Peace Threat," *MSNBC*, 3 November 2003, at http://www.msnbc.com/news/988413.asp?0cv=CB20&cp1=1.

62. Daniel Dombey and Stanley Pignal, "Europeans See US as Threat to Peace," *Financial Times* (London), 1 July 2007.

63. Ibid.

64. Salmon and Shepherd, *Toward a European Army*, 2–3.

65. Brooks and Wohlforth, "Hard Times for Soft Balancing," 92.

66. Andrew Mathewson, Minutes of Evidence Taken Before the Select Committee on the European Union (Sub-Committee C), Question 30, 19 January 2006, at http://www.publications.parliament.uk/pa/ld200506/ldselect/ldeucom/125/6011901.htm.

67. Art, "Striking a Balance," 177.

68. Pape, "Soft Balancing Against the United States," 8–9. A similar argument is supported by Paul, "Soft Balancing in the Age of U.S. Primacy," 46–71.

69. Nye, *Soft Power*, 5.

70. Aysha, "September 11," 193.

71. As quoted in Cogan, *The Third Option*, 104.

72. André Dumoulin, "Les ambitions de l'Europe: de l'après-Kosovo aux indicateurs de coherence," *Politique Étrangère* 2 (2000): 488, as quoted in Cogan, *The Third Option*, 110.

73. European Council Declaration, Strengthening the Common European Policy of Security and Defence (Annex III), European Council, Cologne, 3–4 June 1999.

74. "Capability Improvement Chart I/2005," Council of the European Union, at http://ue.eu.int/ueDocs/cms_Data/docs/pressData/en/misc/84902.pdf.

75. Lord Truscott, Minutes of Evidence Taken Before the Select Committee on the European Union (Sub-Committee C), Question 28, 19 January 2006, at http://www.publications.parliament.uk/pa/ld200506/ldselect/ldeucom/125/6011901.htm.

76. James Kitfield, "Charm Offensive," *National Journal* 37 (2005): 516–520.

77. Sylvie Kauffmann, "France and America Make Up," Special Issue: The World in 2006, *The Economist*: 77.

78. Brooks and Wohlforth, "Hard Times for Soft Balancing," 72–108.

79. As reported in "Solana Outlines Goals of European Security Strategy," Deutsche Presse-Agentur, 22 September 2003.

80. European Security Strategy, "A Secure Europe in a Better World," Brussels, Belgium, 12 December 2003, 1, at www.consilium.eu.int/uedocs/cmsUpload/78367.pdf.

81. Haas, *The Reluctant Sheriff*.

82. See, for example, Kupchan, *The End of the American Era*.

83. Salmon and Shepherd, *Toward a European Army*, 5.

84. Brooks and Wohlworth, "Hard Times for Soft Balancing," 91–92.

85. Salmon and Shepherd, *Toward a European Army,* 3.

86. See, "A Tale of Two Bellies: Demography in America and Europe," *The Economist,* 24 August 2002.

87. *Europe Daily Bulletin* (Brussels), 4 June 2004, 6–7.

88. For a more detailed investigation, see Haltiner, "The Definite End of the Mass Army in Western Europe?" 13.

89. Select Committee on European Union, "European Defence Agency: Report with Evidence," Ninth Report of Session 2004–2005, Chapter 3, 15, United Kingdom Parliament, House of Lords.

90. "NATO-Russia Compendium of Financial and Economic Data Relating to Defence, Defence Expenditures of NRC Countries (1980–2004)," 9–10 June 2005, at http://www.nato.int/docu/pr/2005/p050609e.htm. Only eleven countries have been members of both organizations since 1986: France, Germany, Italy, Belgium, Luxembourg, the Netherlands, the United Kingdom, Greece, Spain, Portugal, and Denmark. Although many other countries joined NATO during the 1990s, they did not join the EU until 2004.

91. Daniel Dombey, "US NATO Chief Chides Europeans over Budgets," *Financial Times*, 9 June 2005, 8.

92. Select Committee on European Union, "European Defence Agency: Report with Evidence."

93. Ibid.

94. Honor Mahony, "Anglo-French Row over EU Budget Worsens," *euobserver.com*, 13 June 2005.

95. Brooks Tigner, "Summit 'Fiasco': Lack of Action on Defense, Security Leaves EU at Risk," *Defense News,* 27 June 2005, 12.

96. Duke, "The European Security Strategy," 463.

97. Ibid., 469, and the European Security Strategy, 10.

98. Admiral Rafael de Morales, "The European Security and Defense Identity," colloquy, Madrid, 5 May 1998, at http://www.nato.int/docu/colloq/c980504/d980505a.htm. Morales was director of the WEU Planning Cell "Multinational Forces and Their Relations with NATO and WEU."

99. US Department of Defense, *Strengthening Transatlantic Security: A US Strategy for the 21st Century* (Washington, DC: Government Printing Office, 2000), at http://www.pdgs.org.ar/featured/fea-sts-indice.htm.

100. Frédéric Bozo, "The Effects of Kosovo and the Danger of Decoupling," in Howorth and Keeler, *Defending Europe*, 73.

101. Tomas Valasek as quoted in his speech, "European Security Strategy: Is It for Real?" from "Security for a New Century: A Study Group Report," The Henry L. Stimson Center,Washington, D.C., 9 February 2004, available at http://www.stimson.org/newcentury/pdf/020904Valasek.pdf.

102. Shada Islam, "The EU's First-Ever Security Doctrine," Yale Center for the Study of Globalization, 2003, at http://yaleglobal.yale.edu/display.article?id=2023.

103. Sten Rynning, "Coming of Age? The European Union's Security and Defence Policy," Odense: CFES Working Paper No. 10, 2003. See also François de Rose, "A European Pillar in the Alliance?" *NATO at Fifty*, The Eisenhower Institute, at http://www.eisenhowerinstitute.org/programs/globalpartnerships/securityandterrorism/coalition/usandnato/NATOatFiftyBook/deRose.htm; and

Charles Kupchan, "The End of the West," *Atlantic Monthly* (November 2002), at http://www.cfr.org/publication.php?id=-5101.

104. Speech by Joschka Fischer, German federal minister for foreign affairs, at the 36th Munich Conference on Security Policy, 5 February 2000, at http://www.germany-info.org/relaunch/politics/speeches/020500.html.

105. François Bujon de l'Estang, "The French-German Relations, Europe and the Transatlantic Partnership," joint conference with the French and German ambassadors, University of Berkeley, 26 February 1998, and University of Stanford, 27 February 1998, at http://www.ambafrance-us.org/news/statmnts/1998/buj2702.asp. See also his speech "France, Europe and the Transatlantic Partnership," San Diego State University, 18 April 1996, at http://www.ambafrance-us.org/news/statmnts/1996/statem2.asp.

106. Duchêne, "Europe's Role in World Peace," 43.

107. Ibid.

108. See Twitchett, ed., *Europe and the World,* 8.

109. Hill, "European Foreign Policy: Power Bloc, Civilian Power—or Flop?" 54.

110. See Ginsberg, *Foreign Policy Actions of the European Community,* 12.

111. Roy Ginsberg, "The EU's CFSP: The Politics of Procedure," in *Common Foreign and Security Policy*, ed. Holland, 14.

112. See Lily Gardner Feldman, "Reconciliation and External Diplomacy," in *Legitimacy and the European Union,* ed. Banchoff and Smith; and David Long, "Multilateralism in the CFSP," in *Common Foreign and Security Policy,* ed. Holland. See also Michael E. Smith, "Beyond Bargaining: The Institutional-ization of Foreign Policy Co-operation in the European Community, 1970–1996," PhD thesis, University of California–Irvine, 1998, as cited in Ginsberg, "Conceptualizing the European Union," 445.

113. See David Allen and Michael Smith, "The European Union's Security Presence in the Contemporary International Arena," in *The European Union,* ed. Rhodes.

114. Piening, *Global Europe,* 196.

115. Senghaas, *Friedensprojekt Europa.*

116. Hettne, "Security and Peace in Post–Cold War Europe," 279–294.

117. Sivonen, "European Security: New, Old and Borrowed," 385.

118. Hill, "Closing the Capabilities-Expectations Gap," 21.

119. Van Ham, "Europe Gets Real: The New Security Strategy Shows the EU's Geopolitical Maturity," *AICGS Advisor* (2004), at http://www.aicgs.org/analysis/c/-vanham.aspx.

120. Eilstrup-Sangiovanni, "Why a Common Security and Defense Policy Is Bad for Europe," 193–206.

121. "Denmark in Europe," document attached to a letter from the Danish prime minister Poul Schluter to the British prime minister John Major, dated 30 October 1992 (photocopy).

122. Bretherton and Vogler, *The European Union as a Global Actor,* 221.

123. Ibid., 222.

124. Alois Mock, "Austria's Role in the New Europe," *NATO Review* (March 1995): 17, as cited in Bretherton and Vogler, *The European Union as a Global Actor,* 222.

125. National Intelligence Council 2020 Project, "Mapping the Global Future," at http://www.cia.gov/nic/NIC_globaltrend2020.html.

126. *Eurobarometer* 57 (May 2002). See also *Eurobarometer* 59 (June 2003) for similar statistics.

127. See *Eurobarometer* 54.1, as cited in *Eurobarometer* special survey by Philippe Manigart, "Public Opinion and European Defence," July 2001, at http://europa.eu.int/comm/public_opinion/archives/ebs/ebs_146_en.pdf.

128. "Globalisation 'Bigger Threat Than Terror,'" BBC News, 9 April 2004, at HYPERLINK http://news.bbc.co.uk/2/hi/uk_news/3613217.stm.

129. "Transatlantic Trends: Key Findings 2006," German Marshall Fund, 7.

130. John Van Oudenaren, "The Solana Security Paper," talking article at the American Institute for Contemporary German Studies, The Johns Hopkins University, at http://www.aicgs.org/analysis/c/solana.aspx.

# 3

# Nation Building and the ESDP

———————■———————

[Security] is not a mechanical problem. . . . [A]n exact balance is impossible . . . because while powers may appear to outsiders as factors in a security arrangement, they appear domestically as expressions of a historical existence. No power will submit to a settlement, however well-balanced and however "secure," which seems totally to deny its vision of itself. ■ HENRY A. KISSINGER[1]

Social constructivism and nation-building theory explain what seems irrational. Why expend so much time, money, and energy on a divisive and controversial policy that could undermine the organization responsible for European defense? The answer lies in sociological understandings of identity. Ronald L. Jepperson, Alexander Wendt, and Peter J. Katzenstein argued that "the security environments in which states are embedded are in important part cultural and institutional, rather than just material."[2] In other words, the ESDP should not be evaluated solely on its material aspects, but also on its cultural, institutional, and symbolic value. When evaluated in terms of its power projection or its ability to balance threats, the ESDP is weak, at best. When evaluated as a tool to create popular support for European integration, the ESDP becomes invaluable. Through a relatively modest investment in the ESDP, the European Union can take steps to strengthen domestic support for European integration while building and reinforcing a sense of shared history and establishing Europe as a major force in world affairs. As a framework, constructivism explains the process through which the ESDP can, borrowing from Benedict Anderson, create an imagined, but by no means imaginary, community.

## The Goal of the ESDP:
## A Tool for Nation Building in Europe

Is the EU, a nonstate actor, pursuing a common security policy for defense reasons, or to separate itself from US security policy in order to enhance and solidify its European identity? Rather than being in a "cocoon," as Henry Hyde (R-IL) put it,[3] the EU has pursued its own security and defense policy as a way to increase its stature on the world stage and among its people at home; in other words, the ESDP is for nation-building purposes[4] and not for defense per se.

The EU needs to broaden its appeal among the peoples of Europe. Too often now, referenda in EU member states are unsuccessful and kill the momentum necessary to integrate. The ESDP can be used to distinguish what is European and to broaden the EU's base of support. US policy is a likely target: one way to make the once fifteen—now twenty-seven—different nations feel "European" is to show and reinforce that they are collectively different from the United States.

Europeans seem to have little to bind them together. To become a member of the EU, the country must have a functioning free-market economy, be a functioning democracy, and be on the European continent. Otherwise, all the current EU countries share is a Christian cultural heritage and a bloody history where, twice in the past one hundred years, the United States has intervened decisively in European wars. The EU's ESDP provides another way to rally its citizens behind European integration. Significantly, of all the institutions, the European populace places the most trust in its countries's militaries; the police come in second.[5] The ESDP not only provides the EU with another attribute of a state, but also serves as a way to create a foreign and security policy distinct from that of the United States, which increases the prestige of the European Union, both among its peoples and abroad.

### Nation Building? In Europe?

"Nation building" must be separated from the concept of "state building," with which it is often confused. Taken in isolation, these two projects differ significantly. State building represents efforts to establish a centralized government organization and to extend that government's authority across the width and breadth of the territory it holds sovereign within the state system. Nation building is more concerned with fostering legitimacy and the formation of a national idea, a national identity among the people living within a defined territory—a national, collective self-awareness.

Nothing in this definition limits nation building to failed states or postconflict reconstruction contexts, despite the emphasis placed on these contexts by recent works on the subject.[6] Similarly, nothing in this definition limits nation building to less developed countries. Admittedly, as a body of literature, nation-building theory expanded tremendously during the political upheaval characterizing new states emerging from colonial empires, especially during the 1950s and 1960s.[7] However, this definition is broadly applicable to any society dealing with a fragmented population exhibiting any number of cleavages. The violence associated with Basque separatism in Spain and the upheaval of Northern Ireland remind one that even ancient, well-established states face considerable nation-building tasks.

Finally, as its emphasis on fostering legitimacy and forming identity would suggest, this definition of nation building does not describe a short-term exercise or event, but a long process. Accordingly, despite the apparent success of the international community's state-building efforts in East Timor, nation building there will take some time. In neighboring Indonesia, for example, nation building remains that state's greatest challenge after nearly sixty years of independence. In the United States, a nation of immigrant communities, nation building is also an ongoing process.

While it is one thing to engage in nation building in individual states, can the concept be applied to such a broad entity as the European Union? In examining the literature of nationalism and national identity, one sees little to suggest that these terms cannot be used in discussing the EU. While Ernest Gellner sensibly cautioned against trying to fix rigid definitions to the terms "nation" and "culture," he did indicate that a nation can be made and held together by a mixture of culture and will. That is, groups that demonstrate an enduring will to live together and are not too culturally diverse can be defined as a nation. However, he asserted that this definition of a nation holds *only* when these elements of will and cultural affinity are shared broadly among the entire population, not merely among elites.[8] Anthony Smith set forth clear requirements for national identity, defining a nation as "a named human population, sharing an historic territory, common myths and historical memories, a mass, public culture, a common economy and common legal rights and duties for all members."[9] The European population has the defined, or at least delimited, territory from the Atlantic to the Urals;[10] decades of economic cooperation and integration have moved Europe toward a common economy; and the integration process has also made great strides in establishing legal rights and duties for Europeans. In terms of culture, Europeans seem relatively homogenous in race, religion, dress, and so on, when compared to populations of other regions—although Europeans might not agree. Still, the integration process provides shared symbols of a common culture, ranging from a flag and an anthem ("Ode to Joy," from Beethoven's Symphony No. 9) to a single currency.

Binding Europeans together with common myths and historical memories presents more of a challenge. From a distance, it may not seem so. European societies share classical philosophical roots, a Christian heritage, as well as other values rooted in their history. In addition, many share histories common to the vast empires that have dominated the continent over the centuries. However, European integrationists are faced with the task of effectively undoing the work of previous generations of nationalists and nation builders in individual European states. As Benedict Anderson observed, in manipulating symbols in the cause of nationalism, nationalists are less inclined to describe the potential glories and accomplishments of a shared future than to evoke memories of the glorious common history of a time when their antecedents made their mark upon the world.[11] One way for European integrationists to solidify a foundation of common historical memory is to make history in the name of Europe, using a truly European security and defense policy.

### Why Nation Building in Europe?

Nationalism has a negative connotation in Europe because of its use by fascists to exterminate people and to foment war. However, nation building need not be limited to creating an "imagined community" only among those of a single race, ethnicity, or religion. Multinational countries such as Canada and Brazil work hard at creating a national identity to bind their countries together. In the case of the United States, a national identity is woven around a civil religion[12] and a creed, rather than the traditional glue of race or language.[13]

Moreover, nationalism is important because it inspires "often profoundly self-sacrificing love. The cultural products of nationalism—poetry, prose fiction, music, plastic arts—show this love very clearly in thousands of different forms and styles."[14] The European Union needs to nation-build in order to build popular support for the integration project; otherwise, the project could well fail.

The integration process may be losing steam. Most decisions regarding the European Union are taken by national parliaments—i.e., the educated elites—with whom the idea of a united Europe has been the most popular.[15] In 2006, more than 75 percent of Europeans polled could not say how many member states there were.[16] Such ignorance can be taken as an indication of apathy. When treaty ratification has been put to a popular vote, the results have been rather underwhelming. The Danes voted no in the first referendum on Maastricht. The French voted yes by only the narrowest of margins.[17] Ireland rejected the Treaty of Nice. Sweden, the UK, and Denmark have refused to join the single currency, the euro. The European Parliament elections of June 2004 reflected this public dissatisfaction with and skepticism toward the EU, with a turnout of just 45.3 percent, the lowest turnout in the history of the assembly. Moreover, in the ten new EU member states, whose populace overwhelmingly voted to join, only 26 percent voted in the 2004 parliamentary elections. To quote parliament spokesman David Harley, it was a "disappointing and pathetically low turnout."[18] Significantly, the Euro-skeptic and right-wing nationalist parties achieved their best results to date across the continent.[19] With regard to the new EU constitution, Spain voted yes, but with a very small turnout. Both France and the Netherlands voted no, putting the constitutional treaty in limbo. Altogether, this public skepticism represents a significant speed bump on the road to European integration.

The European Union faces a daunting nation-building challenge for several reasons: plurilingualism, being an elite-driven project, continuing expansion, and lack of myth. The economic advantages of integration do not sway public opinion. Liesbet Hooghe and Gary Marks believe identity does: "Citizens do indeed take into account the economic consequences of European integration, but conceptions of group membership appear to be more powerful."[20]

Plurilingualism is a serious problem. According to Sue Wright, "Language is a key organising principle of nationalism."[21] She concluded that "the present EU strategy of promoting plurilingualism is admirable in its idealism and concern to maintain equality between groups, but utopian; not all of us will become polyglots."[22] Rather, Wright argued, plurilingualism exacerbates the divide between the people and the elites. She warned, "[W]ithout a community of communication, the European Union must remain a trading association run in an autocratic way by bilingual patrician technocrats."[23]

Simply put, the EU falls short of Gellner's requirement for building a nation out of a sense of shared culture and common will; the European integration process has been and remains an elite-driven project. As a result, as observed by John Peet in *The Economist*, the people are being left behind.[24] Many people believe the European project threatens their own national culture, and even their food. Brigid Laffan pointed out that the

> "European project" itself adds a new dimension to the politics of identity in the Member States and in the wider Europe. The dynamic of integration has implications for how different states and communities define themselves culturally, politically, and economically. The goal of a "Europe without frontiers" changes the nature of borders as system of inclusion and exclusion. Market regulation can threaten long-held traditions (the politics of local beer, cheese or snuff!) in different localities.[25]

In the words of Raymond Aron, a sympathetic critic of European unity efforts, "[T]he name Europe distinguished a continent or a civilisation, not an economic or political unit. . . . The European idea is empty; it has neither the transcendence of Messianic ideologies nor the immanence of concrete patriotism. It was created by intellectuals, and that fact accounts at once for its genuine appeal to the mind and its feeble echo in the heart."[26] Dutch minister for European affairs Atzo Nicolaï noted this problem at the informal ministerial meeting on communicating Europe in 2004. Quoting Jacques Delors, who warned that "you can't fall in love with a single market," Nicolaï recommended using pop stars or sports figures to make Europe recognizable, because the EU lacked personality and "face." The goal was not to replace national identity, but rather to add a European identity.[27] John Bruton, former Irish prime minister, explained, "The EU as a project may engage people intellectually, but it is not engaging them emotionally, in the same way it did in the 1950s. . . . We need to inject emotion."[28]

Nevertheless, the EU has had limited success in developing this second, European identity. In polls, only about 50 percent of EU citizens "feel European." In general, the great majority of Europeans identify themselves with their member states first and with Europe second (see Figure 3.1).[29] Luxembourg is at the highest end, with 27 percent of people polled feeling either "European first" or just "European." At the lowest end are the Finns, of whom only 4 percent feel either "European first" or just "European." On average, only 11 percent of Europeans across the EU feel either "European first" or just "European." National pride has proven itself resilient and is much stronger than European pride.

### Concerns over Eastern Enlargement

Popular enthusiasm for the integration project is further strained by the rapid eastward expansion of the EU itself. At the first anniversary of EU

**Figure 3.1  How Europeans Identify Themselves (percentage)**

| Country | Nationality only | Nationality and European | European and nationality | European only |
|---|---|---|---|---|
| Italy | 20 | 65 | 9 | 4 |
| Luxembourg | 26 | 43 | 13 | 14 |
| Spain | 28 | 60 | 4 | 4 |
| France | 33 | 52 | 9 | 4 |
| Belgium | 34 | 49 | 10 | 5 |
| Denmark | 38 | 55 | 5 | 2 |
| **EU-15** | 38 | 48 | 7 | 4 |
| Germany | 39 | 43 | 10 | 6 |
| Netherlands | 41 | 48 | 7 | 2 |
| Portugal | 43 | 40 | 4 | 2 |
| Austria | 45 | 39 | 11 | 2 |
| Ireland | 47 | 43 | 4 | 3 |
| Greece | 48 | 46 | 4 | 2 |
| Sweden | 54 | 39 | 5 | 1 |
| Finland | 55 | 40 | 3 | 1 |
| United Kingdom | 62 | 28 | 4 | 4 |

Nationality only     European and nationality

Nationality and European     European only

*Source:* Eurobarometer 57, Survey no. 57.1, Fieldwork March 2002–May 2002, figure 4.5.

*Note:* "Don't know" not shown.

enlargement, the *euobserver* headline read, "Mixed Feelings One Year After Enlargement." Despite official assurances of the "happiness" of the day from European Commission president José Manuel Barroso, the *euobserver* wrote that the day was "a milestone that is being greeted with something less than enthusiasm in some older members of the club." Countries such as the UK, Sweden, France, Germany, and Ireland were concerned that eastern expansion meant an influx of cheap labor and the unraveling of their social services.[30]

If one thinks of the *idea* of Europe as an elastic band binding the peoples of Europe to the integration process, that band is being stretched ever thinner by Europe's expansion.[31] Lars-Erik Cederman's work demonstrates that while European identity remained relatively "thick" with an EU membership of fifteen, this sense of common identity grows "thin" as the European Union takes on more member states, especially states of the former Eastern bloc, which many Western Europeans have long thought of as a social and cultural "out-group." Leaving aside the

Nazi-era view of eastern, Slavic peoples as *Untermenschen,* the fact remains that, as recently as the interwar period, Western Europe has viewed Eastern Europe as having economies and even cultures sharply different from those in the West. A Polish member of the European Parliament, Bronislaw Geremek, argued the same for the East: "Europe was very far for us. . . . There was a feeling that what happened in western Europe did not concern us, that western Europe was of little interest to us."[32] The East-West divide has presented a greater number of challenges than foreseen in reunited Germany. As the EU expands to include peoples whose cultures may be considered other than "European," popular will toward integration might erode. To use Cederman's words, EU expansion may not be a matter of just widening versus deepening, but of exclusion versus dilution as well.[33] According to a 2006 poll, a majority of Europeans, with a high in the Netherlands (76 percent) and in France (68 percent)—that is, the two countries that rejected the constitution— believe that further enlargement makes the creation of a common European identity more difficult.[34]

Problems over Turkey's membership are apposite here. Setting aside both Turkish disagreements with Greece over Cyprus and Turkish economic and human rights problems, the European populace has opposed Turkish membership on the basis of values.[35] Can Turks be considered European if they have different values or if they are perceived as having different values? This question of who is European is thus directly related to the EU's political identity because the EU foreign and security policy is informed by European values. As Michel Barnier, former French foreign minister and former EU commissioner, explained, the Turkey debate was directly related to the EU's role in the world. "If we want Europe to count in the world, we need to address the question of Europe's geographical and political identity."[36] In a news analysis, the *International Herald Tribune* elaborated:

> The question of Europe's borders is emerging as a central issue in a quest for a collective identity that can overcome the rift between European citizens and their leaders. Deceptively simple and yet fraught with controversy over how to translate an elusive cocktail of geography, history and common values into frontiers, the debate goes to the heart of the EU's bid to secure its place in the 21st century.[37]

The question of "belonging" is so serious that four French socialist members of parliament (MPs) wrote an article in *Le Monde* in 2001, harking back to the days of the Treaty of Rome and the original six nations, proposing a "core Europe" for those with similar ambitions with regard to

European integration.[38] This proposal would create a two-speed Europe; it was still being discussed during the Austrian EU presidency in 2006.

### Creating a European Myth

Even if some people were willing to exchange one identity for another, since the EU is an intellectual idea framed in economic terms, there is little in the European project to rally people to the idea because there is no EU myth. As Daniela Obradovic explained:

> Myth expresses and maintains social solidarity because it refers to values of belongingness and originality and a sense of shared collective identity and fate. Such a myth of origin as the ultimate source of legitimacy is missing from the European venture. No mythologein is powerfully operative within the Union, no one can win the consent of the entire Union population. The task of firmly and indisputably establishing Union policy legitimacy therefore encounters serious theoretical difficulties.[39]

Anthony Smith argued that the problem is not just the absence of a European myth, but that the age of myth is over.[40] The historical *mytho-moteurs* rooted in religion in the golden age of European Christendom are not appropriate for today's secular society. Smith lamented, "But where else can one look for the necessary political mythology? Is it possible for the new Europe to arise without 'myth' or 'memory'?" He continued:

> Here lies the new Europe's true dilemma: a choice between unacceptable historical myths and memories on the one hand, and on the other a patchwork, memoryless scientific "culture" held together solely by the political will and economic interest that are so often subject to change.[41]

### Ways the European Union Attempts Nation Building

Anderson wrote, "*[I]n themselves*, market-zones, 'natural'-geographic or politico-administrative, do not create attachments. Who will willingly die for the Comecon or the EEC?"[42] Although people do not fall in love with "administrative units," as Anderson calls them, it is possible and has been done. "To see how administrative units could, over time, come to be conceived as fatherlands, not merely in the Americas but in other parts of the world, one has to look at the ways in which administrative organizations create meaning."[43] To create meaning that will resonate with the resident population first the government must define its territory and its people, and what they have in common. For nations where the meaning is clearly apparent, the choice has been to highlight the similarities of religion, race, or ethnicity. In multinational states, the government can stress a creed, a shared history, or shared values. In the European Union, the creed is "unity through diversity."

The idea of European unity or Europeanism has origins that go back as far as the Roman Empire. Granted, most of those who wanted to unite Europe used force—Charlemagne, Napoleon, Hitler—but many intellectuals had visions as well, often with a Christian theme. For example, Pierre Dubois, a jurist and diplomat in both the French and English courts, proposed in 1306 that a permanent assembly of princes be established to keep the peace through the application of Christian principles; and de Béthune, the Duc de Sully, proposed a federation of Christian states to ward off the Turks. The idea of a united Europe became very popular in the 1940s, when resistance groups preached unity to combat the nationalism that had started two world wars. The concept gained currency with politicians of the day, including Robert Schuman. Jean Monnet, who would later be called the "father of Europe," was a leading advocate of this school of thinking.

A vital part of convincing the public of the necessity of European integration was the creation of a narrative; that is, a story around which the citizens could identify.

> To put it in a nutshell, the identity narrative channels political emotions so that they can fuel efforts to modify a balance of power; it transforms the perceptions of the past and of the present; it changes the organization of human groups and creates new ones; it alters cultures by emphasizing certain traits and skewing their meanings and logic. The identity narrative brings forth a new interpretation of the world in order to modify it.[44]

Although Smith may say the age of myth is over, such a declaration may be premature. The EU's identity narrative attempts to create a myth. It is clearly spelled out on the EU's Web page:

> The historical roots of the European Union lie in the Second World War. The idea was born because Europeans were determined to prevent such killing and destruction ever happening again. In the early years, the cooperation was between six countries and mainly about trade and the economy. Now the EU embraces 27 countries and 490 million people, and it deals with a wide range of issues of direct importance for our everyday life.

> Europe is a continent with many different traditions and languages, but also with shared values such as democracy, freedom and social justice. The EU defends these values.[45]

This narrative tells the citizen that he or she is decended from the people who rebuilt Europe out of the ashes of World War II and laid the framework for true peace, based on the shared values of democracy, freedom, and social justice. The EU is the defender of those values.

Despite the power of the narrative, as Jean Monnet reminded us, "[N]othing is lasting without institutions." With this in mind, the designers of the Rome Treaty not only created the European Parliament, the European Commission, the European Court of Justice, and the Council of Ministers, akin to the national branches of government, they also created such "national" symbols for the European Economic Community as a flag and an anthem. Michael Billig explained, in his book *Banal Nationalism*, that although nation building may be punctuated by wars and the like that cause the people to rally 'round the flag, mundane, day-to-day national symbols (flags, anthems, money, passports, etc.) lead people to develop an identity—to recognize themselves as a particular group, out of habit.[46]

To keep the recognition of Europe second-nature to its citizens, the EU has a well-developed educational campaign, with free teaching tools for educators. Coloring books for kindergarteners ask young students to explore "my country Europe";[47] the first task is to "colour Europe as one."[48] Recognizing the lack of common myth, this publication coopts "imaginary characters from myth and legend" for the EU, because "they are all European."[49]

The map is also of vital importance in nation building because the map becomes a logo, a symbol of the territory that people see as their own. Historian Thongchai Winichakul explained,

> In terms of most communication theories and common sense, a map is a scientific abstraction of reality. A map merely represents something which already exists objectively "there." In the history I have described, this relationship was reversed. A map anticipated spatial reality, not vice-versa. In other words, a map was a model for, rather than a model of, what it purported to represent. . . . It had become a real instrument to concretize projections on the earth's surface. A map was now necessary for the new administrative mechanisms and for the troops to back up their claims. . . . The discourse of mapping was the paradigm which both administrative and military operations worked within and served.[50]

The map delineates who is "one of us" and who is an "outsider." The map of Europe, with the hole in the middle for Switzerland, has become a symbol of the European Union and can be seen on publications and even on EU money.

Some academics have argued that there was no economic reason for the euro; rather, that it was an explicit replacement of a national symbol by a European one. On the banknotes, fictitious bridges, tunnels, and archways "link" Europeans to one another. Their fictitious nature means that the citizen holding the note will not be able to link the landmark with any place other than Europe. New Year's celebrations literally centered on the new currency when it was introduced in 2002, as people danced around giant, sparkling euro signs in the middle of city centers. Peter van Ham remarked, "The EU's striking logo—a blue flag with a circle of 12 stars—is already omnipresent. The application of 'euro' to everything from trains and soccer championships to a unit of currency will make it one of the most frequently used names across the continent and one of the world's most popular brands."[51] Martin Feldstein, a Harvard economist, commented, "[T]here is no doubt that the real rationale for EMU [European Monetary Unity] is political and not economic. Indeed, the adverse economic effects of a single currency on unemployment and inflation would outweigh any gains from facilitating trade and the capital flows among the EMU members."[52]

Feldstein's analysis may be correct. In an HSBC report titled "European Meltdown?" Robert Prior-Wandesforde and Gwyn Hacche stated,

> The eurozone's current path is unsustainable. We believe the single currency has helped create significant economic strains which look set to become more and more extreme if nothing is done. In particular, it is probably only a matter of time before Germany and the Netherlands are dragged into deflation, while Italy seems destined to move in and out of recession for years to come.[53]

Frits Bolkestein, the former EU internal market commissioner, has questioned the chances of survival for the euro in the long term. He argued that states "will be forced by political pressure to borrow more and increase their budget deficit, with consequences for interest rates and inflation," so "the real test for the euro is not now, but in ten years['] time."[54] Using the opportunity to attack opposition leader and former European Commission president Romano Prodi before Italy's 2005 elections, Prime Minister Silvio Berlusconi of Italy called the euro a "disaster" and a "rip-off" that "screwed everybody."[55] Feldstein noted that the long-term political effects "would be the creation of a political union, a European federal state with responsibility for a

Europe-wide foreign and security policy."[56] In other words, EMU was a prerequisite for the ESDP.[57]

The draft Constitutional Treaty was yet another tool for nation building. The constitution was not for the elites, but for the people. Jacques Chirac of France put in plain words that there had to be "a feeling of European identity. . . . The adoption of a constitution would contribute to this. . . . Such a text would unite the Europeans by enabling them, through their solemn approval, to identify with a project."[58] Louis Michel, Belgian foreign minister, agreed: "This is of course a key symbolic issue. And symbolism is important in politics."[59] Nevertheless, despite daily interaction with the EU flag and other symbols, a strong educational campaign, and strong support from the ruling parties, the French people, along with the Dutch, rejected the constitutional treaty and the accompanying symbolism.

Few options remain for getting the people on board. In the wake of the constitutional defeat, the Centre for European Reform and the Institut Montaigne wrote "A Manifesto for Europe: 20 Ways to Revive the EU." One of the key ways indicated was "a stronger role in the world," focusing on strengthening and streamlining foreign and security policy decisionmaking and directing more resources to the ESDP in order to make the EU both more effective and popular.[60] Karl Lamers, former Christian Democratic Union (Germany) deputy for European affairs, agreed:

> I would like to remind you that the European Defence Community, that is the idea of a European army, was blocked in 1954 by a negative vote from France. But this impasse led to the Treaties of Rome three years later: instead of defense, it was economics that was allowed to go forward. Why would it not be possible, in 2005 [after a second French rejection], to take the opposite path: for us to concentrate on the perspective of a European defense to fire up the integration process?[61]

## How the Security Realm Is a Useful Tool for Nation Building

Drawing on Anthony Giddens, Billig stated that "nation-states do not exist in isolation, but 'in a complex of other nation-states.'"[62] He continued,

> Nationalism embraces a way of thinking—patterns of common-sense discourse—which make this boundedness and monopolization of violence seem natural to "us," who inhabit the world of nation states. This world—"our" world—is a place where nations have their official armies, police forces and executioners; where boundaries are

rigourously drawn; and where citizens, and male citizens in particular, might expect to be called upon to kill and die in defence of the
national borderpost.[63]

The international arena plays a strong role in nation building. First, it
delineates the boundaries of the territory in question. Everything within
the boundaries can be defined as "we"; those outside the boundaries, "the
other." Therefore, the very act of creating a foreign policy defines the
"in-group." Second, viewing the in-group in international competition
with the other helps to create solidarity and a feeling of belonging among
the citizens—especially if the in-group feels threatened by the outsider.[64]
Third, the international arena provides international recognition. No state
exists without international and diplomatic recognition. Fourth, the international arena provides a reason to act—and action provides meaning. As
a result, action in the international arena creates a narrative and possibly
even a mythos for the people to rally around. Most national narratives
revolve around military valor in a glorious past.[65]

According to Robert Art, military force can be used in four ways:
for defense, deterrence, "compellence," and swaggering. He explained,
"Not all four functions are necessarily well or equally served by a given
military posture. In fact, usually only the great powers have the wherewithal to develop military forces that can serve more than two functions
at once. Even then, this is achieved *vis à vis* smaller powers, not *vis à vis*
the other great ones."[66] In no way could the ESDP be used for defense.
Given the reduction in defense spending in almost every EU member
state and the limited power projection capabilities envisaged, despite
rhetoric to the contrary, the ESDP will not be capable of defending the
European continent. (See Chapter 2.) The rhetoric of the opening of the
Maastricht negotiations, the EU's "rendezvous with history,"[67] shows
that the goal of the security identity of the European Union is not for
defense or deterrence, but rather for swaggering, in order to define the
identity of the EU both at home and abroad.

The ESDP contributes to a collective identity in several ways. First,
it provides prestige on the cheap. As a corollary, the increase in prestige
augments the ability of the EU countries to influence others diplomati-
cally, thus reinforcing the image of the EU as a powerful actor on the
world stage. Third, the security identity opens the door to the possibility
of a new, glorious future created through unity of the people. Every success attained by the CFSP and the ESDP is a reflection of the collective
achievement of the European people.

By *swaggering*, Art explained that a state would create a military force "to enhance the national pride of a people." Ilya Prizel concurred, stating, "Foreign policy, with its role as either the protector or the anchor of national identity, provides the political elite with a ready tool for mass mobilization and cohesion."[68] With an artificial entity such as the European Union, such pride is a necessary tool to encourage cohesiveness. Ole Wæver wrote,

> Asking for a defense identity is less than asking for a defense organization. On the other hand, it points to Europe's need to constitute a political personality, a political subject in international relations, which traditionally has meant sovereignty. . . . Here, defense becomes symbolic of unit-ness; defense and identity become mutually constitutive.[69]

Furthermore, swaggering would allow the EU to be taken more seriously in the eyes of the world. Art asserted,

> A state or statesman swaggers in order to look and feel more powerful and important, to be taken seriously by others in the councils of international decision making, to enhance the nation's image in the eyes of others. . . . Swaggering is pursued because it offers to bring prestige "on the cheap." If swaggering causes other states to take one's interests more seriously into account, the general interests of the state will benefit.

A common sight in the developing world and in communist countries is the military parade, in which tanks and weaponry roll through the capital's thoroughfares, where throngs come to watch. The idea is to demonstrate the country's power to the world, and thereby create a feeling of pride among the country's people. Interestingly, such parades have lost their cachet in the developed world. One exception was in 1994, in France, where the Eurocorps marched down the Champs-Élysées on Bastille Day, the first time German soldiers had marched in Paris since World War II. As Mitterrand pronounced,

> France today honours . . . the European Army Corps, whose presence is testimony to the shared wish of our people to build the future together. . . . If we want to build Europe, we must realise that this Europe needs its own defence. If it simply remains dependent on outside powers, it will not be itself.[70]

Socialist president Mitterrand of France was echoing the views of many third world leaders. To quote Sylvanus Olympio, president of Togo from 1960 to 1966, "We cannot be an independent nation without an army of some sort."[71] French president Jacques Chirac echoed these sentiments with a similar statement, "The European Union will not fully exist until it possesses an autonomous capacity for action."[72] EU leaders want a military for the same reason: a modern military denotes a powerful, modern international actor.[73] In his first oversight of Bastille Day celebrations, French president Nicolas Sarkozy sat in the back of a military vehicle leading military contingents from all twenty-seven EU countries down the Champs-Élysées. He made clear, "It's Europe's party. . . . It was a parade of armies but it is peace that we want to celebrate."[74]

### How to Strengthen European Identity Through ESDP

To quote Erik Ringmar, "We act, not in defence of our interests, but in defence of our identity."[75] Through a relatively modest investment in the ESDP, the European Union can take steps to overcome the perception of "new Europe" as an out-group, while building and reinforcing a sense of shared history and establishing Europe as a major force in world affairs. Constructivism provides a useful framework within which to explore this process.

#### Foreign Policy as a Way of Delineating Actorness

An EU foreign and security policy is vital to creating a European Union because the process of creating such policy determines, simultaneously, what is foreign and what is not (i.e., domestic) and what the whole must be protected from.[76] In other words, the rhetoric has arguably more importance than the substance of the policy because the references to the EU as an actor make the EU itself more "real." This postmodern, international actor may not be a state, but it has power to create policy to influence foreign actors. In addition, discussion of a foreign and security policy demonstrates that new Europe (the twelve new member states) is part of the whole—and not the foreign "other," to be dealt with in the CFSP.

Without the CFSP, there would be no "one voice," no manifestation of European values on the world stage. Since its establishment in 1993, the EU has managed to create hundreds of foreign policy statements with regard to every part of the globe. Together, these documents create a discourse for the EU as an international actor. Thomas Diez argued that discourse vis-à-vis the EU not only describes it, but is part of the process of its ongoing construction.[77] Apart from its locutionary act (i.e., the act of speaking itself) language also has an illocutionary force (i.e., the power to found or to establish).[78] The power of language is evident in that "holiest [of holy] cow[s],"[79] the *acquis communautaire* (EU law and regulations accumulated to date). In his article, "The Social Construction of the Acquis Communautaire: A Cornerstone of the European Edifice," Knud Erik Jørgensen argued that the *acquis* "is one of the key features distinguishing Member States from non-members" and thus defining Europe from non-Europe.[80] The very act of adopting the *acquis* makes a country "European." By the same token, the act of a country using the EU to make a foreign or security policy statement through the CFSP is an illocutionary act, defining both the EU and itself as part of the EU.

The process of writing common foreign and security policy statements encourages the formation of a European strategic culture. Christoph O. Meyer recognized the persistence of national strategic cultures, but also noted their convergence into a common strategic culture, creating European norms. "On the issue of the legitimization of the use of different instruments of power, a preliminary conclusion is that the dynamics of convergence—particularly the impact of the Balkan experience—described above have influenced norms about the authorization of 'out of area' interventions."[81] Sten Rynning argued that although the EU does not have the capacity to create a strong strategic culture, a European consensus, based on good governance and effective multilateralism, does exist with regard to UN rules and norms, thus creating a foundation for an EU strategic culture.[82]

Despite problems converging the different national security cultures, the CFSP and ESDP have been supported by the member states, partly because of the difficulty in defining the new security environment after the end of the Cold War and after September 11.[83] The absence of a clear, definable, imminent threat allows the Europeans to experiment with their security policy. A variable geometry in the security architecture is possible because the threat of full-scale war in Europe is practically nil. Nevertheless, threats in the form of global terrorism require new cooperation and coordination of security strategies. Therefore, a European security strategy is more appealing and practicable to the member states than during the Cold War. Moreover, such an arrangement is appealing to small states, as the EU increases their international influence. As for neutrals, as NATO is unacceptable, the EU is the only organization available to them in which to discuss security issues. Consequently, the CFSP provides good soil in which EU norms can be cultivated.

### Pride and Power

Although the age of myth may be gone, the CFSP and the ESDP have given the Europeans much positive attention. The coming-of-age image is another version of "the rendezvous with history," marking a new era of cooperation for the Europeans and leading to a new, glorious history together. During the Cold War, the Europeans were under the thumbs of both superpowers. The CFSP/ESDP is an opportunity for them to regain some of their pride. Support among the people for security and defense continues to rise (see the Appendix). Although Denmark rejected the Maastricht Treaty partially on the grounds of the CFSP and negotiated an opt-out accordingly, ten years later, 60.1 percent of Danes want Denmark to join the Common Security and Defense Policy (CSDP), with only 23.8 percent opposed.[84]

The top decisionmakers in the EU also look favorably on CFSP/ESDP. According to a poll of European elites, these actors see security and defense as a major concern best dealt with at the European level. Moreover, one of the most important goals, as they see it, for the EU is "to defend European Union interests throughout the world."[85] As one official in Javier Solana's office explained, "[I]t's a Union defined by the money and defense, not the regulation of hairdressers."[86]

## Conclusion

Chapter 1 describes the puzzle of the ESDP: it is a security policy designed at a time of minimal threat. Although most EU members are also members of NATO, some academics have seen the ESDP as a foil to both the Atlantic Alliance and the United States. Despite the rhetoric surrounding the ESDP and its potential, the EU has placed minimal resources in that area. What explains the ESDP's anti-US bent, the great rhetoric which surrounds the ESDP, and the lack of material funds and follow-through? The answer is "nation building."

Although the EU is not a nation, nation-building theory applies to it. For the EU to succeed, it requires the support of the people within its jurisdiction. Foreign and security policy is a powerful tool long used by states to unite and focus the will of the people. Giving the EU a foreign policy delineates what is "European" from what is "foreign." It defines common values to defend and to promote abroad. Even if not operational, a small, token military force can create a rippling effect. As one of the premier symbols of the state, the military stands for power and independence. Although small, the EU battle groups demonstrate before the media that the EU can act abroad. As a promoter and protector of European values, especially compared to US values, the ESDP is a tool for creating pride among the people and support for the European Union.

## Notes

This chapter is based on Stephanie B. Anderson and Thomas R. Seitz, "European Security Policy Demystified: Nation-building and Identity in the EU," *Armed Forces and Society* 33 (October 2006): 24–42.

1. Henry A. Kissinger, *A World Restored: Castlereagh, Metternich and the Restoration of Peace, 1812–1822* (Boston: Houghton Mifflin Company, 1957), 146, as quoted in Ole Wæver, "European Integration and Security: Analyzing French and German Discourses on State, Nation and Europe," in *Diskursteorien på arbejde,* ed. Torben Bech Dyrberg, Allan Dreyer Hansen, and Jacob Torfing (Roskilde, Denmark: Roskilde Universitetsforlag, 2000), 279–318.

2. Ronald L. Jepperson, Alexander Wendt, and Peter J. Katzenstein, "Norms, Identity, and Culture in National Security," in Katzenstein, *The Culture of National Security,* 33.

3. See Chapter 1, note 14.

4. The definitions of *nation building* versus *state building* are discussed in more detail in the next section. In either case, both definitions are problematic, considering that the European Union is a sui generis entity; i.e., an intergovernmental organization with supranational characteristics. Indeed, the European Union is involved both in nation building and state building (at the supranational or suprastate level). For our purposes, rather than come up with a new label appropriate specifically for the EU, this chapter will, in keeping with the relevant literature, refer to "nation building" as the effort to create a pan-European identity.

5. *Eurobarometer* 54.1, as cited in a *Eurobarometer* special survey by Philippe Manigart, "Public Opinion and European Defence," July 2001, at http://europa.eu.int/comm/-public_opinion/archives/ebs/ebs_146_en.pdf.

6. See, for example, Minxin Pei and Sara Kasper, "Lessons from the Past: The American Record of Nation-building," Carnegie Endowment Policy Brief No. 24, April 2003. Also, Marina Ottaway, "Nation-building," *Foreign Policy* 132 (September/October 2002): 16–24.

7. See, for example, Pye, *Politics, Personality and Nation-building;* and Deutsch and Foltz, *Nation-building.* Also see Marquis, "The Other Warriors."

8. Gellner, *Nations and Nationalism*, 5–7, 53–56.

9. A. Smith, *National Identity*, 14.

10. Where the continent of Europe begins and ends is not clear. In general, geographers say it is bounded by the Atlantic and Arctic Oceans to the west and north, by the Mediterranean Sea to the south, and by the Caucasus Mountains and the Black Sea to the southeast. To the east, Europe is divided from Asia by the Ural Mountains and Ural River and by the Caspian Sea. Nevertheless, the political borders have never been clear. Austrian statesman Prince Klemens Wenzel von Metternich is credited as saying, "Asia begins at the Landstrasse," thereby excluding Hungary from Europe. French president Charles de Gaulle famously included Russia but excluded the United Kingdom from Europe by defining it "from the Atlantic to the Urals." The Organization for Security and Cooperation in Europe (OSCE) includes both the United States and Canada, and thereby boasts of a region spanning from "Vancouver to Vladivostok." In the United Nations, the Western Europe and Others Group (WEOG) includes the United States, Canada, Australia, New Zealand, and Israel, which is technically on the continent of Asia. The Eurovision Song Contest also includes Israel. The

political definition of Europe also begs the question of whether Turkey is part of the continent, because only a small portion, Thrace, is in Europe, whereas the rest is in Asia.

11. B. Anderson, *Imagined Communities,* 192–196.

12. Habermas, *The Inclusion of the Other*, 113.

13. B. Anderson, *Imagined Communities*, 47.

14. Ibid., 141.

15. *Eurobarometer* 57 (2002): 12–15.

16. Andrew Rettman, "Most Europeans Don't Know Their Union Has 25 States," *EU Observer*, 11 October 2006.

17. The Maastricht Treaty passed in France with 50.5 percent voting yes and 49.5 percent no.

18. As quoted in Paul Taylor, "Europe's Voters Turn Backs on EU, Governments," *Reuters,* 14 June 2004.

19. William Horsley, "Euro-Skeptics Storm the Citadel," *BBC News,* 14 June 2004.

20. Hooghe and Marks, "Does Identity or Economic Rationality . . . ?" 415.

21. Wright, *Community and Communication,* 61.

22. Ibid., 8.

23. Ibid.

24. John Peet, "Europe's Mid-Life Crisis," *The Economist,* 31 May 1997.

25. Laffan, "Identity and Political Order in Europe," 82–83.

26. As quoted in Haas, *The Uniting of Europe*, 28–29.

27. Atzo Nicolaï, closing remarks, informal ministerial meeting on communicating Europe, 5 September 2004, at http://www.europa-web.de/europa/03euinf/10counc/comeuclu.htm.

28. As quoted in Graham Bowley, "EU Ambassador Finds the Positive in Katrina; U.S. Learned Value of International Aid," *International Herald Tribune*, 16 September 2005, 6.

29. *Eurobarometer* 57, EU 15 report (spring 2002): 60.

30. Honor Mahoney, "Mixed Feelings One Year After Enlargement," *euobserver*, 1 May 2005.

31. Lars-Erik Cederman, "Political Boundaries and Identity Tradeoffs," in *Constructing Europe's Identity*, ed. Cederman, 1–32.

32. As quoted in Mark Beunderman, "'Europe Was Very Far for Us,'" *euobserver.com*, 22 March 2007.

33. Cederman, "Political Boundaries," 3.

34. The German Marshall Fund, "Transatlantic Trends: Topline Report 2006," 15, at http://www.transatlantictrends.org/doc/2006_TT_Topline%20Report%20FINAL.pdf.

35. Masanori Naito, vice director, Centre for New European Research, "Enlargement or Transformation," speech presented at the symposium "Enlargement of Europe and the Islamic World," Tokyo, 22 January 2005, at http://cner.law.hit-u.ac.jp/events/symposia/-europe_islam/naito_speech/view. For a more in-depth discussion, see Bilgin, "A Return to 'Civilisational Geopolitics' in the Mediterranean?" 269–291.

36. As quoted in Katrin Bennhold, "News Analysis: Turkey Debate Key to EU World Role," *International Herald Tribune,* 14 September 2006.

37. Ibid.

38. Jean Noël Jeanneney, Pascal Lamy, Henri Nallet, and Dominique Strauss-Kahn, "Europe: pour aller plus loin" [Europe: How to Go Farther], *Le Monde*, 20 June 2001.

39. Obradovic, "Policy Legitimacy and the European Union," 191–192.

40. A. Smith, "National Identity and the Idea of European Unity," 74.

41. Ibid.

42. B. Anderson, *Imagined Communities*, 53. Emphasis in original.

43. Ibid.

44. Martin, "The Choices of Identity," 7. For more on the importance and role of narrative in identity building, see Ricoeur, *Oneself as Another*.

45. European Commission, "Panorama of the EU: United in Diversity," at http://-europa.eu/abc/panorama/index_en.htm.

46. Michael Billig, *Banal Nationalism*, 8.

47. Mauro, *Let's Draw Europe Together,* 9.

48. Ibid., 11.

49. Ibid., 9.

50. As quoted in B. Anderson, *Imagined Communities*, 173–174.

51. Van Ham, "The Rise of the Brand State," 5–6.

52. Feldstein, "EMU and International Conflict," 60.

53. Robert Prior-Wandesforde and Gwyn Hacche, "European Meltdown? Europe Fiddles as Rome Burns," *HSBC Global Research*, July 2005, at www.nytteuropa.nu/index. phtml?download=true&fid=8166.

54. As quoted in Mark Beunderman, "Ex-Commissioner Questions Survival of Euro," *euobserver.com*, 26 January 2006.

55. As quoted in Filipe Rufino, "Berlusconi Attacks Euro," *euobserver,* 29 July 2005.

56. Feldstein, "EMU and International Conflict," 60.

57. Ibid., 70.

58. As quoted in Lara Marlowe, "EU Constitution in 2004—Chirac," *Irish Times,* 28 August 2001, 8.

59. Foreign Minister Louis Michel, speech on the occasion of the diplomatic contact days, 1 September 2003, at http://www.diplomatie.be/en/press/speechdetails.asp?-TEXTID=9115.

60. Centre for European Reform and the Institut Montaigne, "A Manifesto for Europe: 20 Ways to Revive the EU," 24 October 2005, at http://www.cer.org.uk.

61. Karl Lamers, "L'Europe de la défense en priorité," *Le Figaro*, 31 May 2005. Author's translation.

62. Billig, *Banal Nationalism*, 20, citing Anthony Giddens, *Social Theory and Modern Sociology*, 171.

63. Ibid.

64. Bloom, *Personal Identity, National Identity, and International Relations*, 75, 79.

65. Prizel, *National Identity and Foreign Policy*, 19.

66. Art, "To What Ends Military Power?" 5.

67. Jacques Delors, president of the European Commission, as quoted in Clyde Haberman, "West Europeans Formally Initiate Closer Federation," *New York Times,* 16 December 1990.

68. Prizel, *National Identity and Foreign Policy.*

69. Wæver, "Identity, Integration and Security" (electronic copy). Art, "To What Ends Military Power?" 10–11.

70. As quoted in Beunderman, "Ex-Commissioner Questions Survival of Euro."

71. As quoted in Dana P. Eyre and Mark C. Suchman, "Status, Norms, and the Proliferation of Conventional Weapons: An Institutional Theory Approach," in *The Culture of National Security,* ed. Katzenstein, 79.

72. Chirac in Toulouse, as quoted in J. A. C. Lewis, "Building a European Force: New Key Figure on the European Union Stage," *Jane's Defence Weekly* (23 June 1999): 22.

73. See Eyre and Suchman, "Status, Norms, and the Proliferation of Conventional Weapons," 79–113.

74. As quoted in Lucia Kubosova, "Sarkozy Brings in EU Troops to Celebrate Bastille Day," *euobserver,* 16 July 2007.

75. Ringmar, *Identity, Interest, and Action,* 4.

76. For an in-depth discussion, see Campbell, *Writing Security,* 61–62.

77. Diez, "Speaking 'Europe,'" 599.

78. Ibid., 600.

79. Weiler, "The Reformation of European Constitutionalism," 98.

80. Jørgensen, "The Social Construction of the Acquis Communautaire," 3.

81. Meyer, "Theorising European Strategic Culture," 19.

82. Rynning, "The European Union," 486.

83. Hyde-Price, "European Security, Strategic Culture, and the Use of Force," 323–343.

84. *Europe Daily Bulletin Documents,* 10 September 2003, 6.

85. Jacqueline Spence, "The European Union; 'A View from the Top': Top Decision-Makers and the European Union," *EOS Gallup Europe,* n.d.

86. General Secretariat Official II of the Council of the European Union, interview by author, Brussels, Belgium, 7 December 2005.

# 4

# The Role of the United States

---■---

The question of European identity is tied to Europe's future role in the world, and thus, in particular, the matter of its relationship with America. ■ WOLFGANG SCHÄUBLE, VICE CHAIRMAN OF THE CDU IN THE BUNDESTAG.[1]

One relatively easy and effective way to create a collective identity for a people is to designate an "other" as a referent and measuring stick. As a federation, a superpower, and perhaps even the EU's namesake (the future "United States of Europe"), the United States has played the role of referent to all the member states of the European Union. Especially recently, but also in the past, politicians, journalists, and even academics have sometimes portrayed the United States as an antagonist against which the Europeans—the protagonists—are required to take action. By using rhetoric to create a *Feindbild,* or "picture of an enemy," the Europeans both enhance their unity as well as create the "theological" problems that plague the Atlantic Alliance. As early as 1966, in his book *The Troubled Partnership*, Henry Kissinger warned that "[a] Europe constructed largely on theoretical models might be forced into an anti-American mold because its only sense of identity could be what distinguished it from America."[2]

US foreign and security policy has now become a rallying point for the European people. In 2003, Europeans ranked the United States second, after Israel, as a potential threat to world peace.[3] This trend has continued: in 2007, Europeans ranked the United States as the greatest threat to world stability.[4] During the US invasion of Iraq, Jürgen Habermas and Jacques Derrida noted that 15 February 2003, the date of mass demonstrations against the US invasion of Iraq, could become a "birthday of a European public, the beginning of a new European consciousness of common identity."[5]

This chapter discusses the development and usefulness of the United States as a referent in European integration. Drawing on the theoretical basis for the "minimal group paradigm," the chapter uses historical evidence to demonstrate how conflicts between the United States and Europe in the security sphere have led to the formation of the present-day Common Foreign and Security Policy/European Security and Defense Policy (CFSP/ESDP). In doing so, the author demonstrates that the ESDP has its roots in distinguishing itself from the policies of the United States, and not in defense per se. Next, the chapter discusses the process by which Europe and the United States have exaggerated their differences and how the Europeans have glossed over theirs to strengthen the fragile European identity. Finally, the chapter examines how both sides attribute intent to actions, creating "theologies" that strain NATO.

## "Minimal Group Paradigm" and Nation Building

Each individual holds personal beliefs. At the same time, people generally project or confer beliefs onto institutions as well. To quote Marilynn Brewer,

> [S]ocial identities are not simply individual cognitive constructions; they are based on collective beliefs about shared attributes, values, and experiences which constitute the content of specific social identities. Changes in social identity imply changes in who is seen as sharing common in-group membership with the self and what attributes and values are presumed to be self-defining.[6]

Just as individuals can change their beliefs and views of themselves, so can societies and institutions. The most common way for people to assess their and others' identities is through comparison—an assessment as to who they are like and not like.

Therefore, one of the key ways to create an identity is to create or designate an "other." As Brewer explained in her theory of optimal distinctiveness, there exists a human need to feel both part of a group—that is, included—as well as distinct and special. To use her words, "The theory postulates that social identity is derived from the opposing forces of two universal human motives—the need for inclusion and assimilation, on the one hand, and the need for differentiation from others on the other."[7] Brewer specifically focused on multiple social identities and explained that one can identify with many groups. She discovered that when a person feels left out, he or she will change his/her identities to feel more included, and if a person is made to feel "excessively assimilated to a large collective," the person will seek to distinguish himself or herself more fully, for example, from a Briton to an Englishman or even to a Yorkshireman. She applied her theory to Hong Kong, but it can just as easily be applied to Europe.

In the case of the European Union, the pressure to "become European" has resulted in a backlash, as one might predict from Brewer's theory. Extreme right and nationalist groups, as well as anti-EU political parties, have gained in strength as the EU has enlarged and introduced the single currency. As discussed in the previous chapter, enlargement has hindered the development of a European identity; people are seeking to distinguish themselves because they are in too large a collective. One way to counteract these feelings is to create an out-group to provide distinctiveness.[8]

Cognitive psychologists have discovered that "even when no obvious grounds for categorizing exist, people will invent them." In other words, people naturally divide themselves into groups of "us versus them." Called the "minimal group paradigm," simply dividing people into groups will create the foundations for distinctive identities. Competition sharpens the distinctions. By the same token, nuances and fine distinctions tend to make pigeonholing more difficult. As a result, people will tend to exaggerate their perceptions of others to make the distinctions clearer and more memorable as well as to facilitate categorization, which leads to stereotyping. This process of categorization allows the in-group to minimize differences among themselves and to highlight their similarities. It homogenizes them. At the same time, this process creates negative attitudes toward the different out-group.[9]

The more powerful the out-group is perceived as being, the more likely the in-group will be guilty of attributional bias; that is, seeing any actions by the other as being intentional. Whereas the in-group's actions are seen as being constrained by the situational context (e.g., the weather prevented us from coming), the out-group's actions are explained by intent (they must not have wanted to come; the weather wouldn't have stopped them). After all, if the out-group is perceived as powerful, the group could have used its power to overcome any obstacle.

To sum up: first, the very action of dividing people into groups creates the foundations for a distinct identity within the group, even if people have multiple allegiances. Second, people will tend to exaggerate the differences between the groups in order to make categorization easier. Third, the in-group will tend to explain away their own actions and inactions as being unintentional and constrained by circumstances beyond their control while explaining the out-group's actions as done on purpose. These lessons from cognitive psychology help explain US-European relations in security policy since the end of World War II, especially since the end of the Cold War.

### The United States as "Other"

As Ilya Prizel explained, "[W]hile all nationalist births require a contact with an 'other,' the contact does not necessarily have to be a short and cataclysmic event. . . . National identity may emerge slowly, after incubating for centuries."[10] The United States is the obvious, and convenient, foil to the Europeans and the European Union. The attributes that join Europeans together are weak. They share the same continent, a belief in market economies and democracy, a Christian cultural heritage, and a bloody history. Geographic location only holds so much weight. As to administrative and economic institutions, as established in the previous chapter, they do not tug at people's heartstrings; likewise, with regard to religion and history, memories of the past and religiosity may be fading. However, the citizens of the EU do share another commonality that they are reminded of every time one of them reads a newspaper, hears Britney Spears sing, or watches *The Simpsons*: their relationship with the United States.

The EU member states' relationship with the United States is one of the most potent forces binding them together. While some countries might perceive themselves as superior to other member states because of size or past conquests, all are equal in the eyes of the United States. With very few exceptions, almost all EU member states were conquered, liberated, or significantly aided (after World War II or the Cold War) by the United States.[11] The Marshall Plan and, to a significantly lesser extent, aid after the Cold War helped revive the European economies. The United States has been Europe's benefactor.

Moreover, all European countries are familiar with US products and culture. While Athenians may well be unfamiliar with Finland's biggest television star, almost all Europeans have seen *Baywatch* (dubbed into their local language) and tasted Coca-Cola. Even in France, US products have a strong appeal. Ironically, despite France's world-famous cuisine and strong legacy of anti-Americanism, McDonald's is more successful in France than in other European countries.[12] In France in 2004, Britney Spears was the person most searched for on Google-France.[13]

In a European Union where there are twenty-three official languages, 44 percent of the people are monolingual;[14] and where only 2 percent live in a country outside their country of origin (the European Commission designated 2006 as the "European Year of Workers' Mobility" to encourage citizens to move to find jobs),[15] there is relatively little intermingling among the Europeans. Along with tourism and student exchange, the United States provides an important conduit of understanding among Europeans. Heinz Ickstadt observed,

> Indeed, the US has become instrumental in the creation of a European consciousness and will very likely continue to be needed as an antagonistic Other to bring an as yet divided Europe politically together. On my recent travels through "Euroland," I not only enjoyed the conveniences of a single currency but also realized that "Anti-Americanism" has become Europe's spiritual coin easing communicative transactions across national, even linguistic, borderlines on all social levels.[16]

For decades, the Europeans have used the United States as a way to measure their own progress. One of the first references to European integration was set out in US terms: the "United States of Europe" was suggested by Churchill in 1946.[17] Europe has continued to compare itself to the United States. In the early 1990s, the European Commission produced a claymation video extolling European integration and the single market as the only way to combat the "American cowboy."[18] Airbus was a response to Boeing. Today, at twenty-seven members, the EU exceeds the United States in population and, as of 2005, equaled it in gross domestic product (US$11 trillion).[19] The euro's value at its debut was roughly equivalent to the US dollar, and was widely viewed as a rival to it and to its status as world currency. In his speech to the graduates of the College of Europe, European Commission president José Manuel Barroso complained that the United States seemed to have a monopoly on great universities, while Europe lagged behind.[20] As *The Economist* observed, "No meeting of the European Union's constitutional convention in Brussels is complete without a reference to Philadelphia."[21] Finally, the EU's motto, "United in diversity," is almost identical to the US motto, *"E pluribus unum."* The EU is seeking parity with the United States.

## The Significance of Security and Defense Policy

Of all the aspects of US-European relations, the most significant is security because it involves wounded pride. One of the basic measures of a state is its ability to protect its people. At crucial times during the twentieth century, Europe was not able to defend itself. US cemeteries in Belgium, France, Luxembourg, the Netherlands, Italy, and the UK, along with 294 US military installations on the continent, provide constant reminders of this fact.[22]

Moreover, US foreign and security policy has been one of the most controversial aspects of US politics, causing mass demonstrations both at home and abroad. European countries' security policies have been inextricably intertwined with the United States' security policy because most of those nations are members of the Atlantic Alliance. Although all supposedly have equal weight in this consensus-based organization, the grand marble entrance to the US mission to NATO marks the United States as the de facto leader.

The Europeans have sought and continue to seek equality with the United States. Politicians state this very clearly; European Commission president Barroso has said that the United States needs to treat the EU as an equal partner.[23] According to Jacques Chirac, "To become a real power, the EU must, in their eyes, define itself as a 'balance' against the United States. An independent defence force is a primary condition for confirming Europe's identity as more than an economic bloc."[24] At the Thessaloniki EU Council summit, the member states included a formal statement, under the heading "USA," on the importance of developing "an equal footing" with the United States.[25]

## Seeking Balance and Equality: A Historical Overview of US-European Security Relations

Security has always been a primary concern of the EC. The European Coal and Steel Community of 1952 (ECSC), precursor to the European Community, was established to promote peace between two longtime enemies, France and Germany. Within the ECSC, France and Germany changed their relationship from one based on war to one based on trade. In this way, the ECSC satisfies Karl Deutsch's definition of a security community, in which countries within the community forego war as a means of settling disputes.[26] Even as an economic community without a common security dimension, the EC was a control against internal disturbances to peace.

By the same token, European integration also played a role in the balance of power on the European continent. President Eisenhower supported European integration because he believed it would provide a strong and directed bulwark against the Soviet threat. In his words, "[T]he unity of western Europe today . . . would solve the peace of the world. A solid power mass in western Europe would ultimately attract to it all the Soviet satellites and the threat to peace would disappear."[27] As stated in a once-classified security document from the Eisenhower administration,

> The US policy of encouraging the Western European countries to take steps toward integration, including possible political federation or confederation, stems from a profound desire to achieve certain effects that are accepted as a probable consequence of Western European integration. The US interests lie in the economic, political and military strengthening of Western Europe within the Atlantic Community context, and in support of NATO objectives, that might result from such integration. The creation of European institutions, without achieving this substance of integration, would represent failure rather than success of US policy.[28]

As the European Community was a security instrument and part of the West's struggle against communism, it is not surprising that the EC's and NATO's histories are closely intertwined. Although one of the most difficult areas in which to achieve consensus between all the member states, security policy has been discussed in the European Community since its conception. Within two years of the signing of the North Atlantic Treaty, France, Germany, Italy, and the Benelux, supported by the UK and the United States, attempted to form a European defense force and a European army to play a military role in the Cold War offensive against the Eastern bloc. Through the European Defense Community (EDC), the European Communities would have entered the sphere of traditional security affairs; but the project failed. As a result, European defense policy and security interests were subsumed by NATO during the Cold War.

A historical survey demonstrates that strains in US-European relations during the Cold War spurred incremental increases in European security cooperation. Although the United States and most of the European governments shared common security interests, they often had different security policy objectives and perceptions. As these perceptions and objectives diverged, transatlantic relations became stressed. As Nicole Gnesotto explained:

> At each decisive stage, at each possible turning-point in political integration, the member states are always faced with the same two dilemmas: how can the continuation of an Atlantic Alliance dominated by the United States be reconciled with the emergence of a strategic and political Europe? How can respect for national sovereignty be combined with building a structure to share political power? America or Europe, the nation or integration, these are the two fundamental questions that have never been resolved and still divide the different partners of the Union.[29]

Negatively or positively, European foreign, security, and defense policy reacted to changes in US foreign, security, and defense policy. Richard Eichenberg documented that "[a]lthough support had always been fairly high [for joint European action], it increased significantly in every country as the controversy within NATO raged over the issue of new nuclear deployments and relations."[30] Eichenberg concluded that "the data from the 1980s suggests that dissatisfaction with the United States is one factor that moves Europeans to seek common solutions in the security field."[31] Simon Nuttall concurred, calling the US-European relationship one of the keys to understanding European political cooperation: a consistent feature has been the need to find a way of expressing policies that are not those of the United States.[32]

During the 1950s and 1960s, only the French really grappled with the United States over defense policy. During this period, the United States encouraged security integration as a way to overcome internal distrust. After the failure of Kissinger's Year of Europe in 1973, the Western European countries collectively started to disassociate themselves from US foreign and defense policy. Although maintaining the alliance was necessary as long as the Soviet threat existed, each crisis within NATO led to a corresponding strengthening of foreign, security, and defense policy cooperation within the European Community. Certain trends that come out during the survey show that the European countries had a "cooperation reflex": when a problem arose, they looked to each other for a solution. Often the catalyst for change was a dispute with the United States or a change in the Cold War. Although the countries looked to each other for a solution, agreement on a course of action was often difficult because of differences of opinion among the member states. These trends are also visible in the formation of the CFSP.

### The Founding of NATO and the EDC (1948–1955)

Immediately after World War II, the United States understood that Europe was vital to its security.

> [T]he defence of the United States and Canada in North America and of Great Britain and France in western Europe is inseparable from the combined defence of them all. . . . The opponent would have to show that an assault by our ideological opponents on any one of these nations would not be of vital consequence to the other three nations. No one can show this. . . . This means that the entire area of western Europe is in first place as an area of strategic importance to the United States in the event of ideological warfare.[33]

As a result of the juncture of security interests between the Western European countries and the United States, these countries had reason to cooperate. Alone, France, the Benelux, Italy, and Germany could not defend themselves, especially while in the process of rebuilding. A defense alliance was the only solution.

NATO was a British invention designed to keep the United States in Europe.[34] Some British observers thought that the Marshall Plan's support for European unity was another form of US isolationism, because a strong Europe would not need the US.[35] To ensure that the United States would remain in Europe, a transatlantic alliance seemed the perfect solution. For the UK, NATO would be a loose enough coalition that Britain would not lose its independence as it would in a continental organization, where it would be forced to consort with what David Calleo has termed "former enemies and defeated friends."[36] UK foreign minister Bevin had in mind a "spiritual" federation that would embrace all of Western civilization, covering both the Atlantic and the Pacific, in order to curb Soviet expansion. To quote a cabinet paper to Prime Minister Clement Attlee of the UK,

> Political and indeed spiritual forces must be mobilized in our defence. I believe therefore we should seek to form backed by the Americas and the Dominions a Western democratic system. . . . As soon as circumstances permit we should of course wish also to include Spain and Germany without whom no Western system can be complete. This may seem a somewhat fanciful conception, but events are moving. . . . I can only say that in the situation in which we have been placed by Russian policy half measures are useless.[37]

In mid-January 1948, the Truman administration approved such an alliance, but stressed that the United States could not hand over any security guarantees until the Europeans had taken the initiative. In 1948, the Dunkirk Treaty (originally signed in 1947 between France and Britain) was expanded and changed to the "Treaty of Brussels" with the accession of Belgium, the Netherlands, and Luxembourg. In the event of an armed attack, the signatories promised to "afford the party so attacked all the military and other aid and assistance in their power."[38] No supranational organization was involved. In response to this action, Truman told Congress, "This development merits our unqualified support. I am sure that America will take the measures necessary to provide the free countries with any assistance that their situation might call for."[39] Convinced of the sincerity of the European commitment, the United States signed the North Atlantic Treaty establishing the Atlantic Alliance the next year.

As for the French, the NATO-US presence in Europe guaranteed its borders from both the Germans and the Soviets, leaving their forces free to look after their colonies in North Africa and Indochina and freeing resources for resurrecting the economy. NATO was also possibly a way of breaking into the Anglo-US partnership, which was very strong after the war.[40] Although not part of the Atlantic Alliance at its inception in 1949, Germany, under the leadership of Konrad Adenauer, supported a strong US role in Europe. "While Social Democrats and some Christian Democrats feared NATO would preclude German reunification, the West German Chancellor saw neutralist reunification as an illusory and probably undesirable goal."[41]

The first attempt to establish a specifically European defense identity came after North Korea's invasion of South Korea in 1950, when the United States and others became convinced that they needed a rearmed Germany to secure Europe from the communist threat. France, especially, was unenthusiastic about rearming its neighbor, which had invaded France three times in the previous one hundred years. At the same time, the ECSC was being negotiated with Germany in the autumn of 1950. Although Robert Schuman was hoping to extend European integration gradually, the Korean War intensified US pressure for German rearmament and strengthened Germans' desires for a means to defend themselves.[42]

Jean Monnet, architect of the Coal and Steel Community, designed a European Defense Community along similar lines, with supranational institutions and a European army into which rearmed German units would be integrated. René Pleven, France's prime minister, submitted Monnet's plan, now called the Pleven Plan, to the United States as a compromise to straight-out rearmament. All members except Germany would be allowed to have national militaries outside the European army. Adenauer, as well as Eisenhower, disapproved of the unequal status given Germany in this forum. Once France dropped this requirement, the United States supported the plan wholeheartedly.

The EDC deserves special attention for several reasons. It demonstrates that security and defense were not originally separate from European integration. The trends are also visible in this history: integration was spurred by an external event; the member states looked to each other for a solution; the deal was stymied because not all the states could agree. As with many of the cases in the historical overview, the United States was an important actor in the attempt to establish the EDC. As was also a recurring theme in European security relations, the EDC failed because of French reluctance to get itself involved in such a supranational arrangement and to relinquish its independent defense capability.

The EDC's defeat had wide ramifications for European defense policy. As a result of the inability of the member states to come up with an agreement on security or defense policy, it was excluded from the Treaty of Rome. (Despite the exclusion, the EC member states, gradually over the decades, increased cooperation in the security sphere.) Washington saw the defeat as a great tragedy, because it was "a psychological and political defeat for the proponents of European unity from which they might not recover for two or three years if at all."[43]

After the failure of the EDC, Germany joined the newly established Western European Union in 1954, a product of the revised Brussels Treaty, and joined NATO one year later. Without an EDC, NATO became the focal point for European defense cooperation and policy. Despite having the same security interests, the United States and Europe have had serious differences within NATO. According to Calleo,

> In the military sphere, Europeans have worried about the reliability and dangers of American deterrence for Europe. Americans have worried about the dangers that their European commitment might pose to themselves and have fretted over the inadequacies of Europe's own contribution to deterrence.[44]

The Europeans saw US domestic pressure to bring US troops home as a sign of their lack of a commitment, and the United States saw Europeans as reluctant to share the burden of their own defense.

Another problem with the Atlantic Alliance was the imbalance in influence between the United States and the Europeans:

> The relationship of protector and protected evokes arrogance and condescension from one side; resentment and irresponsibility from the other. The Alliance is not one of equals. The two sides can only reach agreement if they engage in a proper division of labour.[45]

The drive for NATO reform came as no surprise to such intellectuals as Henry Kissinger and David Calleo who had been predicting the Atlantic Alliance's demise for years if major reform did not take place.[46] Although NATO was based on the premise of partnership, the partnership was considerably one-sided, with the United States wielding the most influence and paying the largest share of costs, distorting the relationship and making both sides call for reform—with the French taking the lead. These strains in the Atlantic Alliance bolstered the European countries' resolve to distinguish themselves with an independent foreign and, to a lesser extent, security policy.

### Suez, the French, and the Eisenhower Administration (1955–1961)

Under the Eisenhower administration, NATO underwent two difficult traumas: France's defeat in Indochina at Dien Bien Phu and the Suez Canal crisis. These events created feelings of mistrust between France and the United States, giving impetus to the idea of European independence in the security field.[47] Charles de Gaulle felt that the NATO treaty signed by the weak Fourth Republic did not give the French enough recognition as a great power. The United States' special relationship with the British, characterized by close and constant consultations, reduced France to being a follower and not a leader. Embarrassed by the French loss in Vietnam, de Gaulle apportioned blame on the United States. "The opinion—widespread in France in any event—that American anti-colonialism was merely a pretext for substituting an American for the European presence in the former colonial territories was thus confirmed."[48] These events would affect his policy toward NATO a few years later, when he became president of France.

The Suez crisis only reinforced these feelings. French foreign minister Christian Pineau remarked, "The principal victim of the Suez affair was the Atlantic Pact. . . . If our allies had abandoned us in difficult, if not dramatic circumstances, they were capable of doing so again if Europe in turn found itself threatened."[49] On the day in 1956 when Great Britain and France, under US pressure, abandoned Suez, Chancellor Konrad Adenauer told Pineau, "France and England will never be powers comparable to the United States and the Soviet Union. Nor Germany, either. There remains to them only one way of playing a decisive role in the world; that is to unite to make Europe. England is not ripe for it but the affair of Suez will help to prepare her spirits for it. We have no time to waste: Europe will be your revenge."[50]

Two years later, in 1958, de Gaulle, now in power, asked for "the moon,"[51] demanding a directorate council—an official grouping of France, Great Britain, and the United States as the leaders of NATO. Only France was for it; the other member countries did not like being relegated to secondary status. Eisenhower offered to discuss all relevant issues with the French unofficially, as he did with the British prime minister, but de Gaulle refused. He used the rejection as an excuse for turning away from the military organization of NATO and putting all of his efforts into strengthening the European security identity and an intergovernmentally based *"Europe des patries,"* with France as its de facto head.

After Suez, de Gaulle, now very mistrustful of the US commitment to European security, supported moves for Europe to pursue its own foreign policy goals on an intergovernmental basis outside the European Community. From this point onward, the Western European countries started the process of deeper cooperation in the foreign policy and security fields. In 1959, de Gaulle proposed that the foreign ministers of the Six (France, Germany, Italy, Belgium, the Netherlands, and Luxembourg) should meet on a regular basis in the forum served by a permanent secretariat. Many agreed to explore the proposal at their first summit meeting in 1961 in Bonn. The leaders commissioned a committee, headed by Christian Fouchet, French ambassador to Denmark, to consider ways in which the Six could increase their political cooperation. The Fouchet Plan included a council of government heads or foreign ministers where, in regularly scheduled meetings, they would decide issues by unanimous vote; an intergovernmental, permanent secretariat composed of senior foreign affairs officials based in Paris; four permanent, intergovernmental committees in charge of foreign policy, defense, commerce, and cultural affairs; and a European assembly composed of appointed members from the national legislatures. However, disagreements stymied progress.[52]

The Fouchet Plan was not popular. The original Fouchet Plan, the French revision, and the counterproposals from the other five member states were all abandoned. Italy and West Germany felt the plan's intergovernmental nature would undermine the European Community and compete with NATO; the Benelux countries did not want to deal with such fundamental issues until British membership was resolved. Afraid that the large countries would dominate European Community policy, the small Benelux countries wanted Great Britain in the EC to counterbalance the growing cooperation and influence of the Franco-German partnership. Ultimately, the Fouchet Plan was rejected because it would weaken the Treaty of Rome by giving too much power to the individual countries, especially the larger ones.

## The Kennedy and Johnson Administrations (1961–1969)

By 1961, when John F. Kennedy (JFK) was elected president of the United States, Soviet nuclear technology and rocketry had improved enough to make the United States vulnerable to nuclear attack. "That a vulnerable United States would initiate a nuclear war to stop a conventional attack on Europe seemed implausible to many Europeans and frightening to some Americans."[53] Under the Kennedy administration, NATO established a new strategy of "flexible response," where a nuclear strike would not automatically follow a conventional attack. Such a policy required a buildup of conventional weaponry, especially on the European allies' side. During this time, the United States campaigned to change the Atlantic Alliance into a more equal partnership as a way of extending deterrence and fulfilling the United States' global obligations. Kennedy's "Grand Design," his Atlanticist view of a unified Europe, foresaw more European intervention in out-of-area problems, so long as it followed the US lead. As Kennedy said, "We look forward to a Europe united and strong, speaking with a common voice, acting with a common will, a world power capable of meeting world problems as a full and equal partner."[54]

JFK's intention to treat the European allies as equals seemed insincere when, in May 1962, US defense secretary Robert McNamara presented his strategic conception for NATO at the NATO Council meeting in Athens—without any prior consultation with other members. Such was the US regard for "equal partnership."

Now skeptical of US nuclear assurances and dismayed at the price tag attached to the increase in conventional weapons required for "flexible response," the Europeans balked at the new US policy.

> Whereas the Americans wanted to minimize the likelihood that the US defence of Europe would lead to nuclear war between the superpowers, Europeans believed their safety depended on convincing the Soviets that an attack on Europe would quickly escalate into an all-out nuclear war with the Americans, a war that would not spare the Soviet Union's own territory. For Europeans, the object of deterrence was not to limit a war, but to prevent one.[55]

Charles de Gaulle was particularly skeptical of US nuclear assurances. Both France and Britain pursued their own independent nuclear capabilities, claiming that their nuclear forces would also act as a deterrent to the Soviets. De Gaulle also decried "flexible response" and called for a massive French nuclear strike on Soviet territory if France or its assets came under attack.[56] France removed its forces from

NATO's integrated military structure in 1966, but remained part of the political structure of the Atlantic Alliance.

West Germany was also pursuing its own diplomatic initiatives for détente between itself and the Eastern bloc. Between 1963 and 1966, under Chancellor Ludwig Erhard, Germany opened limited trade relations with its Eastern neighbors. After 1966, Willy Brandt, first as German foreign minister and especially after 1969, when he became chancellor, further developed *Ostpolitik,* cultivating close relations with the East Germans and Soviets. The United States had serious misgivings over West Germany's independent foreign policy. Reflecting the diverging foreign and security policy strategies among the NATO allies, the Harmel Report permitted and codified the practice of individual and collective diplomacy vis-à-vis the Eastern bloc.[57]

With regard to the Third World, European and US policies had very different priorities. The United States was withdrawing troops from Europe to fight in Vietnam. By the end of the Johnson administration, 60,000 troops had been withdrawn.[58] The Vietnam War's unpopularity in Europe meant little European support of the now-US war. Frustrated with Europe, Senator Jacob Javits said in April 1966, "We should remind them [Europe] that we stood by them in their great hour of need when they might have gone down the drain. Why don't we press them on Vietnam? What is wrong with pressing them? Why are we so touchy and so fastidious?"[59] Later that year, in October, Senator Mike Mansfield introduced a resolution advising severe cutbacks in US troops in Europe.[60] Divergent foreign policy perspectives meant that Kennedy's Grand Design, with a unified Europe playing an active role in global security, had evaporated.

Nevertheless, Kennedy's "dumbbell" vision of an alliance balanced between North America and the European powers did make some headway. According to its own literature, Eurogroup was established in 1968 "to strengthen the whole Alliance by seeking to ensure that the European contribution to the common defence is as strong and cohesive as possible."[61] Eurocom, Eurolog, Eurolongterm, Euromed, Euro/NATO-training, and Euronad/Armaments Cooperation are all subgroups to promote interoperability, respectively, in communications, logistics, long-term concepts for the operation of European forces, military medicine, developing joint training facilities, and procurement of defense equipment. In the same spirit, in 1976, eight years after Eurogroup was founded, the Independent European Program Group (IEPG) was established to achieve greater cooperation in armaments procurement.

In late 1969, the heads of state and government at the EC summit at The Hague entrusted the foreign ministers "to study the best way of achieving progress in the matter of political unification, within the context of enlargement."[62] Étienne Davignon, a Belgian official of the Ministry of Foreign Affairs, proposed an informal intergovernmental association without legal obligation, in order "to strengthen their solidarity by promoting the harmonization of their views, the co-ordination of their positions, and, where it appears possible and desirable, common actions" on important foreign policy issues.[63] In order for it to be accepted, European Political Cooperation (EPC) was only to make declarations and begin dialogue; it could not discuss security issues. Without institutional backing, and without being either legally or EC-based, the intergovernmental arrangement had limited impact on world events. Thus, EPC reached its first plateau, "paving the way for a united Europe capable of assuming its responsibilities in the world of tomorrow and of making a contribution commensurate with its traditions and its mission."[64]

### The "Year of Europe"? (1973–1981)

In order to revive the US-European relationship, battered by differences on issues ranging from Vietnam to détente,[65] Henry Kissinger had proclaimed 1973 the "Year of Europe" and called for a "New Atlantic Charter." In a speech to the Associated Press, he recognized the European nations' success in economic integration and in their revival after World War II. However, the United States did not view Europe as an emerging power. According to Kissinger, the "United States has global interests and responsibilities. Our European allies have regional interests."[66] Michael Smith wrote,

> By the end of the year, a combination of established trends and unexpected events had created an atmosphere of recrimination and suspicions which made the idea of a "New Atlantic Charter" seem fairly ridiculous, and in which the idea of a specifically European identity based on political coordination between members of the European Communities (EC) had apparently gained fresh impetus from the Kissinger challenge.[67]

By December 1973, in Copenhagen, the EC member states chose to define their own relations and place in world affairs.

> [T]he time has come to draw up a document on the European Identity. This will enable them to achieve a better definition of their relations

with other countries and of their responsibilities and the place which they occupy in world affairs. They have decided to define the European Identity with the dynamic nature of the Community in mind.[68]

Europe was supposed to take a backseat in world affairs and give its unconditional support to US policy, but splits in foreign policy—for example, with regard to the Arab-Israeli War—demonstrated that the United States and Europe had different interests.

During the Arab-Israeli War of 1973, the United States' traditional allies, France and Britain, rejected the US call for a cease-fire resolution in the United Nations. France actually sent tanks to Libya and Syria during the crisis. Britain, France, Italy, and later Germany refused to allow the United States to use their bases, facilities, or airspace to aid the Israelis.[69] In 1974, the EC established a separate Euro-Arab dialogue through European Political Cooperation to separate themselves from US policy. European foreign policy was taking a turn from Atlantic Alliance policy. In his "Report on European Union" of 1975, Leo Tindemans argued, "The need for Europe to speak with one voice in its relations with the United States is one of the main underlying reasons for the construction of Europe." Only a Europe with a clear identity could "establish relations with the United States based on the principle of equality, free of any sense of dependence. . . ."[70]

In light of the EDC debacle and strong European support in general for NATO, EPC was to keep only to foreign policy issues. However, from its birth EPC dealt indirectly with security affairs. EPC was very successful in coordinating policy within the Conference on Security and Cooperation in Europe (CSCE), dealing with arms control and confidence-building measures. Nevertheless, the avenue to pursue a separate European security policy still did not exist. Although the Nine (the Six, plus Britain, Denmark, and Ireland) were active participants in the negotiation of the Helsinki Final Act, "from 1977 onwards to the end of the decade, cohesion loosened considerably."[71] A higher level of cooperation was needed if the Nine were to make a stronger impact on international events. The Klepsch Report in 1978, the Davignon-Greenwood Report of 1980, and the Delligent Report of 1981 all promoted the idea of a "'Europeanist Security Policy' in which, in the framework of NATO, the exclusive European security interest [could] be pursued, clustered around the EC."[72]

### The "Second" Cold War (1980–1989)

The 1980s continued to see a divergence of European and US security perceptions. Bitter disagreements over the neutron bomb, sanctions on the USSR for Afghanistan, winnable limited nuclear wars under Reagan, Pershing missiles, the "second Cold War,"[73] and the Strategic Defense Initiative (SDI) all "convinced Europeans across the political spectrum that there were indeed separate continental interests."[74] In a speech to the House of Commons and to the Conservative Summer School at Oxford, UK foreign secretary Douglas Hurd suggested strengthening EPC with a firmer commitment to EPC and possibly endowing the presidency with permanent staff.[75] Soon, in October 1980, these and other ideas on how to improve EPC, including whether to enlarge EPC's mandate to include security issues, were discussed with other ministers. Despite Ireland's opposition to the inclusion of security, these discussions led to the London Report of 1981, which allowed "certain important policy questions bearing on the political aspects of security" to be raised within the framework of European Political Cooperation. It also formally approved the role of the Commission in the EPC: "[T]he Ten attach importance to the Commission of the European communities being fully associated with political co-operation at all levels."[76] In this period, EPC reached a third stage, which Elfriede Regelsberger labeled "a new quality of the *acquis*."[77]

Many factors, including strained relations with the United States, Greek accession to the EC, and the fact that it took the member states nineteen days to react to the Soviet invasion of Afghanistan, created pressure for EPC reform. Pauline Neville-Jones explains: "The inability of Europe significantly to influence the course of events and the nakedness of its exposure to external aggression was nowhere more keenly felt than in the German Foreign Ministry."[78] German foreign minister Hans Dietrich Genscher said that possibly the time had come for a Treaty on European Union to strengthen the European Community's political influence on the world stage: "Perhaps Europe's voice would be better heard in Washington if this Europe of ours spoke more with one voice and acted together more decisively."[79] Italian foreign minister Emilio Colombo supported Genscher's views and together they proposed closer cooperation in security and defense. Their draft treaty sought "the co-ordination of security policy and the adoption of common European positions in this sphere in order to safeguard Europe's independence, protect its vital interests and strengthen its security."[80] The Genscher-Colombo initiative sowed a great deal of discord and discontent among the member states. Greece, Ireland, and Denmark all opposed cooperation on security questions. France did not support the proposal, possibly because it was not consulted. Two years later, in 1983, the member states signed a watered-down version of Genscher-Colombo: the Solemn Declaration of Stuttgart. At their council in Stuttgart, the heads of state reaffirmed the European Community's international identity and promised to work more closely together within European Political Cooperation.

At the same time, anti-US sentiment was rising; many people were opposed to the nuclear arms race and US bases in Europe. In October 1983, two million people participated in demonstrations throughout Europe to protest nuclear armaments.[81] Such an outcry probably influenced politicians to take a step away from the United States, and to revive a forum for the European Community countries interested in discussing security issues. The resuscitation of the Western European Union (WEU) was purely political and not institutional: "The significance of the reactivation of the WEU in 1984 lies more in the political will and the wide publicity given to it by its seven members than in its somewhat limited relaunching."[82]

Despite the resuscitation of the WEU, the issue of incorporating security policy into the European Community itself did not die. As well as providing specific duties to the Commission in the framework of EPC, the Single European Act (SEA) codified the discussion of political and economic aspects of security. The British and the Dutch were reluctant supporters, worried that such moves would compete with and, therefore, could undermine the Atlantic Alliance.[83] Ireland, due to its neutrality, and Denmark, with its Nordic identity, desired to keep the EC only to those aspects authorized by the Treaty of Rome; the Papandreou Greek government, which was less critical toward the Soviet Union than were the other member states, concurred, thus hindering the evolution of the EPC. For the countries that wished, the SEA allowed them to pursue "closer co-operation in the field of security . . . within the framework of the Western European Union or the Atlantic Alliance."[84]

### The End of the Cold War and the Birth of the CFSP (1990–1997)

The end of the Cold War seemed the perfect opportunity to change the focus from the United States to Europe, and the rhetoric hit an all-time high. With peace on the European continent, the EC would be able to take its rightful place as leader of the whole of Europe. At the opening of the intergovernmental conference (IGC) in Rome in December 1990, Commission president Jacques Delors declared that the Europeans had "a rendezvous with history."[85] There, the EC formally announced its pursuit of a closer union containing a common foreign and security policy. Alan Clark, the British minister for defense procurement, explained that Europe needed "something slimmer, less set than NATO, something capable of faster response." After all, Clark asked, "what exactly were the 4,000 military and civilian employees doing at NATO headquarters these days?"[86] The secretary-general of the Western European Union, Wim van Eekelen, a former Dutch defense minister, said he would not need such a vast bureaucratic structure to maintain the type of the European defense force he proposed, consisting of a brigade of 4,000 to 5,000 soldiers from each country, with their own staffs, artillery, and logistical support. A single European general would have command. Such a force, van Eekelen reminded his audience, could have been used in the Gulf War.[87]

The Gulf War (1990–1991), the United Nations' effort led by the United States to liberate Kuwait from Iraqi occupation, had underlined the need for a common foreign and security policy in the eyes of many Europeans. The EC's impotence during the war prompted Belgium's foreign minister to complain that Europe was "an economic giant, political dwarf and military worm."[88] Even in one of the clearest cases possible of international misconduct, the European Community could act neither politically nor militarily in unison. Politically, although the EC quickly denounced the Iraqi invasion, the big three, Britain, France, and Germany, soon went their separate ways. The UK immediately identified itself with the United States and even went so far as to put its troops under US command. France sent troops, but kept control while trying in vain, as Christopher Hill put it, "to get its erstwhile Iraqi partners off the hook on which they had impaled themselves."[89] German constitutional restrictions stopped the FRG from sending troops; although they helped fund the mission, they came under a great deal of criticism for not doing more.

The Gulf War brought security cooperation to the forefront of the debate over EC reform and forced the member states to treat EC and NATO reform "as two closely interrelated processes."[90] Jacques Delors blamed the absence of a military dimension for the uncoordinated effort.

It is true that the very first day—2 August 1990—the Community took the firm line expected of it. It confirmed the commitment of its member states to enforce sanctions, the first line of dissuasion against aggressors. However, once it became obvious that the situation would have to be resolved by armed combat, the Community had neither the institutional machinery nor the military force which would have allowed it to act as a community. Are the Twelve prepared to learn from this experience?[91]

The answer was yes. The French learned that its forces "possessed virtually no independent intelligence or airlift capacity and were compelled to rely on U.S. support."[92] Therefore, Europe needed an EC or WEU rapid deployment force with independent logistical support. Even the British agreed something had to be done: "Foreign policy needs security and [there is] no security policy without defence."[93]

Belgian foreign minister Mark Eyskens believed that the addition of a security and defense identity would increase the EC's clout on the world stage. When asked about the minor role the EC was playing in the Middle East, and the possible formation of a US-instigated regional conference with Israel, he answered,

> We in the EC would take offense if a Middle East conference took place with the United States and the Soviets, but without the Europeans. Now Israeli Prime Minister Shamir wants to invite the Europeans as observers. For me it is humiliating if only a folding chair is offered to us. But Europe now has to develop a political identity of its own, including a security and defense dimension.[94]

When the Yugoslav crisis erupted, the CFSP was being hammered out in the 1991 intergovernmental conference. So confident was Jacques Poos, Luxembourg's foreign minister, of the EU's future prowess that he declared, "It is the hour of Europe, not the hour of the Americans." The days of political deadlock were "pre-history."[95]

Nevertheless, the EU member states could not agree on whether or how to intervene militarily or even whether or not to recognize the breakaway republics of Yugoslavia. Lord Owen believed the failure of the EC came from its cockiness:

> There was an air of unreal expectation about the European Community's early involvement. In fairness it was undertaken at the request of all of the parties. But a combination of the United States being unwilling to be dragged in and a European Community being all too ready to prove itself as an independent force in the field of foreign affairs meant that little thought was given to involving from the outset either the UN or the Russian Federation. Yugoslavia we were told in confident terms was a European Community responsibility so much so that many neglected the complex make-up of the country, its Communist legacy and its divisive history itself reflected in past divisions within European Community countries.[96]

The EC continued to be active in the Yugoslav peace process, working in conjunction with the United Nations, but it no longer tried to lead. By February 1993, the Europeans were urging the United States to get more actively involved. As Wim van Eekelen, secretary general of the Western European Union, explained, "[O]ur credibility has fallen very low in the Balkans. . . . We are all looking for the US to take the lead again."[97]

As for similar causes in the past, this failure and the US "win" in the Balkans rallied the member states in the Amsterdam Treaty of 1997 to increase their degree of security cooperation. The treaty charges the EU through the CFSP to "preserve peace and strengthen international security, in accordance with the principles of the United Nations Charter, as well as the principles of the Helsinki Final Act and the objectives of the Paris Charter, including those on external borders."[98] The Amsterdam Treaty gave some meat to the CFSP by establishing a policy planning and early warning unit and a high representative for the CFSP. The unit was responsible for security and threat analysis, along with policy options and recommendations when requested by the council or the presidency.[99] In addition, the Petersberg tasks, formulated under the auspices of the WEU and implying a military component for the first time for the European Union, were formally incorporated into the EU. The Treaty of Amsterdam in no way admitted defeat in the Yugoslav crisis; rather, it convinced the member states, during the IGC negotiations, that the only way to demonstrate they were the equal of the United States was to become yet more coordinated and to take on a military dimension.

### The European Security and Defense Policy (1998–2005)

The Kosovo crisis created a rift between Britain and the United States that the French exploited. The UK very much wanted to intervene in Kosovo, but the Clinton administration, embroiled in the impeachment trial, provided weak leadership and support. For the first time, the UK came on board for a European security and defense policy. A UK Ministry of Defense official explained in an interview that, considering that the UK was neither a member of Schengen nor of the euro, Prime Minister Tony Blair chose to make defense Britain's area of influence in the EU.[100] As a result, Blair became amenable to the idea of an autonomous military capability for the European Union, an initiative that culminated in the Saint-Mâlo Declaration of 1998.

> The European Union needs to be in a position to play its full role on the international stage. . . . This includes the responsibility of the European Council to decide on the progressive framing of a common defence policy in the framework of CFSP. To this end, the Union must have the capacity for autonomous action, backed up by credible mili-

tary forces, the means to decide to use them, and a readiness to do so, in order to respond to international crises.[101]

In the Cologne Presidency Conclusions written in June 1999, the member states echoed Saint-Mâlo, at times word for word, declaring they were resolved that "the European Union shall play its full role on the international stage."[102] Member states pledged not to reduce military spending, and to "bring together national and multi-national European forces";[103] for example, as in the Eurocorps. They stated categorically, "[T]he Union must have the capacity for autonomous action, backed up by credible military forces, the means to decide to use them, and a readiness to do so, in order to respond to international crises without prejudice to actions by NATO."[104] At the December 1999 European Council summit in Helsinki, the EU member states declared unequivocally that they would form their own rapid reaction force of 60,000—the same size as the NATO force in Kosovo—independent of NATO. Although supposed to be operational by 2003, the European Rapid Reaction Force (ERRF) did not come to fruition as envisioned. However, in February 2004, France, Germany, and Britain initiated a joint military force to create several battle groups of 1,500 soldiers to be deployed at short notice. In November 2004, the EU defense ministers pledged to commit up to 165,000 troops to EU battle groups to tackle crises around the world.[105]

Just as during the Gulf War and the Yugoslav crisis, the US invasion of Iraq in 2003 split the EU member states and demonstrated the fragility of the CFSP. Eager to prove themselves good NATO allies, the former Eastern bloc countries and soon-to-be members of the European Union vociferously supported the United States. In reaction to France and Germany's criticism of US foreign policy, US secretary of defense Donald Rumsfeld said the United States could ignore "old Europe" because new Europe was on their side.[106] The Eastern members' vocal support for the United States caused French president Jacques Chirac to suggest publicly that they "be quiet."[107] France, Germany, and Belgium went so far as to reject Turkey's invocation (in expectation of a US invasion of Iraq) of NATO's Article IV, requesting aid in anticipation of an imminent attack from Iraq. All three voted against supplying aid, as a way of showing their displeasure with US foreign policy. Despite France's gift to the United States of the Statue of Liberty and the headlines in the French newspapers after 9/11 declaring *"Nous sommes tous américains,"*[108] the United States blamed the French (who were to be punished) more than the Belgians (who did not even get noticed), the Germans (who were to be ignored), and the Russians (who were to be forgiven).[109]

At the Thessaloniki European Council ending the Greek presidency in June 2003, the Presidency's Conclusions noted, "The European Council reviewed the state of the EU-US relationship and expressed its conviction that the development of the transatlantic relations on an equal footing remains of fundamental importance in every domain not only for the two sides but also for the international community."[110] In order to make such a relationship a reality, Greek foreign minister George Papandreou suggested the creation of a European Security Strategy (ESS) akin to the US National Security Strategy (NSS). Having been constantly criticized as being reactive rather than proactive, the purpose of the ESS was manifold. First and foremost, it demonstrated that the European Union was indeed unified. It was a formal response to the NSS, delineating how European strategic culture differed from that of the United States. As a result, the ESS became a vital tool in creating a European identity.

Seen in this context, the European Security Strategy is not, as Danielle Pletka of the American Enterprise Institute argued, a sign that "Europe is starting to dance to the Bush tune."[111] Rather, according to one EU minister, "[T]his is Europe's answer to the Americans. . . . This is about how we combine all our 'soft power'—the diplomatic, economic, trade and security instruments—and, at the very end, the threat of the use of force. That is some achievement for the Europeans to agree on."[112] The ESS underlined the differences between European and US ways of accomplishing foreign policy goals. Most striking was the ESS's focus on multilateralism. At the same time, this emphasis on multilateralism was an invitation to the United States to collaborate. The first draft of the ESS stated that Europe and the United States can be a "formidable force for good" when acting together.[113] This is the "coming of age" so often invoked: Europe as equal to the United States.

Although perhaps "equal," by definition, "Europe" must differ from "the United States" lest it be merely a poor copy. If the Europeans have gone to so much trouble to create a distinct security identity, it must be informed by different values from those of the United States. How do European values differ from US values?

## Martians and Venusians? Exaggeration of Differences in the Creation of a European Identity

Even before the row over the US invasion of Iraq, Robert Kagan wrote his famous article "Power and Weakness" on why the United States and

Europe disagree on foreign policy. It was widely reported that Javier Solana, the EU's high representative of the CFSP, sent a copy of his more elaborate book on the subject to EU officials and to member state governments.[114] As discussed earlier, his handy catchphrase "America is from Mars and Europe from Venus" encapsulated the warlike tendencies of US foreign and security policy in contrast to Europe's more diplomatic approach. A hardy debate ensued, with pundits across the continents discussing whether the NATO allies still shared the same values and the same worldview.

Although Kagan claimed to take a "psychological" approach, in fact, he took a realist approach: each side's policy is determined by its power position. US policy is all about military power and unilateral action because the United States is very powerful and can follow through; the Europeans, being weak, emphasize diplomacy and solving problems through institutions because they have no other choice. Although an elegant answer, it can easily be broken down. The United States has long used trade agreements, foreign aid, and diplomacy to further its foreign policy goals—much more so than it has used military might. Although the United States may have a penchant for unilateral action, such cases are the exception rather than the rule. Since World War II, it has worked within the United Nations framework and/or with allies—coalitions of the willing, as it were—in the lion's share of its military actions. As to Europe, certainly the UK and France, as Kagan noted, have not been shy to use their military might, especially in their former colonies. Although such European countries as Ireland and Germany have or had constitutional restrictions on how and where troops could be deployed, most of the NATO allies have sent troops to fight together with US troops overseas. Whether in Korea, Vietnam, the Middle East, or, even most recently, Iraq, where many European troops have joined battle alongside US troops, the Europeans have proven themselves ready to fight.

In fact, the main reason why the United States was so angry at the Europeans during the Iraq War was that this time many of the European countries rebelled, whereas in the past they had supported US policy—with troops. Perhaps what is most interesting and significant is that Europe was perceived as having *collectively* rejected US policy in Iraq, despite the fact that of the "old" European countries, the Netherlands, Denmark, Spain, Portugal, Italy, and the UK all sent troops. When one considers the nonparticipants, only Belgium and perhaps France are significant. Ireland, Austria, Sweden, and Finland are neutral and non-NATO members. Nevertheless, Ireland allowed US troops to use

Shannon as a base.[115] Luxembourg has limited capabilities. Greece has long had a reputation for not supporting US policy, despite being a NATO member. Germany, for historical reasons, has a problem with sending troops overseas (the reason why National Security Advisor Condoleezza Rice was willing to "ignore" it). Although French soldiers have usually fought alongside US troops in the past, since France's withdrawal from the military part of the Atlantic Alliance, it has often followed an independent policy. That France should disagree with the United States, therefore, was not surprising. Of these nine countries, only Belgium did an about-face and uncharacteristically rejected the US lead—and Rice did not even take notice.

Especially during the Iraq War, the US people and Europeans alike latched on to Kagan's images, or rather stereotypes, of the United States and Europe. Nicole Gnesotto emphasized the differences, to argue for the need for a separate and distinct EU security and defense policy: "No doubt the European view and practice of power are markedly different from America's."[116] Daniel Keohane, a security specialist at the London-based Centre for European Reform, explained that while "[t]he US rates, analyzes and solves problems very much in military terms, . . . Europe prides itself in using a whole range of means, including aid, economic incentives and civilian police forces."[117] Jonathan Steele, senior foreign correspondent for the UK newspaper *The Guardian,* wrote,

> Europe's social model and parliamentary traditions illustrate the differences that have developed between this continent's values and institutions and those of the US, in spite of common origins. The time has come for Europe to put flesh on this transatlantic division and develop an independent foreign policy. This too can be a rallying point for Europeans, as well as giving the EU a different profile around the world.[118]

Josep Borrell, president of the then–European Parliament, did not mince words when he told an audience at the College of Europe,

> The US today is a country whose logic is IMPERIAL. . . . The American accent is on issues of sovereignty and military security. Europe fights for universal values to make it clear that we do not act believing that "might is right," but, rather, we aim to identify not only the manifestations of terrorism but its CAUSES. . . . This vision that we have of ourselves is a source of irritation to the US.[119]

He went so far as to say that the EU's new mission is to save the United States from itself: "The role of a united Europe today is to help the US overcome its own internal demons and avert the risk of a strong and confident American republic turning into an introverted and arrogant empire."[120]

Although only implied, the original question Kagan was addressing was, "Why do the Europeans no longer support US foreign policy?" This question is flawed on two counts. First, as demonstrated, the Europeans have long had disagreements with the United States over foreign policy. The Iraq example was not special as much as it was vocal. Second, that so many of the EU governments did support the United States despite strong opposition from their publics should be taken as a sign of their loyalty. The true question posed should have been, "Why are Europeans so critical of US policy and seem to set themselves in opposition to it, when they have worked so well with the United States in the past?" The true answer lies with Paul Kowert's psychological analysis rather than with realism: to foster and promote a pan-European identity, the European Union must distinguish itself from the United States, especially in the realm of security policy. When an identity is in the process of forming, both sides will exaggerate the differences to facilitate pigeonholing. This process, which is accelerated during periods of conflict, highlights differences with the out-group while allowing for the glossing over of dissimilarities within the in-group.

### Creating the European "Brand"

Gerhard Schröder, chancellor of Germany, stated that "the emancipation of the country's foreign policy also means that it must sometimes distance itself from America."[121] In a private speech to US officials at a political/military conference hosted by the General Secretariat of the Council of the European Union in Brussels, Robert Cooper, director general for external and politico-military affairs, explained very clearly that although the process "will no doubt be tedious and sometimes irritating for the USA," it is nevertheless necessary for the successful political integration of Europe:

> Europe is a political project. By that I mean that, in part, it is about creating a "we," a group which can and does act together not just when it happens to have a common interests [sic] but because it defines acting together as being a common interest. Europe is a mean [sic] but is also an end. We want to be able to act autonomously because that is what "we" means.[122]

Indeed, the mere existence of the EU creates an alternative to the US model in international relations. Peter van Ham of the Netherlands

Institute for International Relations wrote, "The EU, by its very existence, opens the possibility of a totally different model that downplays
force and realpolitik and upgrades the role of law and trust. The
European integration model is proof that the rule of law, institutional
arrangements and an elaborate diplomatic circus can tame nationalism
and make military might well-nigh irrelevant."[123]

Average citizens both in old and new Europe react positively to this
idea of the United States as the "other." To quote a qualitative
*Eurobarometer* study published in June 2001, before both the 9/11
attacks and the war in Iraq,

> Citizens of all these countries feel, more or less spontaneously, *that*
> *this model, built on the foundations of cultural and humanistic values,*
> *is unique. It sets Europe in opposition to the United States,* whose col-
> lective mentality is broadly perceived as very different and which, in
> some of the countries studied, is lampooned as a people without a his-
> tory, materialist, bereft of these values, and which also arouses intense
> hostility; this is the case not only in France (whose Gaullist tradition
> of distrust of the Americans is well known), and in Germany (whose
> citizens seem to have undergone a sea-change on this front over the
> last 10 years), but even more so in Member States such as Spain or
> Greece, and in many of the candidate countries.[124]

If, indeed, as Cooper puts it, the purpose of the ESDP and its actions is
to define Europe, then, by definition, the European Union must distinguish itself from NATO and delineate how its policy differs from that of
the United States—the federation with which it is most often compared.

In 2005, *Eurobarometer* discovered a continued, positive perception
of the role the European Union played in international affairs, but with a
noted recognition of the role of the United States as the "other." In all
five questions asked, a decided majority of people agreed that the EU
played a more positive role on the world scene than did the United
States. Strikingly, with regard to the question of playing a negative or
positive role in the promotion of world peace, there is a thirty-eight-
point difference among Europeans between the perception of the EU
and the United States (see Figure 4.1).

The report concludes, "Therefore, in general, the role played by the
European Union in these five areas [world peace, protection of the environment, fight against terrorism, growth of the world economy, and
fight against worldwide poverty] is perceived positively by the majority
of the persons interviewed. On the other hand, the role of the United
States is seen far more negatively."[125]

**Figure 4.1 Europeans' Perceptions About the Roles Played by the European Union vs. the United States (percent "positive")**

| | | |
|---|---|---|
| World peace | EU: 63 | US: 25 |
| Protection of the environment | EU: 62 | US: 18 |
| Fight against terrorism | EU: 60 | US: 43 |
| Growth of the world economy | EU: 50 | US: 38 |
| Fight against worldwide poverty | EU: 49 | US: 20 |

☐ European Union   ■ United States

*Source: Eurobarometer* 63 (2005), 69; fieldwork, May–June 2005.
*Notes:* Question A: In your opinion, would you say that the United States tends to play a positive role, a negative role, or neither a positive nor negative role regarding . . . ?
Question B: In your opinion, does the European Union tend to play a positive role, a negative role, or neither a positive nor negative role regarding . . . ?

## Partners or Rivals? Straining Relations in NATO

This desire for "emancipation," as Chancellor Schröder put it, conjures up the image of a slave and a slave owner. It depicts the body that needs to be set free as being in the grips of an all-powerful entity that can choose or not choose to free the other. Kowert explained this view of the other in his third lesson: "Finally, people will tend to attribute the behavior of political out-groups to the intent or desires of these groups; in-group behavior, however, will more often be attributed to the influence of environmental constraints. Perceived increases in the power of out-groups will strengthen the tendency to assume intent (attributional bias)."[126] Nowhere is this "attributional bias," on both the US and European side, so clear as within NATO. Jonathan Steele of *The Guardian* did not mince words when he asserted that the United States intentionally uses NATO to control Europe. "Since the cold war Europe faces no threats that require an automatic triggering of US support, Nato is no longer a crutch. It is a leg-iron preventing Europe from taking action on its own, and a device for US pressure—most recently the bullying of current and would-be Nato members to commit troops to the chaos of postwar Iraq."[127]

NATO has become the unfortunate venue for a rivalry between Europe and the United States, a rivalry whose shorthand is the "theology" debate. As Gnesotto pointed out,

> In addition to the nation-states, the other major structural limit of the ESDP is its relationship to the Atlantic Alliance. Because NATO is identified, in Europe's history and perceptions, with America's protection of Europe, the United States has, since the origin of the ESDP, played a very decisive role in its development and functioning. Right from the start, this role was ambivalent: the American authorities encouraged the development of the ESDP when it meant modernizing European military capabilities, but they also stated very clearly its limits, or even its dangers, when it meant constructing a European political identity.[128]

Gnesotto has hit the nail on the head. Many in the United States, especially the "neocons," are plainly afraid of the construction of a European political identity, which has led to two different perspectives, deemed "theologies," within NATO: does one support Atlanticism and the transatlantic architecture that has preserved Europe's security for fifty years, or does one support the formation of a distinct Europeanist security policy to keep European integration alive? Each side projects an "intentionality" onto the other as to its actions and policies: if Side A supports a particular policy, it is—in the view of Side B—because Side A is actively trying to harm Side B. Cimbalo's "Saving NATO from Europe" clearly encapsulates these feelings.[129]

### Atlanticist Dogma vs. Europeanist Dogma

The theological question asks members to choose between Atlanticism and Europeanism, a difficult and uncomfortable choice for such countries as the Netherlands that identify with both. According to State Secretary for National Defense and Maritime Affairs Manuel Lobo Antunes of Portugal, "Dogmatism has been the real stumbling block for the dialogue between the two sides of the Atlantic."[130]

This Atlanticist dogma prescribes the following: all discussion of security with European allies must take place within NATO; in accordance with Madeleine Albright's speech, there must be no decoupling of Europe or the United States from NATO, no duplication of NATO assets or arrangements, and no discrimination against other non-EU NATO allies; and recognition that the Berlin-plus arrangements give NATO a right of first refusal. "Berlin-plus" is a term used for the comprehensive series of agreements painstakingly negotiated between the Atlantic Alliance and the European Union to allow the EU access to NATO assets, "where NATO is not engaged." Atlanticists interpret these words as meaning that any security questions must be discussed in the NATO context first. All of the above conditions were considered necessary to preserve the integrity and position of NATO or, in other words, a US presence in Europe.

From the Europeanist perspective, although very important, NATO, as a collective defense organization, has both a limited mandate and a narrow military focus. For some countries, led by France, NATO exists only to serve Article V: an attack on one is an attack on all. Very simply, it is less dynamic, and, therefore, of limited use. As one NATO official commented, "What would NATO do with banking experts?"[131] The European Union, however, is a much broader institution whose expertise ranges from banking to development assistance. As such, many, both inside and outside of NATO, see the EU as the more dynamic institution. However, it must be given more attention if it is to thrive. The ESDP components are especially vulnerable, living, as it were, in the shadow of the Atlantic Alliance.

As a result, Europeanist dogma prescribes the following: first, the EU is the preferred organization because it is multifaceted and better able to deal with crises. While the EU can address the developmental, economic, and humanitarian aspects of a crisis, NATO, being a purely military organization, cannot. Second, the EU must evolve if it is to function. One cannot "stifle the baby."[132] Therefore, the EU must be allowed to have military headquarters or whatever else it needs to ensure its growth and competence. As one UK official in the Permanent Representation in Brussels bluntly put it, "But NATO, ahh, that is the US. The EU is 'European.' The point of the ESDP is to be autonomous without having to ask the US. . . . In a nutshell, exchange of information within NATO is all right, cooperation with NATO is all right, transparency with NATO is all right, but *not* coordination with NATO, as that compromises EU autonomy."[133]

### Ramifications of the Theological Divide

The war in Iraq is just one example of the theological divide in NATO. Although the wounds and divisions from the war have been bandaged, since then, relations between the EU and NATO have remained rocky. Despite attempts to codify cooperation and systematize the sharing of military assets, theological problems continue to hound EU-NATO coordination and cooperation.

Beginning with the negotiation of Berlin-plus, the next section examines areas and cases where the two organizations have clashed. These examples are significant in that they show the endurance, pervasiveness, and permeation of theology in EU-NATO relations. They demonstrate the mistrust between the Atlanticists and the Europeanists as each side sees the other as intentionally sabotaging the other. Nevertheless, none of these disputes—even if they had all gone the way the French had wanted—would have hurt NATO militarily. Rather, the focus is on the morale and image of each organization.

*Berlin-plus I: the headquarters issue.* In 1992, the Maastricht Treaty on European Union introduced the Common Foreign and Security Policy (CFSP), which provided the basis for the discussion of security affairs within the EU. Subsequently, in 1994, under the auspices of the NATO Council, the member states recognized the need to define a European identity vis-à-vis security and defense. This agreement led to the development of the European Security and Defense Identity (ESDI) to allow the EU access to NATO assets and planning capabilities to carry out such narrowly defined military operations as peacekeeping and humanitarian tasks, the so-called Petersberg tasks. Although it took another eight years, in December 2002, NATO and the EU approved what is called "Berlin-plus," which

> [w]elcome[d] the European Security and Defence Policy (ESDP), whose purpose is to add to the range of instruments already at the European Union's disposal for crisis management and conflict prevention in support of the Common Foreign and Security Policy, the capacity to conduct EU-led crisis management operations, including military operations *where NATO as a whole is not engaged.*[134]

This wording was carefully chosen to give NATO a "right of first refusal," to be used only "as a last resort," as Nicholas Burns, US ambassador to NATO, had negotiated it. Many UK members of parliament affirmed this interpretation during debate on the issue in the House of Commons.[135] The French interpreted this clause differently. In an interview with the *Daily Telegraph* (London), French General Jean-Pierre Kelche stated, "There is no question of a right of first refusal. If the EU does its work properly, it will be able to start working on crises at a very early stage, well before the situation escalates. Where is the first refusal? NATO has nothing to do with this. At a certain stage the

Europeans would decide to conduct a military operation. Either the Americans would come, or not."[136]

Within five months of this agreement, the French, champions of the ESDP, tried to negate Berlin-plus in two ways. In April 2003, they sought to create a separate military headquarters, although Berlin-plus specifically allowed for the borrowing of the NATO command structure. In May, they initiated an international mission to the Congo under the banner of the ESDP, which included Canada, but without either US or NATO approval—effectively negating any interpretation of Berlin-plus that included a NATO right of first refusal.

In April 2003, taking advantage of the strong anti-US sentiment in Europe with regard to the war in Iraq, the French met with the Belgians, the Germans, and the Luxembourgers at Tervuren, Belgium (later known as the Tervuren Four), to discuss the creation of a new EU headquarters in a suburb of Brussels. Considering that NATO's greatest value-added was its command structure and that four months earlier the EU and NATO had finally concluded arrangements to allow the EU to use that structure, it was seen as a slap in the face to the Atlanticists that these member states would violate one of the three $D$'s—duplication (see Chapter 2). Their proposal to place the EU headquarters in a suburb of Brussels seemed a symbolic foil to NATO, located in a different Brussels suburb. Moreover, they met alone.

Washington derided the meeting as "a little bitty summit" of the "chocolate makers."[137] The Royal United Services Institute for Defence and Security Studies (RUSI) reported, "Overall, Solana's reticence on the Tervuren initiative reflects a feeling that a separate EU headquarters is more objectionable from the point of view of political symbolism rather than potential military duplication. . . . The Blair government strongly suspected that the objective of the April meeting was a political poke at the US rather than a serious military initiative."[138] However, once the UK decided to compromise with the French and the Germans in October 2003, US ambassador Nicholas Burns "described the latest moves by London, Paris, and Berlin as the 'most significant threat to Nato's future.' The French ambassador, Benoit d'Aboville, angrily retorted that the Europeans would do exactly as they pleased and did not have to explain their actions to Washington."[139] French defense minister Michèle Alliot-Marie defended the action by delineating European from US views: "The Iraq crisis has highlighted the need for Europe to express its own world outlook, and we share this outlook with the British."[140]

The US government was critical of the plan because it wanted to avoid duplication of effort. After painstaking negotiations to give the

EU access to NATO planning resources at the Supreme Headquarters Allied Powers Europe (SHAPE) through Berlin-plus, the Tervuren Four proposed duplicating this very asset. Moreover, under such an arrangement, member state militaries would be devoting their limited defense resources to staffing a headquarters rather than to capability deficiencies already identified. Washington was concerned that generals sitting at an EU headquarters would want to justify their existence and prove their worth by coming up with concepts for EU missions. If done without consultation with NATO (as called for in Berlin-plus), this would increase the likelihood that NATO and the EU might produce conflicting operational plans that would draw on the same set of troops and resources.[141] Nicholas Burns, now promoted to undersecretary of state, asserted,

> The answer is NATO. Really. We've had long discussions over ten years about this. NATO has the lead on the security side in the transatlantic relationship. . . . [I]t is possible for the European Union to decide to be involved, but only under the rules of Berlin-plus where the EU borrows assets from NATO to perform the mission. But the EU will not seek to build up permanent security institutions that would duplicate what we have built for over 56 years at NATO. You are getting the theology here, but it's very clear theology.[142]

The UK, France, and Germany tried to explain that such a headquarters was necessary, with a growing EU now composed of twenty-five members for coordination purposes. As one State Department official put it, "The EU member states were mystified: why was the US getting so upset?"[143] US opposition to the headquarters has helped to foster a perception among Europeans that the United States is blocking the ESDP in order to control Europe. If this is true, the argument goes, then, indeed, the EU needs an independent force; if it is not true, then an independent force should not be a problem for Washington. According to one EU official, without a permanent, functioning headquarters to practice coordination, the ESDP is doomed to failure because it requires so much planning to yoke twenty-five (now twenty-seven) member states and their assets together. Therefore, US opposition to such a headquarters is a death knell to ESDP.[144]

*Berlin-plus II: the Democratic Republic of Congo.* Within a few months of the signing of the Berlin-plus agreement, France contacted Washington, bilaterally, about the crisis in the DRC. At first, relations with the United States were very smooth. The United States supported the EU démarche in Bunia. However, Washington said it would give planes to France, but only if done through Berlin-plus. From the French perspective, Kofi Annan had called Chirac and Solana, not Washington. "France had planned everything. If done through Berlin-plus, all the French planning would have been for nothing. Moreover, SHAPE has no African experts and it would have meant a delay of ten days. France withdrew its request."[145] France, being a sovereign country, argued it needed the approval of neither the United States nor of NATO before it sent its troops anywhere. "If it is hard to come to an agreement at 25 [member states], imagine if you have to work with a third country [the United States]."[146]

France, then, led one of the first ESDP missions in cooperation with its own coalition of the willing, including German and British troops. The mission got some very favorable press attention.

> A great deal is riding on French, British and German troops who now stand guard outside the UN headquarters in Bunia or drive bulldozers, extending its airport. This is the first truly European army since the time of Charlemagne—King of the Franks and Emperor of the Holy Roman Empire—twelve-hundred years ago. True, it is no standing army—rather a coalition of the willing, as the phrase goes. But there on the streets of this dilapidated Congolese town are the first stirrings of a force that could, in time provide the European Union with the kind of military that might end America's status as the only superpower.[147]

The question of the "right of first refusal" is now moot. One French diplomat agreed that it was presented as a "fait accompli" to the United States.[148] Considering that the United States truly believed it got the right of first refusal with Berlin-plus, there now exists a lack of trust between Washington and Brussels because the former is afraid that anything it agrees to will be twisted.

*The NATO response force vs. the EU battle groups.* The origins of the NATO Response Force (NRF) and the EU battle groups are tightly interwoven. In 1999, at the Helsinki European Council summit, the EU member states agreed to the creation of an EU rapid reaction force, 60,000 strong, similar in size to the NATO force in Kosovo. Although included in the Headline Goal 2003 (with the goal of being achieved by June 2003), it was never realized. In September 2002, at the NATO Prague summit, US secretary of defense Donald Rumsfeld proposed the creation of a NATO rapid reaction force partly in response to the Berlin-plus negotiations that were taking place at the time, and to the understanding that NATO required agile and mobile forces rather than the massed armies of the Cold War. The NRF would be composed of 21,000 troops, mostly staffed by Europeans, with high-tech weapons to defend against nuclear, biological, and chemical weapons. Individual NATO countries would put NRF trained forces on standby for six-month rotations. These troops were to be deployable within seven to thirty days.[149] In February 2003, at Le Touquet in France, Blair and Chirac met to discuss ways to strengthen European security and defense cooperation. In a joint declaration, the UK and France made the development of a rapid reaction capability "a European priority. Progress here will enable the EU to meet its own objectives and to strengthen the European contribution to the establishment of a NATO Response Force and to ensure compatibility between the two."[150] In November 2003, the UK and France reiterated the need for such a force based on their experience in the first EU-led autonomous military operation—Operation Artemis in the Democratic Republic of Congo. In February 2004, France, Germany, and the UK submitted the proposal for the battle groups to the EU's Political and Security Committee. Similar to the NRF, the battle groups would be composed of highly trained battalions of 1,500 soldiers ready to deploy within fifteen days' notice for thirty days.

Although originally envisioned to work together, relations between the NRF and the battle groups have been tainted by the theology debate. With the demise of conscription, the reduction of European defense budgets, and the aging of Europe's population, there are a limited number of soldiers available to be assigned either to the NRF or the battle groups. Which force should have priority? This competition may impact the military readiness of both groups. In any case, it has caused NATO-EU relations to simmer.

The EU, pressured by the French, seriously considered creating a separate and different certification procedure for their EU battle groups, whose troops would also serve under NATO's reaction force with an already established certification. In other words, the same troops would be forced to learn and train to two different standards for no reason but to demonstrate that the EU battle groups were distinct from NATO's.[151] The rationale was that the battle groups needed a separate certification because the groups might involve participation from countries such as Cyprus and Malta (although they did not volunteer), and they would not be allowed to see NATO classified procedure. The United States was especially disappointed because they had proposed that the NRF be a strategic reserve force for EU battle groups: should the battle groups need reinforcements or need to extend their stay during a crisis, they could draw on the NRF.[152] With different certification standards, the NRF could not play such a role. In the end, NATO decided to declassify the procedures to defuse the issue. In January 2006, the member states chose to use NATO's certification procedures for both groups.[153]

Although formally declared fully operational in 2006 at the NATO Riga summit, military commitments to peacekeeping operations, especially in Afghanistan, have forced NATO allies to withdraw troops and support from the NRF. In a letter to the NATO secretary-general in 2007, General John Craddock, NATO's top military commander, warned that the NRF was no longer at full operational capacity because of a serious lack of troops.[154] NATO spokesperson James Appathurai explained, "We are having problems providing troops for all the NATO, EU and UN missions."[155] In addition, with European troops already in Afghanistan, Iraq, and Lebanon, many European countries are reluctant to volunteer more troops "to a standing force whose use is uncertain."[156] As a result, in October 2007, the NATO defense ministers agreed to scale back the NRF. The issue of troops has also raised the question of loyalties divided between the NRF and EU battle groups. One NATO official explained, "Soldiers that are active for the EU will be missed by us and vice versa. . . . [a]nd in a crisis. To whom do the soldiers really belong? The EU will lose out."[157]

*Relations between the North Atlantic Council and the Political and Security Committee.* In hopes of repairing the EU-NATO rift, in 2004, the new secretary general of NATO, Jaap de Hoop Scheffer, reached out to Javier Solana, the high representative of the CFSP. Since Solana had once been secretary general of NATO himself, Jaap de Hoop Scheffer believed they could work together to rebuild the EU-NATO partnership. However, he was rebuffed; Solana showed no interest in cooperating because his job was to build up the EU's ESDP, not help NATO.[158]

Relations worsened in May 2004 when Cyprus and Malta as well as eight other countries joined the European Union in the largest expansion in its history. As Cyprus and Malta are members neither of NATO nor of Partnership for Peace (PfP), Turkey objects to discussing any classified information during the NAC-PSC meetings between NATO's North Atlantic Council (NAC) and the EU's Political and Security Committee (PSC). According to one Dutch NATO official, "For the EU and NATO, there is no real relationship. With regard to NAC and PSC, it's so bad, you think it cannot last, but it does."[159] Another diplomat called the meetings a "charade."[160] Turkey will only allow issues explicitly designated by Berlin-plus to be discussed—i.e.,

Bosnia, as that is the only item that falls under this rubric. Otherwise, Turkey has refused to discuss any security issue in the presence of representatives from either Cyprus or Malta. In one case, the majority of NAC-PSC countries wished to discuss the political and security ramifications of Ukraine's Orange Revolution at the end of 2004. As Ukraine did not fall under Berlin-plus, Turkey refused to discuss the issue in the presence of Cyprus and Malta, and asked that they leave. The French ambassador then retorted that in the EU, decisions are made at twenty-five; therefore, if the EU is to be represented, all twenty-five member states' representatives must be present. After considering the objection, Solana, who chairs the meetings, did not allow Ukraine as a topic of discussion.[161]

The French argue that the United States must control Turkey.[162] However, Turkey is acting as an obstructionist in hopes of badgering the European Union into accepting its application for membership. Although its membership application was accepted in October 2005, there will probably be no change in Turkish policy until the Cyprus issue is resolved, Cyprus and Malta join Partnership for Peace, or Turkey is finally allowed to accede to the EU.[163]

To get around this problem, the meetings have been adjourned, but continued informally. As one Dutch NATO diplomat explained,

> So, shouldn't Darfur be an NAC-PSC agenda item? Sure, but the French said no. It's not Berlin-plus. To find a way around this, there was fantastic politicking. The Dutch protested saying it was "outrageous." Solana, who is the chair of these meetings, said "[S]ome delegations have made it known to me that they want to discuss the Sudan. So let's close the official agenda, but continue informally after the coffee break." Malta and Cyprus tiptoed into the room and so it worked. This strategy applies to any meeting outside Berlin-plus.[164]

As a result, the meetings have taken place in such other informal venues as châteaux or restaurants hired for the purpose of having more substantive discussions. Nevertheless, these meetings are not always successful. In January 2006, France blocked discussion of terrorism in an informal NAC-PSC meeting, arguing that it was not an official topic of conversation. The meeting was cancelled, with some diplomats wondering whether France truly wanted cooperation between the two organizations. Paris has argued that NATO should not be the world's policeman. Another French diplomat said, "We don't want NATO getting involved everywhere and imposing its agenda on the EU." Solana shared this concern.[165]

*The United States and the EU clash over civilian and military aspects of cooperation.* After US president George W. Bush's reelection in November 2004, both Europe and Washington went on a charm offensive to repair the damage the war in Iraq had inflicted on the transatlantic relationship. In light of Bush's planned visit, the Council of Ministers prepared a US-EU political declaration on improving cooperation in crisis management. This document was supposed to be a symbol of the renewed relationship between the United States and Europe.

> [W]elcom[ing] the existing cooperation between the United States and the European Union in the area of crisis management, from early warning to stabilization and reconstruction, *including civilian and military aspects*, in particular in the Balkans and in Africa. This cooperation is founded on shared values, the indivisibility of our security and out [*sic*] determination to tackle together the challenges of our time.[166]

Consistent with Atlanticist dogma and US policy, the US State Department rejected the declaration on the grounds that it stated "civilian and military aspects." As all military aspects are to be discussed within NATO, they could not be included in the bilateral document. The State Department returned the draft with the word "military" stricken and other offending sections rewritten. Many member states took offense at the deletion. Considering all the military cooperation between the allies and de facto cooperation on the ground between the two organizations in the Balkans and Africa, why was it necessary to delete the word "military" from such a document? In the end, Cyprus vetoed it, and Bush had no declaration to sign before the press on his trip.[167]

### Darfur and Beauty Contests

Deputy Secretary of State Robert Zoellick of the United States told the annual Munich Security Conference he hoped that NATO and the EU would not get embroiled in a long, drawn-out theological debate about which organization was best placed to act in Darfur.[168] Hoop de Scheffer agreed, stating, "Let's not have theology. Let's do it. The African Union came to NATO and the African Union came to the EU. There is no room for competition. There is plenty of work to be done."[169] Yet, the squabbles between the EU and NATO to send desperately needed humanitarian assistance caused a great deal of bad press.[170] Peter Takirambudde, the Africa director for Human Rights Watch, said, "The priorities are profoundly wrong if Nato and the EU let their turf battle come before protecting the lives of civilians."[171]

The conflict in the Darfur region of Sudan began in 2003 after a rebel group began attacking government targets, saying the Khartoum government favored Arabs over black Africans. The government retaliated by mobilizing "self-defence militias." Although the government admits fighting rebels, it denies charges of ethnic cleansing. Nevertheless, many human rights groups as well as the US Congress said genocide was taking place. Hundreds of thousands of refugees were forced to leave their homes, but without enough provisions of water or food in this arid land. In 2005, the African Union (AU) requested aid from both the European Union and NATO to facilitate peacekeeping in the region. *Le Figaro* quoted an unnamed EU official as saying, "Having been on the scene [in Darfur], albeit discreetly, for six months, the EU did not want to see NATO, a newcomer in the region, steal the show."[172]

In a cutthroat beauty contest, each side tried to push the other out of the limelight. According to one Dutch NATO diplomat, the EU should have informed NATO, in the spirit of Berlin-plus, when they were first contacted by the African Union. However, the French did not want to, as they preferred to keep NATO out of Africa; telling NATO could have meant its possible involvement. The issue of merely informing NATO became so heated that, at US behest, the UK called the Dutch, who held the EU presidency at the time, to make sure the subject of Darfur would be brought up in the context of the Atlantic Alliance.[173]

The EU has a serious deficiency in airlift capacity, and therefore leased Ukrainian Antonov 36s (extremely large cargo planes) and requested planes and airlift from every member state to send to Darfur. The AU needed help ferrying its own troops to Sudan. The problem was that the EU simply did not have the capability to organize such a massive operation. As a result, the African Union requested NATO assistance with peacekeeping and because the United States had massive airlift capability. Although the requests were made under the auspices of the EU and NATO, most military assets (e.g., aircraft) were under national control. Countries that were members of both organizations had to choose the banner under which they were to fly. In the case of Germany, Peter Struck, defense minister, said, "This [choice] is completely irrelevant. One should simply agree to help. Who takes the lead in co-ordinating it is secondary."[174] In the end there were divisions: Atlanticist countries, the Netherlands and the UK, went under the NATO flag, whereas Europeanist countries, such as France, Belgium, and Greece, went under the EU flag. The United States provided airlift for the Rwandans, and France for the Senegalese, despite the fact that Washington had wanted to coordinate the entire effort.[175]

As the first NATO mission to Africa, Washington was concerned with the press. Considering the limited number of planes and helicopters, the two organizations involved, and the need for speed, coordination of strategic airlift in Europe was vital.

> The Dutch begged to make use of the European airlift coordination center in Eindhoven. It's not an EU facility, but an ad hoc facility that serves EU member states. It would save money and is apolitical considering that the coordinating machinery for SHAPE has a forward cell there. Some said, "Let's use the Eindhoven facility. We'll just send a few extra guys down." It proved impossible—an unholy alliance between the French and the US. The Dutch kept saying "It's not EU. Let's just use it. Send NATO people." The French said they didn't want to augment NATO and the US didn't want the first NATO mission in Africa sent from a "European" facility.[176]

A single coordination center would have been more efficient. One diplomat said to the press, "Since we were not going to do the operation together, it was not worth moving people from Mons to Eindhoven if they were not even going to sit together."[177]

Once on the ground in Africa, the commanders of the US European Command (EUCOM) had difficulty simply communicating with their EU counterparts because of "stovepiping." As the United States would only discuss security within NATO, if a US commander wanted to speak to his or her counterpart in the EU, the communication had to go through Washington and then to NATO in Brussels, where the US NATO ambassador would send the question to the other European country's ambassador to transmit to the US commander's European counterpart back in Darfur. This stovepiping made communication between the nominal allies very difficult.[178]

One positive effect of embarrassing incidents such as NATO-EU coordination in Darfur is that they are a catalyst for solutions. As one US diplomat explained,

> Things are better because Condoleezza Rice has a pragmatic approach. The Darfur experience was so ugly and uncomfortable over whether it was the EU or NATO to do whichever, the institutional rivalry was so horrible, that now we work with the Europeans to avoid such stovepiping in the future. We just don't pound fists at the table. We [the United States] do defense and security through NATO—you [the Europeans] don't have to [only work through NATO].[179]

Under Rice's orders, US commanders can talk to their EU counterparts in the field when practical and necessary. Although there is no US defense attaché in the US mission to the EU per se, there is a NATO attaché who can therefore speak to the EU military attaché. On the other hand, there is no EU defense attaché in Washington: only the European Commission has representation in Washington, and ESDP does not fall under its purview. The General Secretariat of the Council of Ministers proposed an ESDP exchange with the State Department, but was told the exchange could not deal with security or military issues, as that was done through NATO.[180]

On the other hand, significant progress was made in the 30 April 2007 summit, where the United States and the EU agreed to a "comprehensive approach" toward crisis management "consistent with and building upon cooperation with NATO." In other words, the limiting word, "civilian," which the United States had previously insisted on, has been removed, paving the way toward enhanced "cooperation in the field of crisis management."[181] This declaration may go a long way in salvaging the transatlantic relationship.

The preceding pages seem to describe turf battles and competition. In fact, they do not. The significance is psychological. A NATO without a right of first refusal, an EU with a separate military headquarters, and different battle group certifications would not affect the existence of NATO or the United States' commitment to it. Although the Europeans talk a good show, they have restrained themselves from actually creating a competing alliance for several reasons. First, the rhetoric works; there is no need for a full-fledged European military alliance to compete with NATO. Second, Europeans do not want to spend the money. Finally, NATO is still popular; governments and citizens on both sides of the Atlantic want to keep it.

There is no question that the United States and Europe are allies. However, the "intentionality" each side projects on the other, the idea that policies are pursued on purpose, is undermining cooperation.[182] The United States must understand that if European integration is to succeed, then Europeans have to do everything in their power to solidify a European identity. As Cooper explained, by definition, a Europe acting together means a Europe acting without the United States. The citizens of Europe are reacting positively to the rhetoric. Nevertheless, the rhetoric must be separated from the reality.

## Conclusion

The United States has been a referent for Europe. The Europeans measure their success, their power, and even their values with those of the people of the United States. Jean Monnet called the United States "the arsenal of democracy"; Winston Churchill called for a "United States of Europe"; could a united Europe also become an "arsenal of democracy"? During the twentieth century, European countries had been conquered and/or lost their empires. Pursuing an "ever closer union" seemed the best solution both to achieving peace on the European continent and to regaining lost power and prestige on the world stage.

As a referent, the United States has been the spur of the EU's security policy. Europeans have banded together whenever they have disagreed with US policy and called for increased cooperation in the security field. However, little reform could be achieved so long as the allies had to face off against the Soviets. Although European actions, such as the resuscitation of the WEU, were more symbolic than effective, they set the stage for future cooperation once the Cold War was over and the international environment afforded Europeans more flexibility in their security arrangements. However, the subsequent formation of formal EU structures has strained relations in NATO. Each side has exaggerated the differences between them until they are labeled from different planets.

## Notes

1. Wolfgang Schäuble, "Europe's Strategic Purpose," *Wall Street Journal*, 5 February 2004, 12.

2. Kissinger, *The Troubled Partnership*, 240.

3. "Israeli Anger over EU 'Threat' Poll," *BBC News*, 3 November 2003, at http://news.bbc.co.uk/go/pr/fr/-/2/hi/middle_east/3237277.stm. See also "Iraq and Peace in the World," *Flash Eurobarometer* 151 (8–16 October 2003): 87.

4. Daniel Dombey and Stanley Pignal, "Europeans See US as Threat to Peace," *Financial Times* (London), 1 July 2007.

5. Jürgen Habermas and Jacques Derrida, *"Unsere Erneuerung. Nach dem Krieg: Die Wiedergeburt Europas," Franfurter Allgemeine Zeitung,* 31 May 2003, 33, as quoted and cited in Ickstadt, "Uniting a Divided Nation," 168.

6. Brewer, "Multiple Identities and Identity Transition," 187.

7. Ibid., 188.

8. A full discussion of cognitive psychology is beyond the scope of this project. For an excellent synopsis of minimum group paradigm and the construction of national identity, see Paul Kowert, "Agent Versus Structure in the Construction of National Identity," in *International Relations in a Constructed World*, ed. Vendulka Kubalkova, Nicholas Onuf, and Paul Kowert, 101–122.

9. Ibid., 106.

10. Prizel, *National Identity and Foreign Policy,* 17.

11. Of the twenty-seven member states, eight—Ireland, Sweden, Finland, Slovenia, Malta, Cyprus, Portugal, and Spain—do not fall into this category. Many of the new, former Warsaw Pact countries attribute their liberation and status today to the United States.

12. "McDonald's in France: Delicious Irony," *The Economist,* 25 April 2002. See also "Spot the Difference: French Anti-Americanism," *The Economist,* 20 December 2005.

13. "Spot the Difference," *The Economist,* 20 December 2005.

14. *Eurobarometer* 243, "Europeans and Their Languages," special issue, February 2006, at http://ec.europa.eu/public_opinion/archives/ebs/ebs_243 _sum_en.pdf.

15. "Commission Struggles to Get Workers on the Move," *EurActiv.com,* 20 February 2006, at http://www.euractiv.com/en/innovation/commission-struggles-get-workers-move/article-152787.

16. Ickstadt, "Uniting a Divided Nation," 162.

17. Winston Churchill, "The Tragedy of Europe," 20 September 1946, speech given at the University of Zurich, at http://www.euro-know.org/speeches /paperchurchill.html.

18. This film was shown to school groups touring the European Commission. The video depicted a European businessman, who, with the help of the European Union, was able to defeat both the US and the Japanese karate expert.

19. "Sizing Up Friends (and Rivals)," *New York Times,* 20 February 2005, 3.

20. José Manuel Barroso, speech at the inauguration of the academic year 2004–2005, College of Europe, Bruges, 23 November 2004, at http://www.coleuro be/-template.asp?pagename=speeches.

21. "Charlemagne: Philadelphia or Frankfurt?" *The Economist,* 6 March 2003.

22. "US Troops to Remain in Europe," *BBC News,* 23 February 2005, at http://-news.bbc.co.uk/2/hi/americas/4292269.stm.

23. As reported in Elaine Sciolino, "Europe Is Divided and Wary About the US," *New York Times,* 20 February 2005, 6.

24. As quoted in Charles Bremner, "Paris and Berlin Prepare Alliance to Rival NATO," *Times* (London), 28 April 2003.

25. Presidency Conclusions, Thessaloniki European Council, 19 and 20 June 2003, 11638/03, at http://ue.eu.int/ueDocs/cms_Data/docs/pressData/en /ec/76279.pdf.

26. Deutsch et al., *Political Community and the North Atlantic Area.*

27. "Discussion at the 267th Meeting of the National Security Council," 21 November 1955, National Security Council (NSC) series, Box 7, Eisenhower Presidential Library, Abilene, KS.

28. "Secret Security Information: European Unification in Relation to the Atlantic Community," Whitman Administrative Series, Box 13, File: Draper, William H. Jr., (2) III-5, 13, Eisenhower Presidential Library, Abilene, KS.

29. Gnesotto, "ESDP: Results and Prospects," introduction to *EU Security and Defence Policy,* ed. Gnesotto, 17.

30. Eichenberg, "Having It Both Ways" (electronic copy).

31. Ibid.

32. Nuttall, *European Political Co-operation,* 3.

33. "Top Secret: United States Assistance to Other Countries from the Standpoint of National Security, April 29, 1947," in *Containment,* ed. Etzold and Gaddis, 73.

34. Yergin, *Shattered Peace,* 362–363.

35. Calleo, *Beyond American Hegemony*, 34.

36. Ibid., 35.

37. Yergin, *Shattered Peace,* 362–363.

38. The Treaty of Brussels, 17 March 1948.

39. As quoted in Cahen, *The Western European Union and NATO*, 2.

40. Calleo, *Beyond American Hegemony,* 35.

41. Ibid.

42. Willis, *France, Germany, and the New Europe,* 130–131.

43. "Strengthening Political Basis of Atlantic Community," Confidential File (1953–1961), Subject Series, Box 99, file: United States Special Representative in Europe (2), III-11, Eisenhower Library, Abilene, KS.

44. Calleo, *Beyond American Hegemony,* 4.

45. Coker, *The Future of the Atlantic Alliance*, 50.

46. As early as 1965, a year before the French removal of their forces from the integrated structures, Kissinger wrote *The Troubled Partnership*, stating that the future of the Atlantic Alliance depended on whether NATO could change itself into an equal partnership. See also Calleo, *Beyond American Hegemony*.

47. Calleo, *Beyond American Hegemony,* 42.

48. Grosser, *The Western Alliance*, 137.

49. As quoted in Sherwood, *Allies in Crisis*, 91. The British had the opposite view—that the United States should never be allowed to abandon the Europeans again.

50. As quoted in Kissinger, *Diplomacy*, 547.

51. De Gaulle said, "I was trying to find a means of leaving the Atlantic Alliance and of reclaiming freedom lost during the Fourth Republic at the time of the signing of the North Atlantic Treaty. Thus, I demanded the moon, I was sure that they wouldn't give it to me." As quoted in J.-R. Tournoux, *La tragédie du général* (Paris: Plon, 1967), from which it was cited by Sherwood, *Allies in Crisis*, 106.

52. For a variety of different reasons, including concerns of French and Franco-German domination, desire for British participation, and worry about the shift away from the United States and NATO, most of the other European Community members were reluctant to support the Fouchet Plan. For more details, see Nuttall, *European Political Co-operation*, 37–46.

53. Calleo, *Beyond American Hegemony,* 44.

54. From a speech given by John F. Kennedy in Frankfurt on 25 June 1963, as quoted in Sherwood, *Allies in Crisis*, 113.

55. Calleo, *Beyond American Hegemony,* 46.

56. Ibid.

57. Ibid., 52–54.

58. Sherwood, *Allies in Crisis*, 125.

59. As quoted in ibid.

60. Ibid., 126.

61. United Kingdom delegation to NATO, *Talking Points on the Eurogroup* (Brussels: Eurogroup Secretariat), 2.

62. Elfriede Regelsberger, "Chronology of European Political Cooperation, 1969–1987," in *European Political Cooperation in the 1980s*, ed. Pijpers, Regelsberger, and Wessels, 277.

63. "First Report of the Foreign Ministers to the Heads of State and

Government of the Member States of the European Community of 27 October 1970 (Luxembourg Report)," in *European Political Co-operation*, 5th ed. (Bonn, Germany: Press and Information Office of the Federal Government, 1988), 26–27.

64. William Wallace, "European Political Cooperation: A New Form of Diplomacy," 3–14, as quoted in Elfriede Regelsberger, "EPC in the 1980s: Reaching Another Plateau?" in *European Political Cooperation in the 1980s*, ed. Pijpers, Regelsberger, and Wessels, 5–6. Regelsberger argued that both external and internal events brought EPC to different plateaus of cooperation.

65. Calleo, *Beyond American Hegemony*, 44–64.

66. Henry A. Kissinger, "The Year of Europe," address to the Associated Press annual luncheon, New York, 23 April 1973, in *American Foreign Policy*, 3rd ed. (New York: W. W. Norton, 1977), 104–105.

67. M. Smith, "From the 'Year of Europe' to a Year of Carter," 27.

68. "Document on the European Identity Published by the Nine Foreign Ministers (Copenhagen, 14 December 1973)," in Nuttall, *European Political Co-operation*, 48.

69. Sherwood, *Allies in Crisis*, 138–142.

70. "Report on Europe Union," *Bulletin of the European Communities* (1976): supp. 1, 11–35, as found in European Navigator, at http://www.ena.lu /mce.cfm.

71. Regelsberger, "EPC in the 1980s," 16–17.

72. Jean-Marc Hoscheit and Panos Tsakaloyannis, "Relaunching the Western European Union: An Overview," in *The Reactivation of the Western European Union: The Effects on the EC and Its Institutions*, ed. Panos Tsakaloyannis (Maastricht: European Institute of Public Administration, 1985), 11.

73. Halliday, *The Second Cold War*. Halliday argues that after Nixon's détente, Reagan fanned the flames of the Cold War, creating what Halliday deems a second one.

74. Gambles, *European Security Integration in the 1990s*, 5–6.

75. As reported in Nuttall, *European Political Co-operation*, 175.

76. Report on European political cooperation (London, 13 October 1981), in *Bulletin of the European Communities*, 1981, Supplement No. 3, 14–17.

77. Regelsberger, "EPC in the 1980s," 20.

78. See Neville-Jones, "The Genscher/Colombo Proposals on European Union," 657–699.

79. As quoted in Nuttall, *European Political Co-operation*, 184.

80. The Draft European Act, submitted by the German and Italian governments on 6 November 1981, in *Bulletin of the European Communities*, no. 11 (November 1981): 87–91.

81. John Vincour, "Paris Sees Missile Issue Tied to Germany's Future," *New York Times*, 31 October 1983. These were some of the largest demonstrations in Europe. Mary Kaldor has argued that these grassroots movements were key in getting the governments of the superpowers and of Eastern and Western Europe to end the arms race. See Kaldor, "Avoiding a New Division of Europe," and Kaldor, ed., *Europe from Below*.

82. Hoscheit and Tsakaloyannis, "Relaunching the Western European Union," 16.

83. Wallace, "European Defence Co-operation," 259.

84. Title III, Treaty Provisions on European Cooperation in the Sphere of Foreign Policy, Article 30 of the Single European Act.

85. Clyde Haberman, "West Europeans Formally Initiate Closer Federation," *New York Times,* December 16, 1990, I-6.

86. As quoted in Craig R. Whitney, "A Big Gulf Crisis in Cold War Ended, Questions on US and NATO Roles," *New York Times,* 26 December 1990, A10.

87. Ibid.

88. As quoted in Scott Anderson, "Western Europe and the Gulf War," in *Toward Political Union,* ed. Rummel, 147.

89. Christopher Hill, "EPC's Performance in Crises," in *Toward Political Union,* ed. Rummel, 144.

90. S. Anderson, "Western Europe and the Gulf War," 158–159.

91. Delors, "European Integration and Security," 102.

92. *Europe Daily Bulletin*, no. 5420, 30 January 1991.

93. Ibid.

94. As quoted in "Belgium's Eyskens on Security Policy, Neutrality," FBIS-WEU-91-077, 22 April 1991, 1–2.

95. As quoted in David Gardner, "Crisis in Yugoslavia; EC Dashes into Its Own Backyard—Ministers Making Fresh Trip in Attempt to Salvage Peace Package," *Financial Times,* 1 July 1991.

96. Lord Owen, 1994 Sir Winston Churchill Memorial Lecture, delivered 11 March at the Fondation Pescatore Luxembourg, Reuters, 11 March 1994.

97. As quoted in "NATO's Bosnia Dithering: Waiting for US to Lead," *International Herald Tribune*, 29–30 May 1993, 1.

98. Treaty of Amsterdam, Title V, J.1, at http://europa.eu.int/eur-lex/lex/en/treaties/dat/-11997D/htm/11997D.html.

99. "Declaration on the Establishment of a Policy Planning and Early Warning Unit," Final Act: (6), Treaty of Amsterdam, at http://europa.eu.int/eur-lex/lex/en/treaties/dat/11997D-/htm/11997D.html.

100. Representative from the Permanent Representation of the United Kingdom to the European Union, interview by author, Brussels, Belgium, 11 November 2005.

101. Foreign and Commonwealth Office, "Joint Declaration on European Defence, December 4, 1998," issued at the British-French Summit, Saint-Mâlo, France, 3–4 December 1998, at http://www.fco.gov.uk.

102. The Presidency Conclusions, Cologne European Council, 3 and 4 June 1999, Annex III: "European Council Declaration on Strengthening the Common European Policy on Security and Defence," at http://europa.eu.int/council/off/conclu/june99/annexe_en.-htm#a3.

103. Ibid.

104. Ibid.

105. Andrew Beatty, "EU to Push Ahead with Military 'Battle Groups,'" *euobserver*, 19 November 2004.

106. As quoted in "Outrage at 'Old Europe' Remarks," *BBC News*, 23 January 2003, at http://news.bbc.co.uk/2/hi/europe/2687403.stm.

107. As quoted in Janet McEvoy, "France Warns EU Candidates Risk Membership over Iraq," Agence France Presse–English, 18 February 2003. There is some controversy as to whether Chirac's use of *"se taire"* should have been translated as "be quiet" or "shut up." In any case, the term was widely

quoted in the English-speaking press as "shut up"; see Oana Lungescu, "Chirac Blasts EU Candidates," *BBC News*, 18 February 2003.

108. Jean-Marie Colombani, "Nous sommes tous Américains," *Le Monde*, 13 September 2001, 1.

109. Condoleezza Rice was widely attributed as saying that the US response to its allies' defection would be to "forgive the Russians, ignore the Germans, and punish the French." Colin Powell acknowledged in a press conference that US policy was to punish France over its position on Iraq. The article also reports that Vice President Dick Cheney's office was a strong proponent of such a policy. "US to Punish France over Iraq," *RTÉ News* (Ireland), 23 April 2003.

110. Presidency's Conclusions, Thessaloniki European Council, 19 and 20 June 2003, at http://europa.eu.int/constitution/futurum/documents/other/oth200603_en.pdf.

111. Danielle Pletka, "European Is Starting to Dance to the Bush Tune," *Financial Times,* 4 February 2005, 17.

112. As quoted in Judy Dempsey, "Words of War," *Financial Times,* 5 December 2003, 17.

113. First draft of the ESS, "A Secure Europe in a Better World," June 2003.

114. Steven Everts, "Some Strategies Work Better Than Force: Talking Back to Kagan," *International Herald Tribune*, 1 August 2002, 4.

115. "The European Security Strategy," *Irish Times*, editorial, 13 December 2003, 17.

116. Nicole Gnesotto, "ESDP: The Way Forward," *Military Technology* (December 2002): 19.

117. As quoted in Katrin Bennhold, "EU Urged to Revise Terror Responses," *International Herald Tribune,* 16 September 2004, 1, 8.

118. Jonathan Steele, "A New Kind of Europe: The EU Crisis Gives It the Chance to Shape an Identity and Global Role Independent of the US," *Guardian* (UK), 15 June 2005, Comment and Analysis, 21.

119. Josep Borrell, "A New Europe in a New World," speech at the opening of the academic year, The College of Europe, Natolin Campus, Warsaw, Poland, 3 November 2004 (DI/5478EN.doc.). Emphasis in original.

120. Ibid.

121. As quoted in "European Press Review," *BBC News*, 28 March 2003.

122. Robert Cooper, "ESDP Goals and Ambitions," presentation at the US Political/Military Conference at the General Secretariat of the Council of Ministers, Brussels, Belgium, 12 October 2005.

123. Peter van Ham, "How a Relationship Goes Sour: Trans-Atlantic Tensions," *International Herald Tribune,* 7 February 2006, Opinion, 7.

124. "Perceptions of the European Union: A Qualitative Study of the Public's Attitudes to and Expectations of the European Union in the 15 Member States and in 9 Candidate Countries: Summary of Results," June 2001, 5, at http://ec.europa.eu/governance/areas/studies/optem-summary_en.pdf. Emphasis in original.

125. *Eurobarometer* 63 (2005): 69–70.

126. Kowert, "Agent Versus Structure in the Construction of National Identity," 109.

127. Steele, "A New Kind of Europe," 21.

128. Gnesotto, "ESDP: Results and Prospects," 23.

129. Cimbalo, "Saving NATO from Europe."

130. Manuel Lobo Antunes, "The Portuguese Perspectives on the Evolution of European Security and Defence Policy and the Portuguese and European Defence Industries," speech, at http://www.mdn.gov.pt/secretario_estado/discursos_SE/Manuel_Lobo_-Antunes/2005/portuguese_perspectives.htm.

131. Senior NATO official, interview by author, Brussels, Belgium, 10 November 2005.

132. Representative from the Permanent Representation of France to the EU, interview by author, Brussels, Belgium, 8 November 2005.

133. Representative from the Permanent Representation of the UK to the EU, interview by author. Emphasis in original.

134. "EU-NATO Declaration on ESDP," NATO press release (2002) 142, 16 December 2002, at http://www.nato.int/docu/pr/2002/p02-142e.htm. Emphasis added.

135. House of Commons, Hansard Debates, 29 March 2001.

136. Carey Schofield and Michael Smith, "EU Force Will Not Need Nato, Says French Military Chief," *Daily Telegraph* (London), 28 March 2001, 1.

137. State Department briefing, Federal News Service, 2 September 2003.

138. "Degrees of Separateness: The EU Military Planning Cell and NATO," *RUSI Newsbrief*, 1 October 2003, 111–112.

139. As quoted in Ambrose Evans-Pritchard and Toby Helm, "We Shall Remain Loyal to Both NATO and an EU Army, Blair Tells US," *Telegraph* (UK), 18 October 2003, at http://www.telegraph.co.uk/news/main.jhtml?xml=/news/2003/10/18/weu18.xml.

140. As cited in "European Press Review," *BBC News*, 30 April 2003, at http://news.bbc.co.uk/2/hi/europe/2987439.stm.

141. Author's correspondence with a US State Department official I, Berlin, Germany, 6 June 2006.

142. Press availability by Undersecretary of State for Political Affairs R. Nicholas Burns and Assistant Secretary of State for European and Eurasian Affairs Dan Fried at the Euro-Atlantic Partnership Council Security Forum, Åre, Sweden, 25 May 2005, at http://nato.usmission.gov/PressReleases/Burns_Fried_052505.htm.

143. US State Department official I, interview by author, Berlin, Germany, 26 October 2005.

144. General Secretariat official II of the Council of Ministers, interview by author, Brussels, Belgium, 8 December 2005.

145. General Secretariat official I of the Council of Ministers, interview by author, Brussels, Belgium, 7 December 2005.

146. Representative of the Permanent Representation of France to the EU, interview by author, Brussels, Belgium, 8 November 2005.

147. Martin Plaut, "A Brief Sojourn with Mr. Solana," *From Our Own Correspondent*, BBC World Service (radio), 19 July 2003. This report followed the visit to Bunia, Democratic Republic of Congo, of Javier Solana, European Union high representative for the Common Foreign and Security Policy, on 16 July 2003, at http://ue.eu.int/uedocs/cmsUpload/Martin%20-Plaut%20-%20report.pdf (website of the General Secretariat of the Council of Ministers).

148. Representative of the Permanent Representation of France to the EU, interview by author, Brussels, Belgium, 7 December 2005.

149. "NATO Response Force: More Than a 'Paper Army'?" *NATO Notes: ISIS Europe* 5 (October 2003): note 1.

150. Franco-British summit, Declaration on Strengthening European Cooperation in Security and Defence, Le Touquet, 4 February 2003, at http://ambafrance-uk.org/Franco-British-summit-Declaration,4970.html ?var_recherche=touquet.

151. Representative I of the Permanent Representation of Germany to the European Union, interview by author, Brussels, Belgium, 10 November 2005.

152. US State Department official III, interview by author, Brussels, Belgium, 7 November 2005.

153. Representative II of the Permanent Representation of the Netherlands to NATO, interview by author, Brussels, Belgium, 7 December 2005.

154. Fidelius Schmid, "Nato Commander Warns on Rapid Response Force," *Financial Times*, 28 August 2007.

155. Honor Mahony, "NATO and EU Relations Simmer over Soldiers," *euobserver.com*, 24 September 2007.

156. Schmid, "Nato Commander Warns on Rapid Response Force."

157. Mahony, "NATO and EU Relations Simmer over Soldiers."

158. Representative of the Permanent Representation of the Netherlands to the EU, interview by author, Brussels, Belgium, 8 November 2005; corroborated by Representative I of the Permanent Representative of France to NATO, interview by author, 7 December 2005.

159. Representative I of the Permanent Representation of the Netherlands to NATO, interview by author, Brussels, Belgium, 7 December 2005.

160. Representative of the Permanent Representation of the Netherlands to the EU, interview by author, Brussels, Belgium, 8 November 2005.

161. Representative of the Permanent Representation of Poland to the EU, interview by author, Brussels, Belgium, 9 November 2005.

162. Representative of the Permanent Representation of France to the EU, interview by author, Brussels, Belgium, 8 November 2005.

163. Hans W. van Santen, "EU and NATO," *Merkourios: Utrecht Journal of International and European Law* 23, no. 61 (2005): 35–36. See also Mark Beunderman, "Turkey Pressed to Stop Blocking EU-NATO Meetings," *euobserver.com*, 14 November 2005.

164. Representative I of the Permanent Representation of the Netherlands to NATO, interview by author, Brussels, Belgium, 7 December 2005.

165. As quoted in Alexandrine Bouilet, "Paris bloque une réunion antiterroriste Otan-UE," *Le Figaro,* 26 January 2006, 4.

166. "Annex to the US-EU Political Declaration on Improving Co-operation in Crisis Management," original proposal from the General Secretariat of the Council of Ministers. No date is given, but from an interview with General Secretariat official III, it was either late 2004 or early 2005. Emphasis added.

167. General Secretariat official III, Council of Ministers, interview by author, Brussels, Belgium, 8 December 2005.

168. As reported in "US Pushes NATO, EU to Strengthen Role in Darfur," Deutsche Presse-Agentur, 5 February 2006.

169. As quoted in Judy Dempsey, "NATO Agrees to Lend Its Help in Darfur," *International Herald Tribune*, 9 June 2005.

170. David Mozersky, "EU Must Let NATO Halt Darfur's Nightly Terror," *European Voice*, 7 July 2005.

171. As quoted in Stephen Castle, "NATO Turf War on Airlift Delays Help for Darfur," *Independent* (London), 10 June 2005, 33.

172. "L'UE, étant sur les lieux (à Darfour) depuis six mois de façon discrète, n'a pas envie de voir l'OTAN, nouveau venu dans la région, lui voler la vedette." As quoted in Leo Michel, "NATO–EU–United States: Why Not a Virtuous *'Ménage à Trois'?"* Institute for National Security Studies, National Defense University; also found in *Politique américaine* (Spring 2006).

173. Representative II of the Permanent Representation of the Netherlands to NATO, interview by author, Brussels, Belgium, 7 December 2005.

174. As quoted in Castle, "NATO Turf War," 33.

175. Ibid.

176. Representative II of the Permanent Representation of the Netherlands to NATO, interview by author, Brussels, Belgium, 7 December 2005.

177. As quoted in Castle, "NATO Turf War," 33.

178. US State Department official III, interview by author, Brussels, Belgium, 7 November 2005.

179. Ibid.

180. General Secretariat II of the Council of Ministers, interview by author, Brussels, Belgium, 8 December 2005.

181. "Promoting Peace, Human Rights and Democracy Worldwide," 2007 US-EU Summit, 30 April 2007.

182. Lucia Kubosova, "Fear of US Damaging EU-NATO Relations, NATO Chief Says," *euobserver.com,* 30 January 2007.

# 5

# Politicians and the ESDP: Explaining the Rhetoric

———————■———————

Foreign policy is a way to express your identity. But acting together on the world stage is also a way to progressively shape and enhance a common identity. Identities are not static. They change with different experiences. So the more we act together; the more we have shared successes and the occasional failure; the more our reflexes will converge; the more this idea of a European identity will firm up and become less elusive. ■ JAVIER SOLANA[1]

As demonstrated in the previous chapter, the United States is the main referent for Europeans, and they feel relatively weak in comparison. This feeling of weakness and vulnerability among the people was recognized during the 1970s by EU politicians. According to Leo Tindemans, the way to draw the people to the European Union and to make them feel more in control of their own destiny was to create a foreign and security policy for the European Community. However, at the time, the Nine recognized that the seriousness of the Cold War precluded any experimentation with security organization architecture. Throughout the seventies and eighties, the Europeans took incremental steps to coordinate foreign policy, and to a lesser extent security policy, but no genuinely European approach could be developed until the end of the Cold War. In other words, the formation of a European security policy has had nothing to do with defense; it is the fruition of a thirty-five-year-old desire to connect the EU with its citizens.

By introducing to EU citizens, and to the world, a new actor on the international scene, by defining its values, goals, and missions, a new EU identity is recognized and thus created. Peter van Ham applied marketing strategies and the term "branding" to explain the importance of creating an image that will resonate with the "consumer" or the citizen of the country.

> Over the last two decades, straightforward advertising has given way
> to branding—giving products and services an emotional dimension
> with which people can identify. In this way, Singapore and Ireland are
> no longer merely countries one finds in an atlas. They have become
> "brand states," with geographical and political settings that seem triv-
> ial compared to their emotional resonance among an increasingly glob-
> al audience of consumers. A brand is best described as a customer's
> idea about a product; the "brand state" comprises the outside world's
> ideas about a particular country.[2]

In other words, "branding"—that is, creating an international image of
the EU—can help sell the EU to its citizens and to the world.

Discourse is the construction material of identity. As Ruth Wodak et
al. explained:

> If a nation is an imagined community and at the same time a mental
> construct, an imaginary complex of ideas containing at least the defin-
> ing elements of collective unity and equality, of boundaries and auton-
> omy, then this image is real to the extent that one is convinced of it,
> believes in it and identifies with it emotionally. The question of how
> this imaginary community reaches the minds of those who are con-
> vinced of it is easy to answer: it is constructed and conveyed in dis-
> course, predominantly in narratives of national culture. National iden-
> tity is thus the product of discourse.[3]

Modern mass media greatly facilitate the dissemination of discourse
in the formation of a European identity. The advent of the Internet is
extremely useful, as EU institutions and member states can use or dis-
seminate the same content, but make it available in the appropriate languages. In other words, it allows them to be "on the same page." It also
facilitates the branding that van Ham discussed.

Perhaps the most important aspect of the CFSP/ESDP is how it reinforces the EU narrative. To reiterate, the identity narrative mobilizes a
people and gives meaning to its actions. It creates a framework for understanding a country and for "loving" it. As Denis-Constant Martin stated,

> The elements possessing the capacity to move people are part of their
> culture and organize their world vision. In identity narratives, those
> elements are sifted and the world visions re-organized usually around
> three main poles: relationship to the past; relationship to space; rela-
> tionship to culture.[4]

The ESDP contributes to the EU's identity narrative by changing the
Europeans' relationship to the past, to space, and to culture. The
Europeans are no longer the colonizers of the past when part of the EU's
ESDP. With the ESDP, Europeans control their own space. They are no

longer the protégés of the United States, but rather their own defenders; they export peace, not war.

For methodology, this chapter employs critical discourse analysis, using language found in the media and political documents. This analysis views both written and spoken discourse as a form of social practice. Moreover, "it assumes a dialectical relationship between particular discursive acts and the situations, institutions and social structures in which they are embedded: the discourses influence social and political reality. In other words, discourse constitutes social practice and is at the same time constituted by it."[5] This chapter analyzes how the rhetoric surrounding the ESDP works to create a European identity and a feeling of belonging among its people. The first section traces the origins of the idea of using foreign and security policy as a way for this elite-led project to forge a link with the people. It demonstrates that politicians consciously use the rhetoric for this purpose. The next section discusses how the creation of an ESDP aids in nation building or identity building and in creating a "European."

### Using the Foreign, Security, and Defense Policy to Forge a Link with the People

The first goal mentioned in the Treaty on European Union for the CFSP is "to safeguard the common values, fundamental interests, independence and integrity of the Union in conformity with the principles of the United Nations Charter."[6] This goal raises a couple of questions. First, why is safeguarding "values" the primary objective of the CFSP? Second, if these values are in conformity with the principles of the United Nations, and all the EU member states have already promised to support them—and do—in the UN, why do these values need to be reiterated in the Treaty on European Union?

In answering these questions, Javier Solana recognized that defining European values creates a vital link with the EU citizen.

> [T]he defense and promotion of the values . . . are at the heart of European history and civilisation. We believe in the value of tolerance, democracy and respect for human rights. This must be an integral part of our policy-making process. Because values are our crucial link with the people of the street, who want to understand why we take this or that decision, and whose support we need at all times.[7]

William Bloom maintained that foreign policy is a powerful tool for nation building, whether consciously understood by decisionmakers or not. Foreign policy can create a situation in which the mass of people can perceive a threat to their communal identity, or an opportunity to protect and enhance it.[8] As a result, "the opportunity is always present for a government deliberately to use foreign policy as a method of mobilizing the mass national public sentiment away from internal political dissension, and achieving political integration."[9]

A key component of nation building is creating legitimacy for the governing institutions. Ilya Prizel remarked, "Most modern polities rely on a legitimizing mythology. The conduct of foreign policy, by extension, is one means of affirming that mythology and thereby legitimizing a governing elite."[10] The French and Dutch rejections of the Constitutional Treaty were the equivalent of the EU governing elite losing a vote of confidence from the people. To regain the people's trust, EU politicians emphasized the practicality of a European foreign and security policy. Benita Ferrero-Waldner, European commissioner for external relations, said that the EU had taken advantage of the pause after the constitutional failure

> to reconnect with our citizens' most important concerns—security, stability, prosperity and a stronger EU in the world. We recognize that what our citizens want is results. So we are concentrating on concrete achievements to show that the EU is part of the solution and not part of the problem. And to show that rather than an "old continent," unable to respond to today's challenges we've become a relevant dynamic power.[11]

Presumably, Solana understood the concept when he called for "legitimacy through action" and a "result oriented" pragmatism to gain citizens' confidence.[12] Chris Patten, former commissioner for external relations, concurred, "[T]he EU's credibility will be greatly enhanced if it can demonstrate its contribution to the safety and security of its citizens."[13] He continued, "I am confident this debate will be one of the most appealing to European citizens, one which will make them feel more and more 'euro-activists.'"[14] Leo Tindemans would agree; European Community/Union politicians have explicitly sought to use foreign policy, if not security policy, to nation-build since 1970.

## Past Attempts to Use an EU Foreign and Security Policy in Nation Building

Jean Monnet was not interested in using security policy as a way to unify Europe: "I had never believed that we should tackle the problem of Europe via defence. Although this would no doubt be one task for the future federation, it seemed to me by no means the most powerful or compelling motive for unity."[15] Nevertheless, the onset of the Korean War forced the question of German rearmament. He helped design a European Defense Community (EDC) as a corollary to a European Coal and Steel Community (ECSC) because he had little choice. In any case, defense was still too sensitive a subject, and the proposal died in the French Parliament in 1954.

The idea of using foreign policy as a nation-building tool was first raised by the Davignon Report of 1970. This report was in response to a request by the heads of state or government "to study the best way of achieving progress in the matter of political unification, in the context of enlargement." The report concluded,

> The Ministers therefore felt that foreign policy concentration should be the object of the first practical endeavours to demonstrate to all that Europe has a political vocation. The Ministers are, in fact, convinced that progress here would be calculated to promote the development of the Communities and give Europeans a keener awareness of their common responsibility.[16]

Within three years, the leaders of the Nine published "The Document on the European Identity of 1973." Significantly, this document, although on the subject of identity, dealt almost exclusively with foreign policy. It concluded that a common foreign policy was vital to furthering the integration process and strengthening internal cohesion.

> In their external relations, the Nine propose progressively to undertake the definition of their identity in relation to other countries or groups of countries. They believe that in so doing they will strengthen their own cohesion and contribute to the framing of a genuinely European foreign policy.[17]

The document also stated that if the Nine aimed to "maintain peace" through their role as an international actor, they "will never succeed in doing so if they neglect their own security." However, they (specifically, those members of the Atlantic Alliance; i.e., not Ireland) also agreed that now was not the time for experimentation in this area:

> [I]n present circumstances there is no alternative to the security provided by the nuclear weapons of the United States and by the presence of North American forces in Europe; and they agree that in the light of the relative military vulnerability of Europe, the Europeans should, if they wish to preserve their independence, hold to their commitments. . . .[18]

This statement explains why the CFSP was not launched until the end of 1990; such experimentation in the realm of security was not possible during the Cold War.

Leo Tindemans's Report on European Union (1975) drew upon the above conclusions and explicitly incorporated them as a way to make a link with the common people. He opened his report with a question.

> Why has the European concept lost a lot of its force and initial impetus? I believe that over the years the European public has lost a guiding light. . . . Europe must find its place again among the major concerns of public opinion. . . . We must listen to our people. . . . What do they expect from a united Europe?[19]

Tindemans remarked that, while doing research on the subject, he "was struck by the widespread feeling that we are vulnerable and powerless." At the same time, "Our peoples are conscious that they embody certain values which have had an inestimable influence on the development of civilization. Why should we cease to spread our ideas abroad when we have always done so?" His solution was a European foreign and security policy. Presenting a united front in world discussions would offset public malaise; "our vulnerability and our relative impotence are in the thoughts of everyone." As a result, "external relations are one of the main reasons for building Europe, and make it essential for the European Union to have an external policy."[20] He also proposed significant security cooperation for the benefit of the European Union. Recognizing that a "common defence policy" would not be possible "in the near future," he proposed increased discussion of European aspects of security and defense matters. He asserted that the European Union "will not be complete until it has drawn up a common defence policy."[21]

Public opinion polls reflected Tindemans's understanding of the situation. In 1974 and 1975, an average of over 80 percent of those polled believed that the member states should act jointly through the Common Market rather than individually if they were to "make our presence felt in discussions with the Americans or the Russians."[22] In *Eurobarometer* surveys from 1976 to 1985, an average of 57 percent across the continent agreed that decisions about security and defense should be taken by the member countries of the European Union acting together—even in the United Kingdom, where many citizens were skeptical of the integration process.[23]

*Current Attempts to Use the ESDP in Nation Building*

This new twenty-first-century generation of EU politicians, whether from the European Union or the member states, is in lockstep with the logic of their predecessors. As Solana explained, the CFSP is "also part of a specific project, to know the ambition to promote a model of integration and cooperation."[24] EU Military Committee chairman Rolando Mosca Moschini believed "[t]he ESDP was . . . the main catalyst for the general process of European integration."[25] In its white paper on European governance, the European Commission told how international action could be translated into citizen support.

> The objectives of peace, growth, employment and social justice pursued within the Union must also be promoted outside for them to be effectively attained at both European and global level. This responds to citizens' expectations for a powerful Union on a world stage. Successful international action reinforces European identity and the importance of shared values within the Union.[26]

The member states in the European Council agreed in the Laeken Presidency Conclusions,

> Within the Union, the European institutions must be brought closer to its citizens. Citizens undoubtedly support the union's broad aims, but they do not always see a connection between those goals and the Union's everyday action. . . . Now that the Cold War is over and we are living in a globalised, yet also highly fragmented world, Europe needs to shoulder its responsibilities in the governance of globalisation. *The role it has to play is that of a power resolutely doing battle against all violence, all terror, and all fanaticism, but which also does not turn a blind eye to the world's heartrending injustices.* In short, a power wanted to change the course of world affairs in such a way as to benefit not just the rich countries but also the poorest. A power seeking to set globalisation within a moral framework, in other words to anchor it in solidarity and sustainable development. . . . The image of a democratic and globally engaged Europe admirably matches citizens' wishes.[27]

The words chosen by the leaders of the EU member states—"the role it has to play"—are significant. One of two meanings is possible: that the EU is play-acting or that the EU actually has to be this superman (or, in this case, superstate). Both meanings are problematic, and neither has anything to do with actual defense. The EU is to show its people that it is in a constant battle against evil, defined as "all violence, all terror, all fanaticism" and even worldwide "injustice." Why did the leaders choose such over-the-top language? They used it as a way to engage the people in the EU narrative.

Luxembourg, while holding the EU presidency, made the issue of ESDP promotion a main talking point. Although lengthy, this quotation is instructive.

> The ESDP has become part of everyday life and it is important to underline its indispensability in a globalized world becoming more and more dangerous. *To achieve the goal of an improved and enhanced communication strategy, there is no secret: explain, popularize, envelop it in common language at the same time as debating its objectives and concepts in order to spread it among the public.* In most of the European societies, where armed conflicts have a bad reputation and where the horrors of war are still profoundly anchored, speaking about security and defence often awakens suspicion and provokes a sense of unease which it is difficult to get rid of. Nonetheless, stereotypes and misleading sentiments tend to stay on forever. Therefore, in order to convince, the European Union and the Member States have to become even more active and have to develop a true communication strategy on ESDP. The objective of this strategy should be to rally public opinion around a policy and to legitimate the ESDP by a strong parliamentary and popular support. This support is only possible if those, in charge of implementing the ESDP, will prove to have stamina and teaching skills.[28]

The goal is to increase the visibility of the CFSP/ESDP among the people, even if it means underlining to the public how dangerous the world is becoming. As established in Chapter 2, the defense community finds that there are no significant threats to Europe. In contrast to the Luxembourg document, "Europe has never been so prosperous, so secure nor so free."[29] However, peace and prosperity are not useful for rallying support for a security and defense policy that could be such a useful tool for identity building.

Although substance is important, it is "being seen" that commands the attention of the world. As van Ham explains, it is a question of branding. "Branding acquires its power because the right brand can surpass the actual product as a company's central asset. Smart firms pour most of their money into improving their brands, focusing more on the values and emotions that customers attach to them than on the quality of the products themselves."[30] This model was not lost on Lamberto Dini, former Italian prime minister and foreign minister. He explained that the ESDP could serve an important role, even if not entirely operational.

> Security and defence policy enriches the European Union with new goals, *even if the definition of its conceptual foundations and opera-*

*tional instruments is far from complete. . . .* At the same time, opinion polls in every European country confirm that this is the test-bed for a new legitimacy for the European Union and the formation of a consensus among its citizens with regard to its objectives and ambitions.[31]

In this quotation, below, from Louis Michel, Belgian foreign minister, visibility is the primary role of the EU foreign minister; from the context, the actual impact on world affairs seems secondary.

During the Convention, the prime minister and I called for the appointment of a European foreign minister, who would sit as a vice-president of the Commission and would be the face and voice of Europe. I sincerely believe that this institutional development will considerably enhance the European Union's visibility worldwide. Indeed, it will not only increase its visibility but also its actual impact on world current affairs.[32]

Research suggests that media coverage, provided it is both visible and consistent, can change public opinion regarding the EU.[33]

Not only do EU expeditions provide an opportunity for the EU to be seen internationally, they provide an opportunity for the citizen to become wrapped up in the human element of the story as well. Moral justice plays a large role in the formation of a protagonist for a national—or in this case, European—narrative. In other words, the EU must be seen as the "good cop" in the media and in public statements. As Dan Nimmo and James Combes explained, the news media very often fulfill social and psychological functions more than intellectual or intelligence functions.[34] Laurent Boussié, UK correspondent for France 2 (France's largest public television network), noted at a conference hosted by the Strategic Studies Institute that the "media typically focus on 'sympathy' and 'emotional' issues without much regard for the whole truth."[35] By employing the "melodramatic imperative" in political news—i.e., describing international events as a dramatic story of good versus evil, of us versus them—the news creates an emotive force that can mobilize public opinion. Therefore, the viewer will identify with what is happening to the tourist, company, or diplomat internationally and see it as personally affecting himself or herself. Chosen carefully, the right international event could increase the EU's prestige and therefore enhance its identity.[36]

In any case, Solana's office took the Luxembourg recommendation to heart. Nine months later, the General Secretariat of the Council of the European Union produced the first ESDP newsletter. Its purpose is to create an emotional connection between the ESDP and European citizens: "Beyond the structures and the acronyms lie people, faces and stories. Above all, there is a European ambition. I hope this newsletter will give you an insight into them."[37]

At the same time, the Commission's Directorate General for External Relations (RELEX) and the Council commissioned the European Service Network (ESN) to create a pan-European public relations campaign to promote the ESDP, with large billboards in every member state saying, "Your choice is peace: The European Union is working for peace, security, and stability" (see Figure 5.1).[38]

## The ESDP as the Vehicle for Creating a European Identity: How It Works

Wodak et al. distinguish four different, central content areas in the rhetoric that constructs identities: (1) a common territory; (2) a common

**Figure 5.1** A poster of this billboard was on display at the European Union's information office on Rond-Point Schuman in Brussels, Belgium, on 8 November 2005, and was still on display over a year later, on Europe Day, 5 May 2007, when the billboard was the centerpiece of a huge display advertising the ESDP. This photo is taken of that display.

culture; (3) a collective past, present, and future; and (4) a *homo nationalis,* i.e., a defined national of a country.[39] ESDP rhetoric is extremely useful in constructing a European identity, for a variety of reasons. First, it allows the definition of territory; i.e., what is foreign and what is not. Second, it promotes the defining of common values based on a common culture. Executing the EU's policies creates legitimacy through action; in line with the EU narrative, out of the ashes of World War II, the European Union rises as a force for good in the world. In "branding" EU foreign policy, the EU can create a new label: "a European."

### Creating the Homo Europeus: *The Common Territory*

Foreign and security policy forces the question of what is foreign and what is not. Internally, it requires the definition of the home territory; i.e., who belongs and what is to be protected. Externally, it provides recognition of the EU as an international actor. For example, the EU has a place in the World Trade Organization. When Solana is negotiating with the United States, he can refer to "the identity and specific nature of both partners [EU and United States]";[40] that is, he can refer to Europe as a single entity. In this way, the national borders on the continent fade.

Another major aspect of the identity narrative is to "transform a space into a group's exclusive turf, where they ought to be masters, where their way of doing things should not tolerate any difference or competition."[41] Europeans have not been masters of their own territory. US interventions decided the outcomes of World Wars I and II. During the Cold War, the Europeans were divided and placed into the shadows of the superpowers. They were not the protectors; the United States was, and is, through NATO. Now, the EU can be looked to as a de jure provider of security, although not a de facto one. The ESDP provides symbolic control over European space. Significantly, although the ESDP is geared toward crisis management, it is sold to the public as a way to defend Europe.

It is this protection that Europeans want. In a *Eurobarometer* poll, when asked about what a possible future European army should do, 71 percent of Europeans answered that its number one purpose should be to protect European territory.[42] As a result, much of the rhetoric that surrounds the ESDP is on the protection it provides its citizens, although these assertions are very much exaggerated. The Greek defense minister Yiannos Papandoniou said,

> To us, the crucial issue is not just to promote European security and defense; we need to send the Greek people the message that, through the bolstering of ESDP (European Security and Defense Policy), from

now on they can rely on Europe too for their safety. This message we can convey today, now that the EU goal has been achieved, namely, the operation of the European task force.[43]

Two years later, European Commission president José Manuel Barroso had the same message: "The citizens expect that European actions will contribute to their individual security."[44]

The ESDP was offered as a way to protect European citizens against terrorism. After the 9/11 attacks, the European Council concluded,

> The fight against terrorism requires of the Union that it play a greater part in the international community to prevent and stabilize regional conflicts. . . . It is by developing the Common Foreign and Security Policy (CFSP) and by making the European Security and Defence Policy (ESDP) operational at the earliest opportunity that the Union will be most effective.[45]

However, less than four years later, at a meeting of EU defense ministers, the conclusion was the opposite: "All defence ministers believe that ESDP does not have a crucial role to play in combating terrorism, but rather a back-up role."[46]

In this vein, the Belgians suggested including a mutual defense pact in the Constitutional Treaty, as explained above, to forge a protective link between the EU and its citizens. However, Atlanticist members, such as the UK and the Netherlands, were concerned that its inclusion would tread on the toes of NATO. Still other neutral members felt that it would transform the European Union into a defense organization. "This means that Finland is a NATO member," said one Finnish diplomat.[47]

In the end, a compromise was found in the form of a "solidarity clause": "The Union and its Member States shall act jointly in a spirit of solidarity if a Member State is the object of a terrorist attack or the victim of a natural or man-made disaster."[48] The wording is rather weak; however, the symbolism is strong and important. The solidarity clause encourages a feeling of togetherness and unity; it is an oath to visualize Europe as part of the same territory and to pledge to defend the whole of that territory. This logic was lost on Poland's Jacek Saryusz-Wolski, an EU negotiator for Poland and future member of Parliament and vice president. He "swept aside the proposed mutual defence clause as insubstantial: for Poland (and for its neighbours) the only clause affording solid guarantees was the mutual defence clause in the North Atlantic Treaty; time would tell whether Europe's guarantee was credible or not, but for the time being it was merely empty posturing."[49]

As detailed in Chapter 2, the ESDP would be of limited use in defending Europe. Karl von Wogau, chairman of the European Parliament's Subcommittee of Security and Defense, would agree that the proposed mutual defense pact was mere posturing. Even with regard to homeland security, there is a lack of funds. "If the EU wants to be a real player in security and protection of the citizen, it needs to spend at least one or even two billion euros per year" to begin to achieve the EU's homeland security objectives.[50] However, in a time of tight national budgets, the money has not been forthcoming.

Even after the failure of the Constitutional Treaty, politicians have continued to use security as a way to connect with the people. French defense minister Michèle Alliot-Marie stated that an emphasis on the ESDP's contribution to citizen security could become a rallying point for EU citizens:

> The European Union entered a period of uncertainty after France and the Netherlands rejected the European constitutional treaty last spring. The recent budgetary debates have not lessened that uncertainty. While the Europeans will manage to overcome these difficulties, as they always have, I believe a combined initiative in the defence and security field could help revive both confidence and action in Europe. This, after all, is the domain that attracts most support across the EU, as demonstrated in the constitutional campaign. Not least, the EU's citizens are aware that development of the European security and defence policy (ESDP) contributes to their daily security.[51]

After the tsunami that hit Asia in 2005, Madame Claude-France Arnould, director of Defence Issues and a close collaborator of Javier Solana from the EU Council Secretariat, stressed the importance "of reaching European citizens wherever they were in danger."[52]

### Creating the Homo Europeus: Common Culture and Values

Even if "united in diversity," the European Union cannot represent all of the cultures and values encompassed by twenty-seven countries. Rather, the EU must pick and choose among them for those most emblematic of the EU itself. "If culture is for human groups a system of meanings and understandings underlying a unifying logic, the production of an identity narrative implies a selection of pre-existing cultural traits which will be transformed into emblems of identity."[53]

The first clear iteration of Europe's values comes from the "Document on the European Identity of 1973."

The Nine wish to ensure that the cherished values of their legal, political and moral order are respected, and to preserve the rich variety of their national cultures. Sharing as they do the same attitudes to life, based on a determination to build a society which measures up to the needs of the individual, they are determined to defend the principles of representative democracy, of the rule of law, of social justice—which is the ultimate goal of economic progress—and of respect for human rights. All of these are fundamental elements of the European Identity. The Nine believe that this enterprise corresponds to the deepest aspirations of their peoples who should participate in its realization, particularly through their elected representatives.[54]

As a result, in Paragraph 9, the Nine stated that Europe had a special mission in the world:

The Europe of the Nine is aware that, as it unites, it takes on new international obligations. European unification is not directed against anyone, nor is it inspired by a desire for power. On the contrary, the Nine are convinced that their union will benefit the whole international community since it will constitute an element of equilibrium and a basis for co-operation with all countries, whatever their size, culture or social system. The Nine intend to play an active role in world affairs and thus to contribute, in accordance with the purposes and principles of the United Nations Charter, to ensuring that international relations have a more just basis; that the independence and equality of States are better preserved; that prosperity is more equitably shared; and that the security of each country is more effectively guaranteed.[55]

Twenty years later, the Maastricht Treaty on European Union of 1993 echoed the above sentiments in the drafters' objectives for the CFSP:

- To safeguard the common values, fundamental interests, and independence of the Union;
- to strengthen the security of the Union and its Member States in all ways;
- to preserve peace and strengthen international security, in accordance with the principles of the United Nations Charter as well as the principles of the Helsinki Final Act and the objectives of the Paris Charter;
- to promote international cooperation;
- to develop and consolidate democracy and the rule of law, and respect for human rights and fundamental freedoms.[56]

These values defined the types of missions the European Union was to instigate. Although originally conceived of in the Western European Union, the Petersberg tasks of 1992 were later incorporated into the Amsterdam Treaty (1997). Aside from collective defense, the Petersberg tasks allow Europeans to use military means to perform humanitarian and rescue tasks, peacekeeping tasks, and tasks of combat forces in crisis management, including peacemaking.

The draft constitutional treaty in its first three articles defined Europeans through their values: "The Union is founded on the values of respect for human dignity, liberty, democracy, equality, the rule of law and respect for human rights. These values are common to the Member States in a society of pluralism, tolerance, justice, solidarity and non-discrimination." Moreover, the EU is open to all European states that respect and promote those values; the EU pledges to uphold and promote these values internationally.[57]

These EU values in foreign and security affairs are reiterated in the European Security Strategy (ESS). Geared to the US National Security Strategy, the ESS is significant not so much because of what it says as because it sets "in motion a dynamic that is badly needed if the EU is to become a more effective security provider. This dynamic features a 'top-down' approach to security requirements: i.e.[,] proceeding from a definition of basic interests and goals, to the identification of threats and risks, to the formulation of a set of coordinated policies and thus a security strategy for the EU."[58] Klaus Becher clearly sets out its function in creating European norms:

- An education function vis-à-vis the public in EU states;
- An explanatory function toward the outside world;
- A stimulating function for political debate within Europe with a view to shaping the EU role in the international environment;
- A guidance function for EU and member state officials;
- And an encouragement function for the future of the European integration process.[59]

In other words, the articulation by the member states of a European Security Strategy created European norms to be disseminated for worldwide public consumption. Javier Solana—"M. Pesc"—is the face that represents these values.[60] When the EU gets involved in a peace process and the people see their countrymen with EU patches on their sleeves, they know the EU exists, it is an actor, and it is defending the EU's values everywhere.

Although somewhat vague, the ESS was well received. In Ireland, a neutral country, the ESS got positive press: "The commitment to international law, the United Nations and preventive engagement draws together civil and military crisis management in a way that is quite compatible with Ireland's security and foreign policy—and quite distinct from the Bush administration's foreign policy.[61] As Robert Cooper explained it, "There is something that people perceive about the EU: its peace and prosperity, its idea of a community of democracies."[62] Belgian prime minister Guy Verhofstadt concurred, "Increasingly, the EU is seen as a model of multilateral cooperation, as a mediator and peacekeeper in complex conflicts, as a continent sensitive to social and ecological challenge."[63]

Chris Patten agreed. "The EU, in short, has every reason to strut its stuff: boasting its achievements, shaping events and spreading its values."[64] Solana made clear that the CFSP is not an end unto itself, but rather the "CFSP is the means to an end, namely to promote the values and principles for which the European Union is respected worldwide."[65] He went on to elaborate,

> CFSP is about Europe making a difference in international politics. It is about the European Union being able to project *its values and its interests—the core of its political identity*—effectively beyond its own borders. At the same time, the construction of CFSP is a political project itself. It is the product of continuing debate between the Member States, the European institutions, and the people of Europe.[66]

These values form the core behind the EU's *mission civilisatrice*, i.e., its mission to export the European model as a way to spread peace and prosperity around the world.

### Creating the Homo Europeus: The Common Past, Present, and Future

In May 2005, Javier Solana gave three reasons why Europe needs an ESDP. He noted that among some Europeans, self-doubt and hesitation regarding integration had crept in; as a result, from time to time, one had to remake the case for Europe and its role in the world. The EU needs the ESDP, "first to exercise the demons of our past. Second, to expand the zone of peace and prosperity across our continent. And third to deal with the borderless and chaotic world."[67] This *mission civilisatrice* is vital to the creation of an identity narrative for the European Union. In a nutshell, it explains the EU's need to act. Having suffered collectively from war, and having found the path to peace, the Europeans must act now, collectively, if they are to secure a peaceful future for the world.

The Laeken Presidency Conclusions set out the EU's role:

> What is Europe's role in this changed world? Does Europe not, now that it is finally unified, have a leading role to play in a new world

order, that of a power able both to play a stabilising role worldwide and to point the way ahead for many countries and peoples? Europe as the continent of humane values, the Magna Carta, the Bill of Rights, the French Revolution and the fall of the Berlin Wall; the continent of liberty, solidarity and above all diversity, meaning respect for others' languages, cultures and traditions. The European Union's one boundary is democracy and human rights. The Union is open only to countries which uphold basic values such as free elections, respect for minorities and respect for the rule of law.[68]

Their collective values are based on their collective past. As the "continent of humane values," drawing on examples dating from 1215 to 1989, and even the US Bill of Rights, the member states highlighted the collective journey that has taken Europe to this point in history.

Solana maintained that the CFSP/ESDP is a necessary part of realizing the vision of the European Union's founding fathers:

The European Union was founded by those who sought peace and reconciliation. We must continue to promote these values and principles in our relations with the rest of the world. This can only be a joint undertaking. It requires both commitment and the means to act. I am confident that we can have both. In doing so, we can play our part in living up to the original vision of Europe's founding fathers.[69]

As the European Commission explained, the EU has learned many lessons from its integration process, and the Europeans were ready for its *mission civilisatrice*: "Based on the historic reconciliation of the nations and peoples of Europe, European integration has succeeded in consolidating peace and stability in Western Europe. It is now set to export this stability."[70] Although the individual European countries may have been colonizers who, in the past, exported their cultures with a bludgeon, the EU allows the member states to distance themselves from this history. Now, collectively, the Europeans propagate peace, prosperity, and stability.

In exporting this stability, the European Union has the luxury, to some extent, of being able to choose which areas and issues to become involved in and which not. NATO is still responsible for collective defense and the individual member states still have responsibility for their own national security. Therefore, Solana and the Political and Security Committee can seek out "fair weather" missions that have limited military aspects—because they are the most controversial and most difficult to get through the member states—with high visibility and a high chance of success.[71] Every successful act promulgates the arrival of a new era of European cooperation. Moreover, giving the EU a military gives it the trapping of a state. Each "military" success harkens back to the "glorious" future that awaits the EU as a global defender of peace and security. The news media will tell the stories back home, and the people will respond emotionally.

Italian prime minister Silvio Berlusconi declared that Europe could not play "a central role on the world stage without the back-up of appropriate and adequate military capabilities."[72] That is because without the capabilities, the EU cannot "strut its stuff"; in other words, it cannot be visible on the world stage. Solana spoke of how it would feel to see the European Union in action on the ground: "It is not without some emotion that we will see for the first time our European colours adorn the national uniforms of our police officers in a mission on the ground. [Their presence is a] strong symbol of the collective will of Europeans to act together in this key-task of consolidating stability and security on our continent."[73]

Each EU action was proof of its existence, of its collective present. The EU Council Secretariat went so far as to create a color brochure to promote the EU's leadership in the EU Police Mission in the former Yugoslav Republic of Macedonia (EUPOL Proxima).[74] "Proxima demonstrated the EU's ability to adapt its CFSP instruments to specific situations. Solana said their ability would be one of the conditions for meeting the challenges of the future."[75] Greek foreign minister George Papandreou argued that European defense "will give a feeling of security to citizens and will constitute a step to enable us to tell the universe and the world, on the international chessboard, that the role of the European Union exists."[76] French defense minister Michèle Alliot-Marie made this a talking point, stating that the European Gendarmerie Force (EGF) "once again gives proof of the vitality of European defense at a time when question marks are hanging over European construction."[77] "We are demonstrating in Macedonia, where we took over from NATO, and above all in Ituri where we're operating autonomously, that Defence Europe exists."[78] In a pep talk to French and German soldiers in Kabul, Afghanistan, she told them, "Your presence is proof that Europe exists and is capable of bringing its weight to bear on the great crises shaking our planet."[79]

European soldiers must uphold EU values wherever they are deployed. As Luc Frieden, Luxembourg minister and president-in-office of the EU Council, said, "European soldiers in the world are like our visiting card."[80] Therefore, the Council adopted standards of behavior to be applied to all categories of personnel involved in ESDP operations. Any violation of human rights is to be reported, and all persons are to respect the ethnic, religious, and cultural diversity of the local population. Drug use and sexual exploitation are forbidden. "It is a code of conduct so that EU soldiers are worthy representatives of the EU in difficult missions throughout the world."[81] In pursuit of this goal, the EU created a European Security and Defense College with the goal of forging a European security culture and fostering a common understanding of the ESDP for civilian and military staff of the member states and European institutions.[82]

The ESDP allows the EU to support the United Nations actively. Although sending peacekeeping troops to the DRC was "difficult and risky," it not only made it possible to protect the populations of Bunia and strengthen MONUC (UN Mission in the Democratic Republic of Congo), but also opened the way to "closer cooperation" between the EU and the UN.[83] Solana "noted that without the ESDP and the development of military capability and ability to decide, they would never have been able to respond to the appeal."[84] This achievement was recorded in the ESDP Presidency Report: "The EU has demonstrated that it could intervene in a timely manner, at the request of the [UN Secretary-General], in support of the United Nations."[85]

The sending of troops also allows the EU to rewrite history, with itself as the main protagonist. Italian prime minister Silvio Berlusconi pronounced, "For the first time in its 50-year history, the EU will have the chance for autonomous defence and can become an authoritative figure on the world stage."[86] This is especially important in the EU's backyard: the Balkans. At the time of the initial breakup of Yugoslavia in 1991, the Europeans took the lead. Luxembourg's foreign minister Jacques Poos declared, "If the Yugoslavs want to enter the Europe of the twentieth century, they have to follow our advice."[87] These words came back to haunt the Europeans, who were divided and unable to make progress in the region, forcing them to call in the United States.[88] However, ten years later, the ESDP allowed the EU to rewrite its role in the history of the Balkans. "The shift in world politics has caused a transfer of leadership in the Balkans: it is the European Union that is to set the agenda for the future."[89] Just as significant, it was the EU's first substantial military mission. Geoff Hoon, UK defense minister, pronounced, "Bosnia is a demonstration in practice that this [EU defence policy] can work."[90] *The Economist* noted with irony,

Almost a decade after Srebrenica, the EU is now trying again in Bosnia. It could be argued that the switch from NATO to EUFOR [EU Force] is more cosmetic than real. Although a large contingent of American troops has been replaced by Finns, some 80 percent of EUFOR's troops previously served in the NATO force. They simply took off their old NATO badges and replaced them with EU insignia. Nor has NATO left

Bosnia completely; it retains a small force under an American general, and it even shares a headquarters building and facilities with EUFOR.[91]

Nevertheless, Admiral Rainer Feist reiterated, "The EU 'will be very visible' on the ground. . . . ALTHEA [EU Military Operation in Bosnia and Herzegovina] will be the main actor in Bosnia-Herzegovina, even if NATO keeps a presence in the field."[92] As British general David Leakey explained to a journalist, "Bosnia has come from Dayton and now it needs to be on the road to Brussels."[93] According to Solana, ALTHEA will show that "Europe is capable of taking sensible, coordinated and robust steps to obtain a security environment that benefits its own citizens and those of its neighbours."[94]

In general, the press the EU got for the mission was quite favorable. One article highlighted how "troops at the sharp end of the EU's peace-keeping mission in Bosnia and Herzegovina need tact and listening skills more than they need rifles and ammunition."[95] With EUFOR's goal of "reassuring the population and winning hearts and minds," the EU's vision of itself as a peacekeeper and humanitarian was also assured. As one anonymous EU official explained, "There is a more integrated EU structure than ever before. In a quiet way, this is demonstrating that Europe is taking its responsibility seriously."[96]

As of 2007, the EU has launched nearly twenty missions under the auspices of the ESDP since 2003. These missions have taken place all over the world, but mostly in Europe and Africa. At Solana's behest, in 2005 the EU went to Asia for the first time. The Aceh mission was considered a resounding success and has whetted the Political and Security Committee's appetite to demonstrate the EU's worldwide influence. "This meant that the EU could be in Asia. The next stop? South America! Partly because of the Monroe Doctrine and partly so the EU could have a truly round-the-world presence. The Dutch Foreign Minister proposed it in the GAERC [General Affairs and External Relations Council of the Council of the EU] and suggested the Colombian Peace Process."[97] In late 2005, the United States asked the EU if it could monitor elections in Haiti. They were not able to, but were nevertheless thrilled with the US invitation and the attention.[98]

### The Homo Europeus: Who Is He/She?

What does a *Homo europeus* stand for? Certainly, the *Homo europeus* is very different from his/her counterpart, the *Homo americanus*. He or she does not seek either power or to project its power upon others. As

Solana explained, the CFSP/ESDP "is not about the projection of power. Europe's imperial days have long since past [*sic*] into history."[99] Unlike *Homo americanus, Homo europeus* is not materialist and does not believe that "might makes right." The European does not invade to impose its version of democracy. He/she uses diplomacy rather than force, carrots instead of sticks. The European cares about people, poverty, and development. His/her approach is the comprehensive one: through foreign aid, development assistance, training, and policing, the European can tackle the causes of problems rather than simply treat their symptoms. Troops provide an umbrella under which development can take place free from external threat.

Javier Solana characterized the European when he declared, "We are pro-peace, pro-security, pro-justice."[100] The European does not take sides; as the Belgian foreign minister explained, Belgium, like the European Union, "is neither pro-Palestinian nor pro-Israeli: we are simply pro-peace."[101] The European vigorously supports international law.[102] According to Jim Cloos, director for General Political Questions in the General Secretary Secretariat of the Council of the European Union, the way to export these values and stability is by fostering a "circle of friends" around its borders. The tool it uses to attract these friends is the prospect of closer ties and a share in the EU's prosperity and political stability. "We have enormous power of attraction."[103] As a result, unlike the United States, the European Union is viewed as an honest broker ready to monitor elections, moderate peace talks, and provide police training or developmental assistance whenever requested by either the state in question or the United Nations.

Europeans are willing to die for their beliefs. In a response to the question "Who will die for Europe?" German foreign minister Joschka Fisher answered, "European soldiers are facing danger in Afghanistan, Bosnia and Kosovo. . . . They are there as members of national contingents, but they are serving a wider interest—Europe's. There is a soul . . . [t]here is a spirit. And people die for Europe, and have died."[104] As Lieutenant General Rainer Schuwirth, chief of the EU's military staff, made clear, a true European army is not out of the question "provided the political process develops towards a more binding and deeper Union."[105]

Most importantly, the *Homo europeus* will support and create the institutions necessary to follow through to defend these goals and values. "Thus we are rapidly building a Europe that is actively engaged in the world and that is capable of using the full range of its instruments, including crisis management capabilities. This is what Europeans demand. This is also increasingly what the world insists upon."[106]

## Conclusion

Through the hardship of war, the Europeans have learned how to create a EUtopia.[107] This is the basic narrative of the European Union, the story told and retold to remind its citizens what they have in common and what they have accomplished through cooperation. This European identity has remained remarkably stable since the 1970s. To be a European, one must be dedicated to peace and the promulgation of international law. The European believes in economic progress and human rights. This characterization of the European is pervasive in EU rhetoric.

Whether in the form of a treaty or a document or a declaration or in Presidency Conclusions, member state leaders over the decades have signed on to the idea of "European values," and the need to promulgate them around the world. However, the member states have never been able to agree upon how to promulgate them. Some member states are interventionist; others are loath to intervene; others are restrained from intervention because of their constitutions. Some have little to contribute to a military expedition; almost all are unwilling to dedicate the money necessary to fund the ESDP adequately, very simply because their voters are unwilling. As Wolfgang Wagner put it, "This sympathy for the *project* of an ESDP does not necessarily extend to an ESDP *in practice*."[108] As a result, when analyzing the ESDP, one notices that the rhetoric far outreaches the reality. The following chapter analyzes the CFSP/ESDP structures and explains how they are a reflection of public attitudes in this area.

## Notes

1. Solana, "Identity and Foreign Policy," *ESDP Newsletter* 3 (January 2007): 9.
2. Van Ham, "The Rise of the Brand State," 2.
3. Wodak et al., *The Discursive Construction of National Identity*, 22.
4. Martin, "The Choices of Identity," 6 (electronic copy).
5. Wodak et al., *The Discursive Construction of National Identity*, 8.
6. Treaty on European Union, Title V, Article 11.
7. Javier Solana, "Where Does the EU Stand on Common Foreign and Security Policy?" speech delivered at the Forschungsinstitut der Deutschen Gesellschaft für Auswärtige Politik, Berlin, 14 November 2000, at http://www.consilium.europa.eu/-cms3_applications/applications/solana /details.asp?cmsid=246&BID=107&DocID=63975&insite=1.
8. Bloom, *Personal Identity, National Identity*, 81.
9. Ibid., 82.

10. Prizel, *National Identity and Foreign Policy,* 20.

11. Benita Ferrero-Waldner, "The European Union: A Global Power?" speech delivered at the George Bush Presidential Library Foundation and Texas A&M University EU Center of Excellence, College Station, Texas, 25 September 2006.

12. As quoted in "EU Leaders Seek Legitimacy Through Action at 'Elitist' Event," 30 January 2006, at http://www.evropa.bg/en/del/info-pad/news.html ?newsid=1761 (website of the European Commission Representation in Bulgaria); source: *euobserver.com.*

13. Patten, "A Security Strategy for Europe," 15.

14. Ibid., 16.

15. Monnet, *Memoirs,* 338.

16. "The Davignon Report" (Luxembourg, 27 October 1970), *Bulletin of the European Communities* 11 (November 1970): 9–14, as found at European Navigator, http://www.ena.lu/mce.cfm.

17. "The Document of the European Identity of 1973," *Bulletin of the European Communities* 12 (December 1973): 118–122, as found at European Navigator, http://www.ena.lu/mce.cfm.

18. Ibid.

19. Leo Tindemans, "Report on European Union" (29 December 1975), *Bulletin of the European Communities* (1976): supp. 1, 11–35, as found at European Navigator, http://www.ena.lu/mce.cfm.

20. Ibid.

21. Ibid.

22. Eichenberg, "Having It Both Ways," 627–628.

23. Ibid.

24. "Mais, [la PESC] fait aussi partie d'un projet spécifique, à savoir l'ambi-tion de promouvoir un modèle d'intégration et de coopération" (author's trans-lation). Javier Solana, "CFSP: The State of the Union," speech at the annual conference of the EU Institute for Security Studies, Paris, 1 July 2002.

25. Moschini, chairman of the EU Military Committee and head of the European Defense Agency, "Improving the Link Between ESDP and Public Opinion," speech at the WEU assembly meeting with EU PSC ambassadors, Paris, 10 February 2006; press release, WEU Assembly Press and Media.

26. European Commission, "European Governance: A White Paper," DOC/01/10, 25 July 2001, at http://europa.eu.int/rapid/pressReleasesAction.do ?reference=DOC/01/-10&format=HTML&aged=0&language=EN&gui Language=en.

27. European Council Presidency Conclusions, Laeken, Belgium, 14–15 December 2001, Annex I. Emphasis added.

28. Luxembourg Presidency, "Working Document Relating to Point 5 of the Agenda; Presidency Non-Paper: Promoting the European Security and Defence Policy (ESDP)," 11 March 2005, at http://www.eu2005.lu/en/actualites /documents_travail/2005/03/-18definfo/index.html. Emphasis added.

29. European Security Strategy, "A Secure Europe in a Better World," Brussels, Belgium, 12 December 2003, 2.

30. Van Ham, "The Rise of the Brand State," 3.

31. As quoted in Gnesotto, ed., *EU Security and Defence Policy,* 203. Emphasis added.

32. Foreign Minister Louis Michel of Belgium, speech on the occasion of the diplomatic contact days, 1 September 2003, at http://www.diplomatie.be/en/press/speech-details.asp?TEXTID=9115.

33. DeVreese and Boomgaarden, "Media Effects on Public Opinion," 419.

34. Dan Nimmo and James E. Combes, *Mediated Political Realities* (New York: Longman, 1983), 16, as cited in Bloom, *Personal Identity, National Identity,* 177.

35. As quoted in Douglas V. Johnson II, "The Test of Terrain: The Impact of Stability Operations upon the Armed Forces," conference brief, Strategic Studies Institute, 16–18 June 2005, 2–3.

36. Bloom, *Personal Identity, National Identity,* 84.

37. Javier Solana, "Foreword," *ESDP Newsletter,* December 2005, 3, at http://www.consilium.europa.eu/uedocs/cmsUpload/051214_NewsletterFinal.pdf.

38. See the European Service Network, 28 November 2006, at http://www.esn.be/index_en.cfm?page=tools%7Cnews.

39. Wodak et al., *The Discursive Construction of National Identity,* 4.

40. Javier Solana, preface, in *EU Security and Defence Policy,* ed. Gnesotto, 10.

41. Martin, "The Choices of Identity," 6.

42. Philippe Manigart, "Public Opinion and European Defense," July 2001, 18. This is a translation of "Public Opinion and European Defense," a paper presented at the international symposium organized by André Flahaut, Belgian defense minister, Brussels, Belgium, 3–4 April 2001, at http://ec.europa.eu/public_opinion-/archives/eb/ebs_146_en.pdf.

43. As quoted in "Greek Defense Minister Says PASOK Cannot Take Election Victory for Granted," *Ependhitis* (Athens), in Greek, 7 June 2003, 16, as found in the Foreign Broadcasting Information Service, translated texts.

44. "Les citoyens s'attendent à ce que l'action européen contribue à leur sécurité individuelle." José Manuel Barroso, speaking notes at the press conference, "European Parliament–Europe 2010: A Partnership for European Renewal, Prosperity, Solidarity, and Security," European Parliament, Brussels, Belgium, 26 January 2005, SPEECH/05/44, at http://ec.europa.eu/external_relations/news/barroso/sp05_44.htm. Translated by the author.

45. "Conclusions and Plan of Action of the Extraordinary European Council Meeting," part 3: "The Union's Involvement in the World," Brussels, Belgium, 21 September 2001.

46. "Defence Ministers Admit ESDP Does Not Play 'Crucial Role' in Combating Terrorism," *Europe Daily Bulletin,* 22 March 2005, 6.

47. As quoted in Judy Dempsey, "Neutral Countries Challenge Mutual Defence Plans of EU's 'Big Three,'" *Financial Times* (London), 8 December 2003, 1.

48. Article I-43 of the EU Constitutional Treaty.

49. Ferdinando Riccardi, chapter 18 (untitled) in *EU Security and Defence Policy,* ed. Gnesotto, 228.

50. Karl von Wogau, interview, *Defense News,* 9 May 2005, 30.

51. Michèle Alliot-Marie, "Security Could Be Europe's Great Rallying Point," *Financial Times* (London), 5 December 2005, 23.

52. Madame Claude-France Arnould, speaking at the WEU Assembly seminar on the role of parliaments in shaping public opinion on European security and defense, Paris, France, 28 April 2006; press release, WEU Assembly Press and Media.

53. Martin, "The Choices of Identity," 6.

54. "Document on the European Identity."

55. Ibid.

56. Treaty on European Union, Article 3.1.

57. "Definition and Objectives of the Union," Articles 1, 2, and 3, Title I, Part I, EU draft constitutional treaty, at http://europa.eu.int/constitution /futurum/constitution/part1/title1-/index_en.htm.

58. Roberto Menotti, "European Security Strategy: Is It for Real?" in Federov et al., *European Security Strategy,* 12.

59. Becher, "Has-been, Wannabe, or Leader," 354.

60. Javier Solana is the high representative for the CFSP—in French, *la Politique Étrangère et de Sécurité Commune* (PESC). Sometimes he is referred to as "Monsieur Pesc."

61. "The European Security Strategy," *Irish Times,* editorial, 13 December 2003, 17.

62. As quoted in Graham Bowley, "In Europe, a Shared Foreign Policy, Too," *International Herald Tribune,* 19 February 2005, 1.

63. As quoted in Tomas Valasek, "Europe-US Separation," *Defense News,* 26 May 2003, 29. Valasek was the director of the Center for Defense Information in Brussels.

64. Chris Patten, "A Voice for Europe? The Future of CFSP," 2001, at http://www.europa.eu.int/comm/external_relations/news/patten/speech01_111 .htm.

65. Solana, "Where Does the EU Stand . . . ?

66. Ibid. Emphasis added.

67. Javier Solana, "Give Europe More Weight in the World: The Three Reasons for Europe," *NRC Handelsblad* (the Netherlands), 17 May 2005, 9.

68. European Council Presidency Conclusions, Laeken, Belgium, 14–15 December 2001, Annex I.

69. Solana, "Where Does the EU Stand . . . ?"

70. European Commission, "Defining the Common Objectives and Coherence of Outside Action," Commission Communication on the Institutional Architecture, 1.3.3: Common Foreign and Security Policy, Brussels, Belgium, 4 December 2002.

71. Representative from the Permanent Representation of the Netherlands to the EU, interview by author, Brussels, Belgium, 8 November 2005.

72. As quoted in Judy Dempsey, "Blair Plays Down Rift over Defence," *Financial Times* (London), 18 October 2003, 2.

73. As quoted in "EU/Balkans: Beginning of First Mission Under Aegis of ESDP: Union Succeeds UN in with 'EUPM' Police Mission," *Atlantic News,* 8 January 2003, 1–2, emphasis deleted.

74. At http://www.consilium.europa.eu/uedocs/cmsUpload/Proxima Brochure.pdf.

75. "EU/CFSP: Javier Solana Marks End of Concordia and Launch of Proxima," *Europe Daily Bulletin,* 16 December 2003, 7.

76. "Greek Foreign Minister Addresses PASOK's European Conference," *Athens News Agency,* 5 December 2003.

77. As quoted in "EU/ESDP: European Gendarmerie Force Completes First Exercise," *Atlantic News,* 23 June 2005, 3.

78. Michèle Alliot-Marie, interview by "RTL," Paris, France, 4 August 2003, at http://www.ambafrance-us.org/news/statmnts/2003/-alliotmarie_rtl080403.asp.

79. As quoted in Craig S. Smith, "A Distinctly European Defense Corps Takes Shape," *New York Times*, 23 September 2004.

80. As quoted in "UE/Defence: Progress Expected in Military Capabilities Field," *Europe Daily Bulletin*, 24 May 2005, 4.

81. Ibid.

82. "European Security and Defence College Has Been Established," press release, 27 June 2005, at Luxembourg Presidency website, http://www.eu 2005.lu/en/actualites/-communiques/2005/06/27cesd/index.html.

83. "EU/ESDP: Javier Solana Takes Stock and Stressed Attachment to Propose Civil-Military Planning Unit," *Europe Daily Bulletin* (Brussels), 13 October 2004, 8.

84. As reported in "EU/CFSP: Solana Illustrates EU Security Strategy in Dublin," *Europe Daily Bulletin*, 9 January 2004, 5.

85. ESDP Presidency Report, 15814/03, Council of the European Union, Brussels, 9 December 2003.

86. As quoted in Luke Hill, "EU Defence Surge Despite Constitutional Collapse," *Jane's Defence Weekly*, 24 December 2003, 4–5.

87. As quoted in David Gardner, "Crisis in Yugoslavia; EC Dashes into Its Own Backyard—Ministers Making Fresh Trip in Attempt to Salvage Peace Package," *Financial Times* (London) July 1, 1991.

88. See S. Anderson, "EU, NATO, and CSCE Responses."

89. Martti Ahtisaari, untitled chapter in *EU Security and Defence Policy,* ed. Gnesotto, 163.

90. "Back to Bosnia," *The Economist*, 17 March 2005.

91. Ibid.

92. As quoted in "EU/Bosnia-Herzegovina: Admiral Feist says ALTHEA will be 'very visible' in Bosnia-Herzegovina," *Atlantic News*, 3 September 2004, 2. Emphasis deleted.

93. As quoted in Nicola Smith, "EU Troops Strive to Pass Bosnia Test," *European Voice*, 31 March 2005, 16.

94. As quoted in "EU/Bosnia-Herzegovina: Javier Solana Presents Althea Mission in Bosnia," *Europe Daily Bulletin* (Brussels), 16 July 2004, 4. Emphasis deleted.

95. Andrew Beatty, "Nation-Building on the Ground in Bosnia," *European Voice*, 14 July 2005, 16.

96. As quoted in Nicola Smith, "EU Troops Strive to Pass Bosnia Test," *European Voice*, 31 March 2005, 16.

97. Representative from the Permanent Representation of the Netherlands to the EU, interview by author.

98. General Secretariat officials II and III of the Council of Ministers, Defence, interviews by author, 8 December 2005, Brussels, Belgium. Although one official was visibly pleased that the United States had asked, the other said that some diplomats believed the United States asked for the help in full knowledge that the EU force was not yet operational, as a way to embarrass the EU. This interpretation may be another example of "attributional bias" described in the previous chapter.

99. Javier Solana, "Europe: Security in the Twenty-first Century," Olof Palme

Memorial Lecture, Stockholm, Sweden, 20 June 2001, at http://about.sipri.se/activities/-opml_solana.html.

100. Javier Solana, speech for the CFSP, given at the German Marshall Fund Peter Weitz Awards dinner, Washington, D.C., 20 May 2002.

101. Louis Michel, speech on the occasion of the diplomatic contact days, 1 September 2003, at http://www.diplomatie.be/en/press/speechdetails.asp? TEXTID=9115.

102. Presidency Conclusions, Thessaloniki, Greece, 19–20 June 2003, section 54.

103. Cloos as quoted in Bowley, "In Europe, a Shared Foreign Policy, Too," 1.

104. As quoted in Richard Berstein, "Europe Is Still Europe," *New York Times,* 7 June 2005.

105. As quoted in Judy Dempsey, "General Parades Vision of European Army," *Financial Times* (London), 24 September 2003, 2.

106. Javier Solana, foreword, *ESDP Newsletter,* no. 1 (December 2005): 3.

107. Borrowed from Nicolaidis and Howse, "'This Is My EUtopia . . . ,'" 767.

108. Wolfgang Wagner, "The Democratic Legitimacy of European Security and Defence Policy," Occasional Paper No. 57, Institute for Security Studies, April 2005, 29. Emphasis in original.

# 6

# The ESDP's
# Institutional Structure

◼

We are moving towards a defence Europe with planetary objectives
and it is clear that our capacities are not properly adapted. ◼ ITALIAN
DEFENSE MINISTER ANTONIO MARTINO[1]

## The Capability-Expectations Gap

Despite the rhetoric, the EU seems to lack the wherewithal to follow
through with its ambitions. In 2002, Anne Deighton remarked, "[T]he
EU has neither the means nor the political will to create an autonomous
foreign policy with military capabilities."[2] Simon Duke agreed, stating,
"Currently the EU faces a rhetoric-resources gap whereby the political
pronouncements and aspirations exceed the resources available for crisis
management operations, most notably those involving the use of military force."[3] Julian Lindley-French has also criticized what he called
"the gap between rhetoric and reality." Referring to the EU's military
capabilities, he noted that the draft Constitutional Treaty supported an
expansion of the Petersberg tasks, despite the fact that the EU had been
unable to meet the Helsinki Headline Goals necessary to carrying out
the Petersberg tasks in their original form.[4] Even Javier Solana has publicly complained, "There is a contradiction here: we do not want to
spend more but we want to be morally correct and act on the world
scene. But how can we act if we do not have the means to do so?"[5]

These observations are correct. The European Parliament has cata-
loged three areas of material deficiencies that could seriously impact the
EU's "ability to conduct both civilian crisis management operations and
humanitarian intervention operations of high-intensity dimensions using
mainly military means." Specifically, these are:

- Lack of deployable forces required for maintaining the rotation needed (1/3 on deployment, 1/3 on training, 1/3 resting) in such long-term/high-intensity operations
- Lack of permanent large-scale airlift capabilities for transporting forces abroad
- Lack of sufficient deployable command, control and communications capabilities as well as intelligence, surveillance and reconnaissance resources within the collective framework of ESDP.[6]

General Secretary George Robertson of NATO called the EU a "military pygmy." Later, he changed his mind, adding, "I'm quite prepared to say I made a mistake when I called Europe a military pygmy. In fact, it's not. It's a giant, but it's a flabby giant with no muscle and unable to do anything when trouble comes upon it."[7] As he put into plain words, many European states simply refuse to invest in the military hardware needed to project the EU's strength globally.

What explains what Christopher Hill deemed the "capability-expectations gap"?[8] Why does the gap exist? Why is it that the politicians have not followed through with resources to make the ESDP more capable and able to fulfill the EU's ambitions? How can the member states be accused of having no political will to proceed when they had the political will to put the CFSP/ESDP in motion in the first place?

Nation building explains this gap between rhetoric and reality. The gap is not a reflection of the insincerity of the member states with regard to security and defense policy, or a lack of follow-through. Nor is it a case of getting the cart before the horse; i.e., talking about all the EU can do before it has the means to do so. The horse is exactly where it belongs: the rhetoric is the spur that drives security policy.

Rhetoric is necessary to heighten expectations and excitement about the European Union. As discussed earlier in this volume, the rhetoric creates the rally-'round-the-flag effect, thus stirring public support. However, as opinion polls demonstrate, while people like the idea of a European Union security and defense policy, they are nervous about it, too. Many do not want to spend the money necessary to create a defense force; others do not want to compromise their national forces; and still others are concerned that such forces will militarize the European Union. The expectations-capability gap exists because of the sensitivity of member state politicians to the people's wishes. If the member states are going to use a European security and defense policy to nation-build and create popular support for the European Union, they must not get too far in front of the people—a common criticism. Although expectations are heightened by the promise of ESDP, the reality of it must proceed at a much more cautious pace lest the politicians lose the public support they have taken such care to cultivate. Form follows function: ESDP structures create the veneer of an active European Union abroad, but leave the national governments in charge.

While public support for the ESDP, in particular, is strong, it is also quixotic. Support drops when citizens are asked to choose between their national security and European security, and when asked to increase defense spending. Moreover, many people are concerned about whether the European Union should be—or should have been—militarized in the first place. Finally, would or should the EU have a European army? If so, would there be a draft? Public support, and therefore political will and financing, hinge on the answers to these questions.

This quixotic nature of citizen support has put politicians in a bind. The people want to see Europe as equal to the United States, even as another superpower with a common security and defense policy. Top decisionmakers have similar feelings.[9] However, if they spend the money, which is in short supply in any case, they risk losing public support, as well as one of the best ways, to borrow a term from Chris Patten, to create "Euro-activists."

National control of the ESDP is vital to the success of this policy as a nation-building tool. It allows for European security policy to be bought at a very low political and economic cost. If something were to go wrong in an ESDP mission, or if a member state had a particular reason not to participate, a member state could refrain from any specific mission. Otherwise, if participation were required, the ESDP could actually alienate public support rather than generate it. By making capability contributions bottom-up and on a voluntary basis, the cost of the force can be kept low. Finally, by carefully choosing missions on a case-by-case basis that all the member states agree upon, the European Union significantly increases its chances of success. Every small victory or successful mission is another opportunity to persuade people that the choice for Europe is the correct one.

This chapter carefully examines public opinion in four areas: citizens' desire for a common defense; citizens' preferences for decision-making; citizens' views on increased defense spending; and citizens' views on an EU with a military dimension. In each case, the ESDP structures reflect public opinion, for better and for worse. In other words, the ESDP structures do not reflect the security environment; rather, they reflect public support for the idea of ESDP, but the lack of support for the ESDP in practice—hence, the rhetoric with little to back it up.

## Public Support for a Common Defense

While the idea of a *Homo europeus* is enticing, the Europeans are still a diverse group with a myriad of beliefs. In Europe, strong cleavages exist over issues such as religion, homosexuality, and the price of freedom at the cost of order, thereby compromising the idea of a single set of European values.[10] Europeans also disagree on the role of the European Union; support for the EU is stronger in some countries than in others, and stronger among some social groups than others.

Richard Eichenberg argued that one of the most important lessons politicians took from the antinuclear protests of the early 1980s "was that security policy would henceforth require a solid basis of domestic support."[11] *Eurobarometer* polls from 1990 to 2004 show steady and strong support for a European security policy. Nevertheless, support varies from country to country; in general, support has been the highest in France, Belgium, Germany, and Italy. Support has been lowest in Great Britain and the neutral countries: Austria, Ireland, Sweden, and Finland (see the Appendix).

At the same time, Europeans have continued strongly to support the Atlantic Alliance. Despite the high numbers for a European security and defense policy, historically and today, polls reveal that substantial majorities of citizens in all European states consider NATO "essential" to European security, even in France. From 1967 through 2003, on average, 65 percent of Europeans have strongly valued NATO.[12] Therefore, EU politicians must be careful that EU military missions and assets do not look as if they are competing with or sapping strength from the Atlantic Alliance.

Support for the ESDP falls further when people are asked to choose between national and European defense. Although the ESDP still gets more support, the margin is smaller. In some years, specifically autumn 1993, spring 1999, and autumn 2000, citizens preferred a national policy to a European one.[13]

The EU treaties reflect the mixed feelings Europeans have had over "Defense Europe." The compromise language agreed to under Maastricht states, "The common foreign and security policy shall include all questions related to the security of the Union, including the eventual framing of a common defence policy, which might in time lead to a common defence."[14] In the EU draft Constitutional Treaty, written more than a decade later, the wording is almost identical: "The Union's competence in matters of common foreign and security policy shall cover all areas of foreign policy and all questions relating to the Union's security, including the progressive framing of a common defence policy that might lead to a common defence."[15] For Atlanticists and neutrals, the question of a common defense is problematic; hence the wording that acknowledges the possibility, but promises nothing. Until the people in all the member states feel comfortable with the idea, politicians will not commit their governments to a common European defense. Unfortunately, by not doing so, the member states give the impression of not being able to agree on the most fundamental of issues regarding the ESDP.

## Citizens' Preference for Intergovernmentalism

One of the most difficult questions for EU politicians is how to decide when to send troops. In 2001, nearly half of all Europeans believed that it should be a purely national decision. Eleven percent believed that troops should be sent only when all countries agree; that is, unanimous decisionmaking. A further 17 percent believed in the use of majority voting in making such decisions, but only when member states are assured an opt-out if they disagree. Taken together, 75 percent of Europeans believed that the member states should have a veto when it comes to sending troops on a European Union mission. Only 7 percent agreed with the idea that a majority vote should force the state to send troops; 18 percent did not know.[16]

In light of these poll results, not surprisingly, almost all decisions regarding security and defense are taken intergovernmentally and by consensus. To ensure that security and defense policy would not be "Communitized," the member states placed the ESDP in its own separate pillar. While such a policy has the advantage of reflecting the public's desires, it has also had unintended consequences. Without qualified majority voting, the EU is not able to react quickly to a crisis situation requiring any sort of diplomatic or military action. Moreover, crisis management is not easily split between pillars I and II, resulting in turf battles in Brussels over which institution has competence.

Under the Maastricht Treaty, the Twelve agreed that "the Council shall act unanimously, except for procedural questions and in the case referred to in Article J.3." Concerned that unanimity would stymie the nascent CFSP, the Fifteen (the Twelve plus Austria, Finland, and Sweden) agreed a few years later under the Amsterdam Treaty that although most decisions should be made "by the Council acting unanimously," when possible, decisions would be taken through qualified majority voting, but only if all countries unanimously agreed.[17]

The constitutional convention made little progress on this issue. According to *The Economist*'s analysis of the EU Constitution, "Confusion reigns on foreign policy. Asked recently if the constitution lets foreign-policy decisions be made by unanimity or majority vote, the convention's spokesman refused to answer and invited journalists to work it out themselves."[18] Under the draft Constitutional Treaty, a general rule of consensus would apply under the CFSP.[19] However, under some circumstances, and when agreed upon by unanimity, decisions could be made by qualified majority voting (QMV), but never questions with defense or military implications.[20] If a decision normally designated to be taken by QMV is opposed by one member state because of "vital" concerns, then no decision shall be taken by a qualified majority. Instead, the decision will be referred to the European Council to be decided by unanimity. In this way, each member state retains a veto over foreign, security, and defense affairs. The draft Constitutional Treaty also provided for "structured cooperation," which would allow a smaller group of so-inclined member states to cooperate more closely on military issues.

If the European Security and Defense Policy were the result of a coming of age or a logical progression of integration, then one would expect to see streamlined structures and a significant role for the European institutions such as the European Commission and the European Parliament. Instead, the CFSP/ESDP was placed in a separate pillar to prevent this policy from being "Communitized"; the member states refused to let the European Community method apply. The overarching goal was to make sure that a country was not drawn into war by majority vote in the European Union. As Nicole Gnesotto explained,

> The method for taking decisions on CFSP and defence . . . is governed by an almost universal rule of unanimity among the 15 and now 25 member states, and thus the possibility [exists] for each state to use its right of veto on any decision in this area. Finally the institutional arrangement governing the implementation of the ESDP also demonstrates the burden of national constraints on the development of a European defence policy. The greatest obsession of the majority of member states is, in fact, to exclude from it any reference to, any borrowing from, or any concession to the Community method—in other words to keep the ESDP and the CFSP as a whole outside the scope of the powers of the Commission and the European Parliament.[21]

Therefore, the CFSP/ESDP was put into a separate pillar of the European Union, away from the prying hands of the other, nonintergovernmental European institutions. Security policy was simply too sensitive; national interests in this area could not be horse-traded or regulated by the Commission, the Court of Justice, or the European Parliament. One EU member state diplomat characterized the MEPs as "loose cannons" with no knowledge of foreign, security, or defense policy.[22] Yet, for visibility and publicity's sake, the European foreign, security, and defense policy must appear "European"; i.e., the Commission and the Parliament need to be seen as being involved. If it appears that the CFSP/ESDP is only a caucus for the member states, then this policy will not be seen as a natural extension of the EU.

Although perhaps well designed from the member state perspective, the decisionmaking mechanisms are ill-conceived for the Union itself and for conducting ESDP operations. A mission must be designated pillar I or pillar II or an interpillar mission, when most missions are not so easily pigeonholed. In any of these cases, a division of labor must be established between the Commission and the Council. The problems of interpillar management even affect the day-to-day workings of the permanent representations of the member states.

### Turf Wars: Ramifications of the Pillar System

Although both the Commission and the Council have powers in security policy decisionmaking, the cultures in the two pillars are decidedly different. In pillar I, the Commission has the exclusive right of initiative. Since all the member states begin with the same Commission proposal, 60 to 80 percent of the final decision is already made. In pillar II, the climb is considerably more difficult because several different member state proposals are circulated and must be reconciled. In other words, discussions begin at zero. Most importantly, the Commission is subject to oversight by the European Court of Justice, the European Parliament, and the Court of Auditors. Therefore, the Commission is often characterized as very slow and cautious in its policy formation. It also tries to be seen as neutral in its more technical intervention, looking for apolitical and long-term solutions to develop regions.

In contrast, the General Secretariat of the Council of the European Union has few personnel, few financial resources, and no power of initiative. The office of Javier Solana, the high representative of the CFSP, tries to exert its influence by being the first with the most; that is, trying to set the agenda of the PSC by providing the member states with premade foreign and security policy initiatives. Ironically, the Commission is supposed to have a mind of its own, but it is being quashed; and the

General Secretariat, which is not supposed to have one, does, and expresses it willingly. These differences in cultures and in resources have created institutional turf battles in Brussels in the security arena, which the institutions are supposed to resolve themselves.

The Commission's RELEX existed long before the CFSP. Before 1999, which saw the establishment of both Solana, as high representative, and the Policy Planning Unit, only the Commission existed to deal with the CFSP. The Commission was very active during this period, employing a variety of instruments at its disposal, including technical assistance; development assistance; humanitarian assistance (ECHO); mechanisms for civil protection (dealing with disasters and so on); and the rapid reaction mechanism, to close financial gaps in emergencies. Traditionally, the Commission has provided training, technical advice, mentoring, election monitoring, and more to foreign countries. As a result, it employs 20,000 people and has a several-billion-euro budget; naturally, compared to Commission action in all pillars, the CFSP/ESDP is much more limited in scope.

To help the fledgling policy unit and the CFSP, and to quash rumors that there would be a rivalry between them, Chris Patten, the EU commissioner for External Relations, deferred to his friend, Solana, and let the latter's office take the lead in foreign and security affairs. From 1998 onward, the Commission has refrained more and more from activity in this area.[23] Instead, the Commission has been relegated to "flanking measures" to support ESDP missions.

Around this time, the Council began taking these civilian aspects of foreign policy out of the hands of the Commission. Originally, under Maastricht, the member states foresaw that civilian aspects would remain under the Commission while hard security and military aspects would be placed in pillar II. In 1995, with the accession of Sweden, Finland, and Austria, three neutral countries, the new members took the opportunity to have the Petersberg tasks of 1992 incorporated into the revised Amsterdam Treaty on European Union to keep the CFSP more civilian in nature.[24] Further complicating the distinction between pillars I and II, the Feira Presidency Conclusions of 2000 explicitly placed four areas of civil crisis management (police, civil administration, civil protection, and judicial development) under the auspices of the ESDP, despite the fact that, heretofore, they had been managed by the Commission.[25] To make matters worse, the conclusions did not specify whether the European Community method or intergovernmental method should be used, thereby creating a no-man's-land of how to handle such crises.

This no-man's-land means that many operations that could have been done under pillar I are being done under pillar II because there is no clear definition as to what development assistance is or what is covered by the Petersberg tasks. The rule-of-law missions in Georgia and Iraq should or could have been defined as part of pillar I, yet were designated pillar II. Although technically they are border monitoring missions, the EU's missions to Rafah and to Transdniestria/Moldova have fallen under the ESDP, and therefore do not take full advantage of the Commission's expertise in the area. As a Swedish diplomat explained, the Commission has argued that some operations should be theirs. For example, the EU's mission to Rafah on the Gaza Strip, as it is a customs project, could have been done the old-fashioned way, in and by pillar I. Others argued that it should be done in pillar II because the ESDP needed to gain ground and stature. In this view, Rafah belonged in pillar II because it has been a sensitive political issue and required rapid deployment. Member states feel more comfortable when in control and can send their best people.[26]

The issue of policing, the most popular aspect of the ESDP's crisis management, straddles three pillars. If police are told not to police, but to monitor or to train others, the mission falls under pillar I; if the police are military police who actually police, then it falls under pillar II; if the police are not military police, but under the command of the interior ministry, then the mission falls under pillar III—Justice and Home Affairs. To further complicate matters, German police are forbidden from serving under a military command.

In general, the member states prefer to put all operations, both civilian and military, under ESDP so they can keep a tighter rein on their personnel and resources. If they did not, there would be very few ESDP missions. Only two ESDP missions have been military; all the rest have been civilian. For example, the Aceh monitoring mission in Indonesia was clearly civilian, but was manned by unarmed military in civilian clothes and therefore designated pillar II.[27] However, the no-man's-land creates duplication and anomalies. For example, with regard to Moldova, both the Commission and the General Secretariat were working on position papers to be approved by the College of Commissioners and the Council, respectively. As one Commission official pointed out, "It goes without saying that there needs to be close contact so that the papers are not contradictory."[28]

Both the Commission and the high representative can appoint an ambassador. The Commission ambassadors represent EU trade and development policy, while the high representative's special and personal representatives (EUSR) stand for the CFSP and ESDP. Occasionally, one representative will be appointed who represents both entities; for example, Erwan Fouéré, the special representative to Skopje, Macedonia. In the case of the ALTHEA mission in Bosnia, the EUSR was placed ahead of the Commission delegation in terms of chain of command. This subordination of the Commission was deemed unacceptable because the Community method makes the Commission accountable to the Court of Justice, the Court of Auditors, and public opinion. "How could the Commission accept that another entity would make decisions on their behalf when they are responsible for the policies?"[29]

The competition in this area has created tension in Brussels; each side has felt it was operating as a minority in a foreign environment.

> Colleagues working in the General Secretariat of the Council are relatively few compared to the Commission. On the ESDP side, specifically, we are very few to interact with the Council. There are very few of us present in their meetings. It is totally different [i.e., the opposite] when mainstream issues are discussed involving Commission and Council geographical services. There are good people on both sides of the street. Still more can be done to get rid of infighting and project our energies outside. In crisis response, the key is joint planning.[30]

As another Commission official put it, "The question of 'who does what' is demotivating and distracting. The member states want the Commission and the General Secretariat to sort it out themselves."[31]

The pillar problem affects the Union's ability to react to international crises by hindering coordination of the different elements needed. Development aid and humanitarian assistance fall under the Commission and pillar I; foreign, security, and defense policy falls under pillar II; and policing and rule-of-law missions fall under Justice and Home Affairs in pillar III. In a joint report to the UK presidency of the EU, two nongovernmental organizations, Saferworld and International Alert, wrote,

> *The EU's institutional structure inhibits coherent action towards fragile states.* Due to its problematic "pillar" structure, the EU continues to lack the necessary coordination to maximise the potential of its instruments. This institutional disconnect between the Commission and the Council means, for example, that complementary conflict prevention and development programming is not integrated into the strategic and operational planning of ESDP crisis management operations.[32]

This question of "which pillar?" will, in some part, be decided by the Court of Justice. In 2005, the Commission brought an action against the Council for a lack of competence (under Article 230 of the EC treaty) for the implementation of a joint action, with a view to an EU contribution to the Economic Community of West African States (ECOWAS) in the framework of the Moratorium on Small Arms and Light Weapons. The Council argued that the governing Cotonou agreement covers actions among the member states themselves against the spread of small and light weapons. The Commission argued that the Council decision infringes upon the Commission's powers in the field of development aid.[33]

The pillar question also hinges on the success or failure of a revised Constitutional Treaty and whether an External Action Service will come into effect. Both the Constitutional Treaty and the Lisbon Reform Treaty provide for the creation of an External Action Service, or EU diplomatic office and corps drawing from resources from the Commission, the Council, and staff from the national diplomatic services. Both treaties merged the posts of the Council's high representative for the CFSP and the commissioner for external relations into one called the EU foreign affairs minister under the Constitutional Treaty, now renamed the high representative for foreign policy and security in the Lisbon Treaty. The person in this position will have one foot in the Council and one foot in the Commission, allowing him or her to take advantage of the strengths of both institutions and to bypass some of the pillar problems. Nevertheless, having the European Union speak with one voice may continue to be an elusive goal. The Reform Treaty also creates a standing president of the European Council. This person will have significant clout as will the president of the European Commission. These three positions will all claim to speak for the EU internationally.

*The no-man's-land in COREPER: the problem of two ambassadors.* Even the member state permanent representations (COREPER) have difficulties with the pillar issue. As there are two pillars, each pillar has its own ambassador. Considering the different cultures of the two pillars, one of horse-trading and the other of standing by national interest, each is represented by a different person in the member state missions to the EU. Nominally, the Community ambassador is senior to the Political and Security Committee (PSC) ambassador, but neither has to answer to the other. PSC decisions are finalized by COREPER; however, only as a line item to be approved and not discussed. According to interviews with several PSC officials and ambassadors, the problem is minimal when the chemistry is good between the two and each allows for give-and-take. In other cases, as one Polish diplomat said, "The two ambassadors issue has been very troublesome. During the first presidency when Poland arrived, it was well-known that in one member state, the two ambassadors did not speak to each other. When you prepare a meeting of ministers, it can have an impact."[34] The political role of the PSC ambassadors has been improving presidency by presidency. Rumor has it that in the near future, they will be COREPER-free and will have this equality formalized.[35] However, the member states are in an awkward situation: they must keep separate ambassadors because of the intergovernmental quality of the CFSP and ESDP; yet, having two ambassadors, with formalized equality or not, creates a duality of voice for the state and opens the door to "who's in charge" in the permanent representatives.

*The civilian and military cell.* The only truly interpillar agency is the Civilian and Military Cell (Civ/Mil Cell) within the EU Military Staff in the Cortenbergh building in Brussels. In December 2003, the Brussels European Council reached an agreement on a paper presented by the Italian presidency, entitled "European Defence: NATO/EU Consultation, Planning and Operations," which was based on proposals drawn up by Germany, France, and Britain. One year later, the European Council approved a set of detailed proposals on how the agreement should be implemented. The main objectives were twofold: to improve the planning of EU operations drawing on NATO assets and capabilities, by setting up an EU defense planning cell based at NATO's Supreme Headquarters Allied Powers Europe (SHAPE) and by seconding SHAPE liaison officers to the EU Military Staff; and to strengthen the EU's capacity to plan and conduct autonomous EU-led operations (i.e., without recourse to NATO assets and capabilities). This second task led to the development of the Civ/Mil Cell.

This cell has a small, permanent nucleus that, if the Council so decides, can also serve as an operations center and be expanded to a maximum of eighty-nine staff ("double-hatted" personnel drawn from the EU Military Staff, the Council Secretariat, and EU member states). The operations center will plan and conduct autonomous EU-led operations in the event that no national headquarters has been designated for this purpose.[36]

The Civ/Mil Cell is the first standing EU body that fully integrates military and civilian expertise, bringing together diplomats, officers, civilian experts, and officials from both the Council and the Commission. One senior official called it "the great white hope," but recognized a big disconnect between rhetoric and reality. In his words, the two functions—civilian and military planning—are usually done in parallel rather than together, although they "look beautiful on paper."

However, that was the political compromise struck.[37] The Civ/Mil Cell will do strategic planning with fifteen planners, eight from the military side and seven from the civilian. These include national experts representing the navy, army, and air force as well as medical, intelligence, logistics, and CIS (communications) experts. Of the seven civilians, two are from the Commission and report directly to it. Psychologically, the goal is to keep the Commission officials connected to the Commission. The added value is the combined planning with the Commission, thereby eliminating stovepiping.[38]

The Civ/Mil Cell also houses the Operations Center, although it is not permanent. It is limited in size and military ambitions, but can be activated. It provides the physical infrastructure, offices, computers, and IT infrastructure. It also identifies the human resources needed if the Operations Center is called into operation. The Civ/Mil Cell is to identify the augmentees, train them, teach them the procedures, and familiarize them with EU concepts.

As the civilian missions grow both larger and riskier (for example, Rafah and Aceh), the goal is to create a common structure to accommodate both the needs of the Commission and the Council, as well as those actually doing the crisis management. The cell became operational on 1 January 2007, and the Operations Center was first activated in June 2007 for the MILEX 07/CPX military exercise. The Operations Center is deemed the "Ferrari in the garage"[39] (although a US official dubbed it a "Peugeot"),[40] and many officials are looking forward to its first activation in a real crisis situation. Solana has said that the Civ/Mil Cell will be the center of gravity.[41] Clearly, expectations for the cell are high. Nevertheless, its success is not assured, for the same reasons that have always stymied European cooperation in the security area: the process. Getting support from all the member states is difficult, and there is still competition among the directorates.

The Civ/Mil Cell's mandate is contingency planning in comprehensive management using an interpillar approach and a civilian-military approach. This comprehensive management naturally involves Commission resources and views. The Commission's influence has provided a new element: prudent, advance planning. A significant part of the planning is in the fact-finding mission to determine the potential medical, logistical, security, communication, and force-protection needs. This information is vital for quick action in a crisis. Moreover, considering that ESDP forces are generated from the "bottom up," on a voluntary basis, being able to identify the legal, practical, and financial needs of an ESDP mission in advance is critical to its success.

However, diplomats do not usually plan in advance; they normally juggle crises as they emerge. Many member state representatives are reluctant to discuss a crisis that has not yet materialized, because of the democratic element: who decides which strategic interests in which crisis regions according to whose priority list? These questions are difficult enough to answer within one member state, let alone among twenty-seven. For example, one senior EU official said in 2005 that the cell should have begun planning for Zimbabwe because it could become a humanitarian disaster (though it had not).[42]

Another fundamental problem with the Civ/Mil Cell is that the member states do not like the military aspect in conjunction with the civilian. The military aspects are not only more controversial but also more difficult to coordinate alongside a civilian mission, and not as easily fundable. Neutral countries are especially reluctant to participate in missions with a military dimension. For other member states, the problem is not so much the military aspect as the difficulty in coordinating military and civilian missions; there is no clear chain of command. Ultimately, the question comes down to whether military or civilian commanders, coming from different organizational cultures, should coordinate operations on the ground. Finally, all missions must have a legal basis for the budget; as discussed below, getting money for military missions is extremely difficult and a political hot potato in and of itself. In the end, the official interviewed predicted more missions such as Aceh, which had strong military support of a civilian-directed mission, which was very successful.[43] The Civ/Mil Cell is not likely to become a cure-all for the ESDP, because these very talented people are forced to work within a straitjacket of political considerations.

## Public Opinion and Ramifications for ESDP Financing

Although public opinion strongly supports an ESDP in general, the devil is in the details. Ironically, public support for an ESDP drops significantly once people are asked whether they are willing to pay for it. In 2004, although 71 percent of Europeans wanted the EU to become a superpower like the United States, 47 percent of the 71 percent withdrew their support if securing that goal meant an increase in military spending.[44] In other words, people want the prestige of an EU force, but not the cost. Therefore, where the money should come from to pay for the EU's ambitions is a politically sensitive issue in Brussels. With three pockets of varying depth to choose from—the Community budget, the

CFSP budget, and member state national budgets—deciding who pays for what becomes very difficult, especially in light of whether missions are designated pillar I or II and who gets the credit.

The European Commission oversees a multibillion-euro budget. The 2006 CFSP budget was only 102.6 million euros.[45] Although Solana's office has developed into a genuine secretariat, it has few human and budgetary resources, resulting in little budgetary management. When an ESDP operation is desired, even if done under the CFSP budget, it is still managed by the Commission. In principle, all civilian mission costs should be borne by the CFSP budget, specifically the operational costs and the per diems for the staff. However, member states pay for the bulk of any military missions out of their own pockets because Article 28.3 of the Treaty on European Union forbids the spending of CFSP money on operations with military implications. Regular staff salaries are also footed by the member states they are attached to. As a result, as "costs fall where they lie" with regard to military aspects, the countries that contribute the most in terms of manpower and equipment also have to pay the most. The one exception is for common costs such as headquarters. The ATHENA mission mechanism for military expenditures defines common costs and how member states pay into the mechanism based on their gross national product.[46] For example, Germany pays 22 percent of the common costs.[47] If the Council decides that the per diems should also come out of the CFSP budget, then funds are used up that much more quickly. Many member states feel in a bind. Most put a significant amount of money into the Community budget;[48] however, the CFSP budget is so small that if they want to fulfill the ambitions of the ESDP, they must contribute a second time.

Solana has lobbied very hard for more financial support, but few options are available. One option is that the member states can simply pick up the bill. This option is very unpopular at home, especially in light of national budget crunches owing to, in some cases, bankrupt pension schemes and high unemployment. A second option is to work with the European Commission so it can pay for the ESDP mission on a mainline budget category—for example, MEDA (Mediterranean line items) or the ALAT budget (Asia and Latin America line items) or other regional aid lines. The problem is that the Commission is often considered slow, with a different culture from the Council of Ministers, hence the decision to create the second pillar in the first place. Finally, member states can vote to expand the general budget and have more money appropriated to the CFSP, upon Commission initiation and European Parliament approval. This option has two major problems. First, the budget has been one of the most controversial and embarrassing issues in EU politics. The UK failed to come up with an acceptable budget during its presidency. Issues such as rebates, agricultural subsidies, and structural funds for new members have proven intractable. Second, if, indeed, the member states could agree on an increased budget for CFSP, then the larger the line item, the more control the European Parliament would demand for the sake of transparency and oversight.

Members of Parliament Elmar Brok and Norbert Gresch disapproved of the ATHENA mechanism precisely because they saw it as a way around the European Parliament.

> The EP [European Parliament] therefore takes an extremely critical view of the establishment of an additional budget to finance the joint costs of EU military operations by the member states. The "Athena" fund does not come within the parliamentary scrutiny of either national parliaments or the EP. Different financing mechanisms of this kind for the joint costs of civilian and military operations do nothing for the coherence and transparency of European crisis management.[49]

It is no wonder that "[a]t present the EU's autonomous military capability (and the European contribution to NATO) is only being remodeled where no increase in defense expenditure is necessary."[50]

## Public Opinion and Ramifications for the ESDP Military Capability

Many criticize the European Union for having stellar aspirations without the military capacity to follow through. The European Union has no military assets of its own; rather, the member states place their national assets, on an ad hoc and voluntary basis, at the disposal of the Union. Moreover, many of the military assets offered are still geared toward the Cold War and/or are not state-of-the-art. As explained above, EU politicians seem unwilling to increase defense spending, a necessary prerequisite for the Union's ambitions. As a result, the EU seems weak.

Yet, EU politicians have relatively few options as they are constrained by public opinion. There is a general uneasiness among EU citizens with regard to "defense Europe"; the public prefers to keep troops under national control, and the public does not support an increase in defense spending. Again, ESDP structures reflect public opinion. The ESDP provides a European shell for national military assets. In this way, the EU can acquire military assets at a low political and economic cost.

Such a policy puts the EU at the mercy of national parliaments, however; when the EU needs either more or more modern assets, it forces the question of "guns versus butter."

While many Europeans feel an aversion to war, which sometimes makes the ESDP a tough sell, they also wish for an engaged Europe, as polls reveal. The question of militarizing the EU has been problematic on many levels. Although the EU may well need a military to be taken seriously as an international actor, as explained in Chapter 2, the EU has long had a reputation as a civilian power, which many prized as a way of distinguishing Europe from the United States and as a way of separating themselves from a violent past of war and imperialism. For the Germans, especially, many felt more comfortable in a civilian Europe. Dr. Dietrich Baeuerle, Catholic theologian and activist in Pax Christi's international peace movement, wrote, in the mainstream *Frankfurter Rundschau*, that the EU was on its way to becoming a military union that was no friend of peace.[51] The neutrals were also uncomfortable with the idea of a military Europe. It was they who pressured the other member states into incorporating the humanitarian Petersberg tasks into the Amsterdam Treaty to keep the EU from becoming more militarized. Sweden was afraid their people might reject a European security and defense policy, as Denmark did, which would force them to negotiate an opt-out.[52] Moreover, the Atlanticist countries worried about the EU as a competitor to NATO.

To allay the public's fears, Solana asserted that "the ESDP is not a process of militarization of European construction."[53] Stef Goris, WEU assembly president, argued, "[T]he EU must become a provider of external security, but not a world policeman."[54] If not a civilian power, a military power, nor even a policing power, what kind of power is the EU? Solana's office said, "We are not a military organization, we are a civilian organisation that makes use of military assets."[55] One newspaper dubbed the EU *"Friedensmacht"* or "peace-power."[56] The Schröder government deemed it "a civilian power with teeth."[57]

Whether the EU should create a European army is also disputed among the public and politicians alike. Only 19 percent of people surveyed preferred a single European army to replace national armies. The most popular proposal was that of a permanent European rapid reaction force in addition to national armies (37 percent). Eighteen percent preferred an ad hoc European rapid reaction force that would come into play when needed; 12 percent wanted no European army, but only national ones; and 13 percent did not know.[58]

Among politicians, there is no agreement on whether the EU will acquire an army. In 2001, the Göteborg European Council Presidency Report stated categorically that developing the capacity to act "does not involve the establishment of a European army."[59] Since then, there has been much talk otherwise. Two years later, Lieutenant General Rainer Schuwirth, chief of the EU's military staff, discussed openly the possibility of a European army.[60] Finnish minister for European Affairs Erkki Tuomioja publicly talked about whether the term "common defense" meant setting up a European army or not, and whether it meant that UK and French nuclear weapons would come under European responsibility.[61] Laurent Fabius, former prime minister of France, believed the EU needed an army.[62] Luc Frieden, Luxembourg minister and president-in-office of the Council, explained, "Europe does not wish to become a Europe with a military dimension. It does, however, want a foreign policy in which the defence dimension plays an important role."[63] This statement contradicted one made by Frieden only a year earlier: "This increase [in defense budgets] will be combined with reform of the armed forces in order to provide the EU with a 'small' but 'specialised' army."[64] In September 2006, Kurt Beck, leader of the German Social Democrats, called for the formation of a European army with a single command.[65] After the completion of its mission in the Democratic Republic of Congo to oversee elections, French general Christian Damay said that EU troops were well on their way to being able to work as a common EU army.[66]

Understandably, considering public opinion, issues such as the creation of a European force, or even force generation, remain sensitive. How can the European Union acquire the necessary military and civilian assets to perform the tasks assigned to it while keeping public support? The EU uses a bottom-up and voluntary approach, where member states place military assets at the request of the European Union to be used when needed. In other words, the ESDP creates a European shell for national military capabilities. Moreover, the EU seeks to keep the force generation process as transparent and public as possible in order to encourage public support for an increase in spending.

### The State of ESDP Military Capacity

The Yugoslav crisis and the inability of the European Union to take the lead in their own backyard deeply impressed EU politicians. The Europeans' reliance on the United States and NATO in former Yugoslavia and especially in Kosovo demonstrated the need for an autonomous EU capacity to respond to international crises. The French-British rapprochement, codified by the Saint-Mâlo agreement of 1998, paved the way for the Helsinki Headline Goal agreed upon at the Helsinki European Council meeting in December 1999.

Using the number of troops in Kosovo as a guideline, the headline goal required the European Union countries, by the year 2003, to create a rapid reaction force of 50,000 to 60,000 troops capable of implementing the full range of Petersberg tasks. The member states also promised to develop the collective capability goals with regard to strategic transport, command, control, communications, and intelligence so as to make these forces deployable within sixty days and sustainable for up to one year. However, these numbers were chosen without military consultation, as there was no EU military staff at the time.

The EU rapid reaction force provided a shell for a pool of national units that the EU could, in principle, draw from should the Council decide unanimously to use military force in response to an international crisis. Such an arrangement would satisfy public demands at a low cost. British Conservative Geoffrey Van Orden correctly observed, "In the EU, we don't create new troops, we rearrange existing ones."[67]

Although the EU member states committed up to 100,000 men, 400 aircraft, and 100 ships, these commitments were only on paper and a rapid reaction force never materialized. Karl-Heinz Kamp of the Konrad-Adenauer-Stiftung lamented,

> Alas, the intended crisis management capability of 60,000 men was a Potemkin's village. In half recognition of the failure in June 2004 a new goal was set—this time named "Headline Goal 2010," including the Battle Groups as one component. It is not to be excluded in view of scarce means that the EU will again follow the same pattern: declare immediate objectives reached, although the necessary "hardware" only exists on paper.[68]

The Helsinki Headline Goal did spawn the Headline Goal Task Force and the Capabilities Commitments Conference in November 2000, which created the Helsinki Force Catalogue. The catalog measured the national contributions member states were willing to make on a voluntary basis toward the rapid reaction force. It also uncovered serious shortfalls.

To address the shortfalls, the EU defense ministers created the European capabilities action plan (ECAP) in 2001. The ECAP panels of experts meet independently to develop solutions to the shortfalls. Their work is guided by four core principles:

1. The improvement of the effectiveness and efficiency of European defense efforts, enhancing cooperation between member states or groups of member states.
2. A bottom-up approach to European defense collaboration, relying on voluntary national commitments.
3. Coordination between EU member states as well as coordination with NATO.
4. Public support through ECAP's transparency and visibility.[69]

Broad public support is vital because

> The public in the member states must have a clear vision of the context in which CFSP development is situated, of the existing shortcomings and the efforts to be made to achieve the objectives set. This transparency of the Action Plan will help to make the Action Plan more effective and back up the political action and political will underpinning it.[70]

In this vein, General Rolando Mosca Moschini, Italian chair of the EU Military Committee, emphasized the "vital role of the media" in building public support for the ESDP.[71]

Therefore, shoring up public opinion for the ESDP has been a key objective for the Belgian, Spanish, and Luxembourg presidencies. Belgian prime minister Guy Verhofstadt wrote an open letter to UK prime minister Tony Blair and French president Jacques Chirac, stating, "Now, we must act" to make the European Union more credible in this area, or lose public support for EU defense spending.[72] The Spanish presidency actually went so far as to list a group of "public opinion objectives" for the ESDP: "In order to obtain the people's support, it is necessary to inform them and make them participants in our achievements and, likewise, in our failures. Only in this way will we gain their trust and support."[73]

The ECAP concluded in May 2003 that there were certain significant shortfalls that prevented the EU from implementing the Petersberg tasks. Without public support, there would be no way of addressing them. Burkard Schmitt identified five key areas the EU must address if it is to implement the Petersberg tasks: deployability, mobility, sustainability, effective engagement, and $C^4ISR$.[74]

On paper, the member states have approximately 1.8 million armed forces, but only 10 to 15 percent are deployable for missions overseas because of limits on where conscripts can serve and/or because of a focus on territorial defense. The need to rotate forces (one-third on deployment, one-third training, one-third resting) limits the EU capacity even more.

The EU is also unable to transport its troops. As one US military officer put it, the EU's military assets were akin to a "beached whale":

impressive to look at, but very difficult to move.[75] The British "food for thought" paper explained that initial deployment of a single battle group would require approximately 200 flights by C-130 transport airplanes or 30 flights with the C-17 Globemaster transporter. The UK is the only EU country with any Globemasters; it has four, and a fifth ordered.[76] To close the gap in the short term, the EU can lease transport planes. In the long term, many countries are working to acquire A400Ms, Airbus's military transport planes.

Sustainability is also an issue. Once deployed, troops need provisions, medical support, and refueling options. The goal is to be able to send troops 6,000 kilometers from Brussels. Therefore, the EU will either have to stretch its supply lines or use host nation agreements to arrange for refueling stations and landing rights.

Effective engagement is the ability to withstand a hostile environment on the ground. To effectively engage, the EU needs precision guided weapons, offensive electronic warfare, suppression of enemy air defenses, etc. The Cold War required defensive tactics; until recently, Germany had exclusively a defensive force. The EU needs these offensive tools for effective crisis management far from home.

Finally $C^4ISR$ is necessary for a modern military. While some EU member states have the above, there is also the issue of interoperability. The $C^4ISR$ of some member states is sometimes not compatible with those of others.

In response to the shortfalls, and with much fanfare, in 2004 the EU defense ministers approved an initiative to create battle groups or tactical groups to give the EU rapid reaction capability. Composed of 1,500 troops and the appropriate supporting element, these mostly multinational groups will be ready for deployment within fifteen days and capable of higher-intensity operations. These groups have been operational as of 2007, and although under national command, will be available to either NATO or the EU if requested. To quote Solana, "We begin 2007 ready to take up our responsibilities if needed—which I sincerely hope won't be the case—but we are in a position of readiness."[77]

Nevertheless, the intergovernmental nature of the ESDP has made it extremely difficult to overcome the shortfalls. Schmitt elucidated, "The restructuring of armed forces is almost inevitably slow and cumbersome, because it requires important financial investment, runs against deeply rooted traditions and mentalities and may raise serious social and economic problems."[78] The member states have refused to give up sovereignty in this area; armed forces restructuring is done on a bottom-up and voluntary basis.

The European Defense Agency (EDA) was established to coordinate information sharing among Europe's defense ministries and to find ways to overcome the shortfalls. One of their tools is an inventory map that, as one EDA official "circuitously admitted . . . will offer justification for coordinated cross-border defense industrial policy."[79] The official was reluctant to admit it because many member states resist such a policy. Although there is an abstract need for coordination, no one wants to be coordinated. Defense spending is not a popular initiative because it forces the question of guns versus butter in the parliament. As a Finnish diplomat described the situation,

> Creating a common defence industrial policy would mean that the national parliaments would lose control over their budget and the final decision of what to spend money on. Such a policy would destroy the "bottom-up" approach agreed upon for the ESDP, in other words, the voluntary aspect. A common industrial policy could impose requirements on national parliaments to "buy more helicopters at the expense of new school buses."[80]

As a result, some national governments have been loath to turn over the required information.[81]

The EU's military capacity is weak because public support for an EU military capacity is weak. Ultimately, the power either to increase defense spending or to modernize militaries lies with national parliaments. Without public support for increased defense spending, the ESDP will remain a shell for donated national capabilities.

## Conclusion

Considering the public's preference for intergovernmentalism vis-à-vis sending troops overseas—combined with the difficulty the EU has had in gathering the appropriate military assets—finding the right mission that all member states can agree on and that fits the EU's military instruments (i.e., that the EU is capable of taking on) sometimes presents a challenge. Solana pointed out four significant hurdles in the way of an effective ESDP and challenged the states to overcome them: (1) reconciling some member states' interventionist tendencies with other member states' abstentionist tendencies; (2) the EU principle of absolute equality among the member states; (3) lack of flexibility in the present system; (4) determining the most effective level for managing crises; i.e., individual state action versus collective EU action.[82]

In response to the above, one German diplomat believed little could be done to overcome these difficulties.[83] In fact, these difficulties explain the necessity of consensus rule within the CFSP/ESDP. With regard to the first hurdle named by Solana, some member states, such as France, have both the means and the political will to get involved in civil unrest overseas, as they have done many times in Africa (for example, Sierra Leone and Côte d'Ivoire). Other countries, such as Ireland, have neutrality clauses in their constitutions and/or are uneasy with the idea of sending their troops overseas, especially without a UN mandate.

The rhetoric has created high expectations, so the stakes are high; the EU must demonstrate its success as an international actor. As of October 2007, the EU has had nineteen successful missions, ranging from border control, policing, and humanitarian assistance to rule-of-law missions and a limited number of military missions. Interestingly, no ESDP mission to date has included all of the EU member states. Rather, the ESDP has provided an EU label for European-led multinational missions.

In general, ESDP operations have been de facto coalitions of the willing. Although nominally EU operations, both ALTHEA and the EU Police Mission (EUPM) in Bosnia and Herzegovina (BiH) do not include all the EU members, but do include many others. ALTHEA, the EU Force in Bosnia and Herzegovina that took over from NATO's Stabilization Force, had troops from twenty-two out of twenty-five EU member states and troops from other countries, including Albania, Argentina, Bulgaria, Canada, Chile, Morocco, New Zealand, Norway, Romania, Switzerland, and Turkey.[84] In the EU Police Mission to Kinshasa, only five EU member states contributed officials, along with Canada and Turkey.[85] The EU's response to the crisis in Darfur cobbled together personnel from Austria, Denmark, France, Italy, the Netherlands, Sweden, and the United Kingdom. Financing was also cobbled together from the EC's Rapid Reaction Mechanism (850,000), in addition to funding from Sweden (1 million), the Netherlands (300,000), Germany (€250,000), and Italy (€32,000).[86] These coalitions of the willing are a result of the veto national governments hold in this area; not all member states have been willing to contribute to any or all EU interventions.

The "absolute equality" principle Solana criticized was a prerequisite for cooperation in the security and defense field. National governments are held responsible for foreign policy, especially when the nationals sent overseas could be shot at. National interests must not be compromised. All members are viewed as equals and each holds a veto, creating the rigid system Solana must work under. Finally, considering the lack of flexibility in the system and the reluctance of many member states to become involved, determining the most effective level for managing crises will remain difficult. Solana's critiques are accurate, yet they cannot be overcome as long as security policy is ruled by intergovernmentalism.

## Notes

1. As quoted in "Positive Welcome for the Italian Suggestion of Pooling Rapid Intervention Capacity and for the French Suggestion of a 'European Police Force': Progress on 'Structured Cooperation'?" *Atlantic News*, 8 October 2003, 3.

2. Anne Deighton, "The European Security and Defense Policy," 720.

3. Simon Duke, "The Rhetoric-Resources Gap in EU Crisis Management," 2.

4. As quoted in "WEU/ESDP: Call for Interparliamentary Forum on European Defence," *Europe Daily Bulletin*, 27 September 2003, 5.

5. As quoted in "EP/ESDP: Javier Solana Presents His European Security Strategy to EP Committee on Foreign Affairs," *Europe Daily Bulletin*, 11 September 2003, 6.

6. European Parliament Resolution on the European Security Strategy, P6_TA-PROV(2005)013314 April 2005, written by Helmut Kuhne.

7. As quoted in Gareth Harding, "Analysis: EU Talks Tough, Goes Global," United Press International, 17 June 2003.

8. Hill, "The Capability-Expectations Gap."

9. Jacqueline M. Spence, *The European Union: "A View from the Top": Top Decision-Makers and the European Union* (Wavre, Belgium: EOS Gallup Europe), 51–53.

10. Mark Beunderman, "Religion and Homosexuality Divide Europeans," *euobserver.com*, 18 December 2006.

11. Eichenberg, "Having It Both Ways," 627–628.

12. Ibid., 633.

13. Wagner, "Democratic Legitimacy of European Security and Defence Policy," 13.

14. The Maastricht Treaty on European Union, Article J:4.

15. EU draft Constitutional Treaty, Title III, Article I-16.

16. Philippe Manigart, "Public Opinion and European Defense," Special issue, *Eurobarometer* 146 (July 2001): 13.

17. Treaty of Amsterdam, Article J:13.

18. "Europe: Questions and Answers," *The Economist*, 23 June 2003.

19. EU draft Constitutional Treaty, Title V, Chapter II, Article III-201.1.

20. EU draft Constitutional Treaty, Title V, Chapter II, Article III-201.2–4.

21. Nicole Gnesotto, "ESDP: Results and Prospects," in *EU Security and Defence Policy,* ed. Gnesotto, 19.

22. Representative from the Permanent Representation of the Netherlands to the EU, interview by author, Brussels, Belgium, 8 November 2005.

23. European Commission RELEX official III, interview by author, Brussels, Belgium, 7 December 2005.

24. Representatives I and II from the Permanent Representation of Sweden to the EU, interview by author, Brussels, Belgium, 7 December 2005.

25. Feira Presidency Conclusions, 19–20 June 2000, at http://www.europarl.eu.int-/summits-/fei2_en.htm#an1.

26. Representative I from the Permanent Representation of Sweden to the EU, interview by author, Brussels, Belgium, 7 December 2005.

27. Interview with German Ministry of Defense official III, Brussels, Belgium, 10 November 2005.

28. Lars Lundin, European Commission RELEX official, interview by author, Brussels, Belgium, 9 November 2005, and e-mail correspondence, 5 May 2006.

29. European Commission RELEX official III, interview by author.

30. Lundin, interview by and e-mail correspondence with author.

31. European Commission RELEX official I, interview by author, Brussels, Belgium, 8 November 2005.

32. Saferworld and International Alert, "Enhancing EU Impact on Conflict Prevention; Developing an EU Strategy to Address Fragile States: Priorities for the UK Presidency of the EU in 2005," executive summary, June 2005, 3. Emphasis in original.

33. Action Brought on 21 February 2005 by the European Commission Against the Council of the European Union (Case C-91/05), OJ 2005/C 115/19, 14 May 2005.

34. Representative from the Permanent Representation of Poland to the European Union, interview by author, Brussels, Belgium, 9 November 2005.

35. Ibid.

36. For more detail, see Brigadier General Heinrich Brauss and Roland Zinzius, "Remarks to the European Parliament Sub-Committee on Security and Defence," Brussels, Belgium, 1 March 2007, at http://consilium.eu.int/uedocs/cmsUpload/070227Briefing-CCMBrausstoEP.pdf. Brauss is the director of Civ/Mil Cell; Zinzius, the deputy director.

37. Senior EU official, interview by author, Brussels, Belgium, 8 December 2005. This official preferred not to have the department named.

38. Ibid.

39. Ibid.

40. US State Department official III, interview by author, Brussels, Belgium, 30 April 2007.

41. Senior EU official II, interview by author, Brussels, Belgium, 8 December 2005. This official also preferred not to have the department named.

42. Ibid.

43. Ibid.

44. German Marshall Fund of the United States, "Transatlantic Survey Shows Continued, Significant Split in U.S.-Europe Relations," 9 September 2004, at http://www.-gmfus.org/press/article.cfm?id=12&parent_type=R.

45. The European Commission on the CFSP budget, see http://ec.europa.eu/external_relations/cfsp/fin/index.htm.

46. Council Decision 2004/197/CFSP, 23 February 2004, establishing a

mechanism to administer the financing of the common costs of European Union operations having military or defense implications, OJ L63/68, 28 February 2004, at http://europa.eu.int-/eur-lex/pri/en/oj/dat/2004/l_063/l_06320040228 en00680082.pdf.

47. German Foreign Ministry official, interview by author, Berlin, Germany, 25 October 2005.

48. The European Community budget has a redistributive function: some member states are net contributors; others are net receivers.

49. Elmar Brok and Norbert Gresch, untitled chapter in *EU Security and Defence Policy,* ed. Gnesotto, 187.

50. Salmon and Shepherd, *Toward a European Army,* 143.

51. Dietrich Baeuerle, "Die EU ist auf dem Weg zur Militärunion," *Frankfurter Rundschau,* 29 June 2004, 8.

52. Representatives I and II from the Permanent Representation of Sweden to the EU, interview by author, 7 December 2005.

53. Javier Solana, preface to *EU Security and Defence Policy,* ed. Gnesotto, 6.

54. As quoted in "(EU) WEU/Defence: Stef Goris Emphasizes Three Key Words: Ambition, Power and Autonomy, Which Will Enable Europe to Find Its Place on International Stage," *Europe Daily Bulletin* (Brussels), 12 May 2005, 9. Emphasis deleted.

55. As quoted in Luke Hill, "EU Defence Surge Despite Constitutional Collapse," *Jane's Defence Weekly,* 24 December 2003, 4–5.

56. Hans-George Ehrhart, "Europa in neuer Rolle: Als 'Friedensmacht,'" *Das Parlament,* 2 May 2005, 16.

57. German Parliament, 15th legislative period, Answer of the Schröder administration to the parliamentary inquiry from the representatives, Dr. Friedbert Pflüger, Christian Schmidt (Fürth), Ulrich Adam, and other representatives of the CDU/CSU faction, government document number 15/2888.

58. Manigart, "Public Opinion and European Defense," 16.

59. Göteborg European Council Presidency Report on the European Security and Defence Policy, from the General Secretariat, 9526/1/01, Brussels, Belgium, 11 June 2001.

60. As reported in Judy Dempsey, "General Parades Vision of European Army," *Financial Times* (London), 24 September 2003, 2.

61. As reported in "EU/WEU: In Address to Assembly, Irish and Finnish Ministers Express Reservations About Mutual Defence Clause Proposed at Naples—Parliamentarians Seek Explanations from Javier Solana on Security Strategy," *Europe Daily Bulletin* (Brussels), 6 December 2003, 7.

62. Véronique Roger-Lacan, "Où va la défense européenne?" *Le Monde,* 21 June 2005, 13.

63. As quoted in "EU/Defence: Progress Expected in Military Capabilities Field," *Europe Daily Bulletin* (Brussels), 24 May 2005, 4.

64. As quoted in "EU/Defence: Luxembourg to Contribute to EU's Civil and Military Capabilities for Allowing Intervention in Strategic Zones, Where Necessary, to Ensure Security," *Atlantic News,* 7 December 2004, 1.

65. As reported in Dempsey, "German Proposes a European Army."

66. As reported in Honor Mahony, "General Eyes 'European Army' After Congo Mission," *euobserver.com,* 1 December 2006.

67. As quoted in "EP/CFSP: EP Sub-committee on Security and Defence Proposes to Send Parliamentary Delegation to Bosnia-Herzegovina," *Europe Daily Bulletin* (Brussels), 4 August 2004, 2.

68. Karl-Heinz Kamp, "European Battle Groups: A New Stimulus for the European Security and Defense Policy?" *Analysen und Argumente aus der Konrad-Adenauer-Stiftung*, no. 15/2004, 17 December 2004, 4.

69. Burkard Schmitt, "European Capabilities: How Many Divisions?" in *EU Security and Defence Policy*, ed. Gnesotto, 93.

70. Conference on EU Capability Improvement, Brussels, 19 November 2001.

71. As quoted in "EU/Defence: EU Chiefs of Defence Welcome New Chairman of Military Committee, Discuss Capabilities and EU Take-Over of SFOR," *Europe Daily Bulletin*, 14 April 2004, 6. Emphasis deleted.

72. Letter from Guy Verhofstadt, prime minister of Belgium, to Tony Blair and Jacques Chirac, 18 July 2002, at http://www.grip.org/bdg/g4502.html. He wrote: "There is, however, no doubt that public opinion in our countries is convinced of the need for a European defence. Indeed, all opinion polls confirm this. Now we must act. The total defence budgets of the member states of the European Union add up to approximately 150 billion euro. Our citizens will no longer accept a situation in which we spend so much money on our defence effort without making our Union any more credible or more operational in this area. . . . I consider it of utmost importance to develop the solidarity between the member states of the European Union. This could be done by means of a mutual security guarantee in the event of an attack calling for a collective response."

73. Federico Trillo, Spanish minister for defense, "Presentation of the EU Spanish Presidency's Objectives for ESDP," speech presented in Madrid, Spain, 10 January 2002.

74. Schmitt, in *EU Security and Defence Policy,* ed. Gnesotto, 95–96. C⁴ISR stands for command, control, communications, computers, intelligence, surveillance, and reconnaissance.

75. Raymond Millen, LTC, US Army, director, Regional Security Issues, USAWC-SSI, interview by author over the telephone, 8 September 2005.

76. As cited in Kamp, "European Battle Groups."

77. As quoted in Andrew Rettman, "EU Ready for More Military Operations, Solana Says," *euobserver.com,* 18 January 2007.

78. Schmitt, "European Capabilities: How Many Divisions?" 97.

79. As quoted in Brooks Tigner, "EU Plans to Map Europe's Defense Capabilities: Inventory Could Be Used to Create Defense Policy," *Defense News*, 25 July 2005, 20.

80. Finnish representative from the embassy of Finland, interview by author, Berlin, Germany, 24 October 2005.

81. Brooks Tigner, "EU Plans to Map Europe's Defense Capabilities: Inventory Could Be Used to Create Defense Policy," *Defense News*, 25 July 2005, 20.

82. Ibid.

83. German Foreign Ministry official, interview by author.

84. ALTHEA fact sheet, at HYPERLINK http://ue.eu.int/uedocs/cmsUpload /051210Althea7.pdf. At that time, Romania and Bulgaria were not members of the European Union.

85. "EU POL" fact sheet, at HYPERLINK http://ue.eu.int/uedocs/cms Upload/DossierUPI_EUPOL-_mars_2006.pdf.

86. "EU Response to the Crisis in Darfur" fact sheet, at HYPERLINK http://ue.eu.int/uedocs/cmsUpload/-Darfur_Update_6.pdf.

# 7

# Security Policy and the Future of the European Union

---

[Europe] may become more cautious about military intervention. The "CNN effect" and associated casualty aversion are already familiar. Military operations will be subject to ever-increasing scrutiny by elected officials, media and populations. Governments and societies increasingly concerned for internal security and social cohesion may be even more hesitant to undertake potentially controversial interventions abroad—in particular interventions in regions from where large numbers of immigrants have come. ■ EUROPEAN DEFENSE AGENCY, 3 OCTOBER 2006[1]

## How Nation-Building Theory Explains the Paradoxes

After the French and the Dutch rejected the Constitutional Treaty in May and June of 2005, Javier Solana was sorely disappointed. However, he quickly rallied and promised to make the ESDP the crowning achievement of the EU, despite the setback. In a press release after the French rejection, Solana told the world,

> What is of crucial importance now is that we keep on working as we did before and that we do not get into a psychological paralysis. Let me assure you that this will undoubtedly not happen to me!
>
> There is no doubt that the European people as well as the European leaders wish the EU to become an increasingly important actor in the international arena. In the meantime, our work has to continue and we need to explain [*sic*] our partners around the world that the EU will remain an active global player. Our partners need a strong Europe that acts with determination on the international stage. Life continues and the course of the world will not stop. The world's challenges will not change because of yesterday's vote and there are many

175

problems of the world that keep on challenging us. We as the EU have to face these problems and we have to keep on working on their resolution 24 hours a day. This is what we will have to do and this is what I will certainly do.[2]

The failure of the constitution makes the ESDP more important than ever. Solana understood that successful ESDP missions could rally the public once more, and renew faith in the EU. ESDP missions could regenerate momentum for the European project that had once again veered off the path because of citizen suspicion. The ESDP is a tool for nation building.

The introduction of this book posited several paradoxes. Why did the EU integrate in the area of security and defense—the area that theorists said was the least likely to accommodate such integration? Why did integration in this area happen so much later than in other areas? Considering the fanfare that has accompanied the ESDP, why have the member states refused to give it the resources necessary to fulfill its goals?

Traditional security analysis did not predict European integration in this area of "high politics" because such analysis does not foresee the use of security policy for anything else besides security and defense. The EU member states, following on the recommendations of European Community leaders during the 1970s, are using foreign security and defense policy to nation-build; i.e., to create pride and popular support for the European project. Although they endorsed the plan, these same EC leaders understood that experimentation in the security realm could not happen in the hostile Cold War climate; hence the delay in its implementation. A modest investment in European security structures, combined with a flexible geometry with regard to troop placement, has created the image of an active European Union working to promulgate European values and its recipe for peace around the world. As Theo Sommer stated, "Such military body-building does not in any way amount to a 'militarisation' of the European Union, as some critics have it. It is a matter of self-esteem."[3]

Self-esteem is a major issue for Europeans, especially with regard to their own security. Although a great number of European countries are former colonial powers, these countries were not able to guarantee the security of their own borders during World Wars I and II, or during the Cold War. Using the United States as a measuring stick, the European countries are weak in comparison. Moreover, Europeans have had little success influencing US foreign and security policy—a policy that has dominated their own. The only way to attract the United States' attention was for the European countries to speak with one voice; the European Union provides that voice.

As dictated by the EU narrative, that voice speaks out against militarism and unilateralism. The EU "myth," discussed earlier, is a mantra: out of the ashes of World War II, the European project was born as a way to encourage the growth of peace and prosperity throughout the continent. In fifty short years, war between France and Germany is unthinkable and, through cooperation, Europe has become one of the most economically prosperous areas of the world.

And yet, despite Europe's fabulous economic successes, its people are much more lukewarm toward the European project than are its elites. The Danes, the Irish, the French, and the Dutch have all rejected EU treaties. Denmark, Sweden, and Britain have refused to join the euro. Moreover, support for the European Union varies significantly from country to country. How can the EU create the popular support it needs to ensure its survival?

Nation-building theorists place great emphasis on foreign and security policy as a tool for rallying the people: it makes people masters over their own territory; it promises to rewrite the past and to create a glorious new future, as well as to cultivate common values and experiences among the citizens. In other words, it enhances the narrative that connects a people to their country.

However, although popular will supports the general principle of a European security and defense policy, the public has not been as supportive of the ESDP in practice. Some Europeans worry about a militarization of the EU, while others refuse to support the necessary accompanying increases in defense expenditure. As a result, the rhetoric does not match the reality of the ESDP.

## Has the ESDP Proven Itself to Be a Viable Nation-Building Tool?

How successful has the ESDP been? To answer this question, one must break it down into two parts: Has the ESDP increased international recognition of the European Union as a world player? And, has the European citizenry taken more pride in the EU thanks to this increased international recognition? Measuring the success of the ESDP is problematic for two main reasons. Considering that the first ESDP mission began in 2003, the time frame in which to assess the success of the ESDP as a nation-building tool is quite short. Nevertheless, the EU has mounted, to date, nineteen ESDP missions. Have these missions had any impact on the EU's image abroad or at home? The internal and the external recognition are two sides of the same coin, and they reinforce one another. Much of the justification for the ESDP comes from the need to create the image of the European Union as the United States' equal. By "asserting its identity on the world stage," the ESDP is supposed to define European values and demonstrate the "value added" that European integration provides. Therefore, to determine the success of the ESDP, one can measure whether or how much the EU has increased in *external* recognition; in other words, whether other countries and organizations recognize the EU as a significant international actor. Next, to determine the success of the ESDP, one can measure whether or how much the EU has increased in *internal* recognition; in other words, whether or how much EU citizens now recognize the EU as a significant international actor.

External—i.e., international—recognition can be measured through other international leaders' language and actions. If other countries, especially the United States, have called on the European Union to help in world policing since the first ESDP mission, then the ESDP has succeeded in increasing the EU's clout internationally. In the largest survey of public opinion in the world, the Gallup International Association's Voice of the People poll asks directly whether the EU's global influence should increase. Moreover, both Pew and the German Marshall Fund have tailored their opinion polls specifically to ask Americans about their view of the European Union. Has US public opinion about the EU improved since the beginning of the ESDP?

The German Marshall Fund and *Eurobarometer* have also polled European citizens on a regular basis as to their views of both the European Union and the ESDP, specifically. Do these polls show any increase in internal—i.e., domestic—support for the European Union?

The answer is yes. The EU has increased in prestige as a world actor, albeit modestly. The next section documents these increases. Significantly, EU politicians are disappointed in the results. In 2006, the UK hosted a conference on ways to increase public support for the ESDP, especially with regard to defense spending as a way to shore up the policy.

However, the problem may be the contradictory image of the EU as a *Friedensmacht* or "peace power." Although this image is both favorable and popular among Europeans, it raises expectations. Can the EU be effective as a peace power? Can and will the EU behave as one would expect a peace power to behave? If the answer is no, then the ESDP will be less effective as a nation-building tool.

*External Recognition*

The CFSP/ESDP has already provided results. Kofi Annan addressed the United States and EU as equals when he called on "Europe and America to do something more this year: to think ahead, and to help plant the seeds of long term global collective security."[4] The United Nations has not been shy to ask the European Union to help stabilize crises throughout the world. The EU has assisted the United Nations in its missions throughout the countries of former Yugoslavia and in Africa. Most recently, European Union member states are contributing around 7,000 troops to a new UN peacekeeping force in Lebanon. According to Solana, Kofi Annan was "very grateful" for the EU's efforts. Annan attributed the 11 August 2006 UN resolution that produced the cease-fire to the EU's engagement.[5]

This close relationship with the United Nations continued with the new secretary general, Ban Ki-moon. The first trip he made outside the United States was to the European Union to speak to Solana. Not only did he recognize that "the United Nations and the European Union have been maintaining a special partnership," but he also expressed his "deep admiration and appreciation of what the European Union has been doing in terms of peace and prosperity as well as the protection and enhancement of human rights, climate change and the fight against terrorism."[6]

Aside from the United Nations, other organizations and countries have requested EU assistance, thereby recognizing the latter as a formidable actor. The Democratic Republic of Congo formally requested an EU advisory and assistance mission for security reform. The African Union requested EU assistance in Darfur. For the Indonesian government, the European Union was the international organization of choice to monitor the implementation of various aspects of the peace agreement on the island of Aceh between the government and the rebels. The Indonesian government preferred the European Union to the United Nations because of Indonesia's negative experience with the UN in Timor Leste.[7]

Even the United States is taking greater notice of the European Union. In a 2001 Commission report to the Council of Ministers, the Commission attributed the launching of the New Transatlantic Agenda to recognition by the United States of the growing role of the EU as an international actor, thanks to the CFSP and the ESDP.[8] In areas where it has limited influence or diplomatic relations, the United States has leaned on Europe to represent its views. For example, the EU has been vital to the United States' strategy toward Iran's nuclear program. In late

2005, the United States asked the EU whether it could monitor elections in Haiti. The EU was not able to, but was nevertheless thrilled with the US invitation and the attention.[9] The 30 April 2007 US-EU summit produced an understanding in which the United States acknowledged the EU's role in crisis management (not just "civilian" crisis management), and agreed to put 200 civilian police under an ESDP police mission should the UN mission in Kosovo end.[10]

During the same period, popular support for the EU in the United States either remained strong or increased. Among those polled, at least 60 percent said a stronger EU would be a good thing for the United States; among the elites, the number was 77 percent.[11] The German Marshall Fund's yearly poll, Transatlantic Trends, shows that from 2003 to 2007, in response to the question "How desirable is it that the European Union exert strong leadership in world affairs?" between 73 and 80 percent of US respondents said such leadership would be desirable. This number was highest in 2003, at the beginning of the Iraq War. In general, US residents think more highly of the European Union today than they did in 2002. The German Marshall Fund asked people to rate their feelings toward particular countries or institutions on a scale of 0 to 100, with 50 being neutral. In 2002, Americans gave the European Union a score of 53; this score shot up to a high of 62 in 2004, and in 2007 was recorded as 59.[12]

The ESDP has created a great deal of attention for the European Union on the world stage. There has been no shortage of requests for EU assistance for a variety of missions. The EU has been a great friend to the United Nations, and even the United States has started to lean on the Europeans. US support for the European Union, as shown above, remains strong among the people of the United States. The ESDP has not had a negative impact on the US public's view of the EU. According to the Gallup International Association's Voice of the People 2007 poll, more world citizens across the continents want to see an increase in the power of the European Union than in any other great power. The European Council on Foreign Relations concludes the world "seems to be crying out for greater European leadership."[13]

*Internal Recognition*

Most importantly, has the European public's perception of the European Union or the ESDP improved since the first ESDP mission in 2003? Opinion polls show a slight downward trend on perceptions of the EU as a whole, and steady support for the ESDP. When asked the question in

2007, "How desirable is it that the European Union exert strong leadership in world affairs?" 78 percent of Europeans answered "desirable," which was the same percentage as measured when asking people in the United States.[14] This number is down slightly from the 2005 figure of 79 percent and the 2002 figure of 81 percent.[15] When asked how Europeans rate the European Union on a scale of 0 to 100, the average score was 69, down slightly from 2002.[16] When asked specifically about support for a common security and defense policy, public opinion in the EU has remained extremely high and extremely steady for the period from 1992 to 2004 (see Figure 7.1). *Eurobarometer* reports the 2006 approval rating for the ESDP at 75 percent; there has been no significant change from 2003 to 2006. Interestingly, despite the support "new" Europe had for the United States during the Iraq crisis, the 2006 *Eurobarometer* report shows the highest approval ratings for the ESDP among the ten new members.[17]

The series of successful ESDP missions may have had an impact on some of the more cynical member states. In 2001, fewer than 50 percent of Finns supported the ESDP; in 2006, 62 percent of Finns approved.[18]

**Figure 7.1 Approval Rating for a Common Security and Defense Policy Among European Union Member States, October 1992–April 2004**

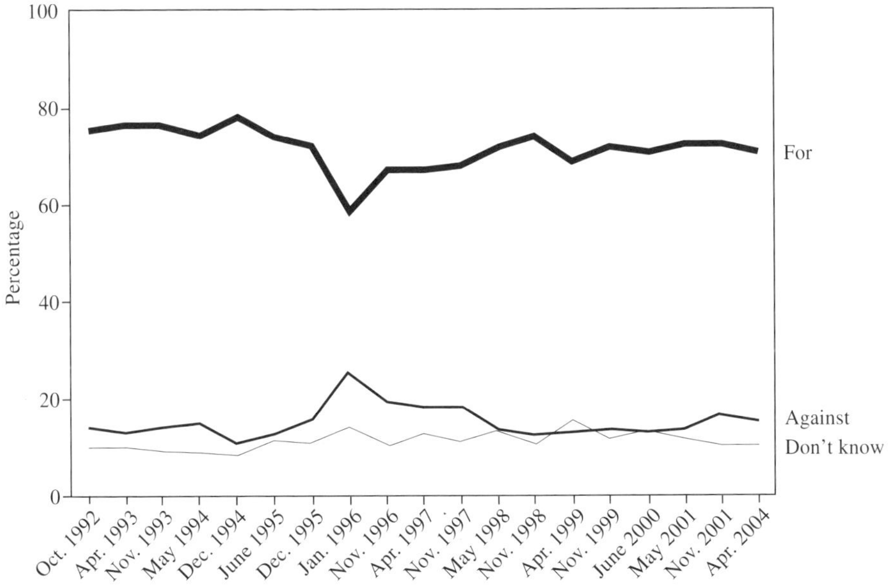

*Source:* Based on survey information from *Eurobarometer* 38–61.

The Finnish defense minister Seppo Kääriäinen believed that promoting "the real achievements of the European Union—peace, stability, and security" and the "added value" factor could bring Europe closer to those citizens "critical" of European integration.[19] During the same time period, public opinion in Denmark on the ESDP increased significantly, to 68 percent, in 2006. (A significant portion of the increase occurred between May 2001 [59 percent][20] and November 2001 [65 percent].[21]) Nevertheless, by April 2004, Danish support had dipped to 61 percent, marking a 7 percent increase in just a two-year period.[22] However, the change in Irish and Swedish public opinion has been negligible (only a 2 percent increase);[23] public support in the UK increased 3 percent during this time period.[24]

## EU Politicians' Concern with Lack of Public Support

EU politicians were very concerned about public attention and opinion regarding the ESDP in 2006. Referring to *Eurobarometer* data, Franz Kernic, from the Institute for Strategy and Security Policy in Vienna, said, "[T]he polls should not only be used to bolster current EU policy but also as an early warning device in policymaking."[25]

According to a report to the WEU assembly, the problem was that people were simply not paying enough attention. The rapporteur concluded, "[T]he EU's role in the security of the region [during the ALTHEA Mission to Bosnia] had not contributed as much as might be *hoped* towards enhancing the way in which the ESDP was perceived by the public at large."[26] Therefore, "tangible results" needed to be made "clearer and more accessible to the public."[27] Just a few weeks later, the UK Parliament hosted a two-day seminar, "Building a Secure Europe in a Better World: Parliamentary Responsibility and Action in Shaping Public Opinion on Security and Defence." As WEU assembly president Jean-Pierre Masseret (France, Socialist group) explained, national parliaments "must address the security concerns of European citizens and at the same time educate public opinion on security and defense issues. Parliaments must explain that Europe's future position in the world was at stake if its common foreign, security and defense policy stagnated." He even suggested that *Eurobarometer* ask a new question in its polls: "How much more are you prepared to pay for your security?"[28] Rob de Wijk, director of the Clingendael Institute in The Hague, argued that parliamentarians needed to "convince public opinion that the stagnation of Europe would inevitably lead to its marginalisation."[29]

## Nation Building as a Civilian Power

Although 82 percent of Europeans want a European foreign policy independent of that of the United States,[30] and 76 percent want the European Union to exert strong leadership in world affairs, 79 percent believe the European Union should concentrate on its economic power and not rely on its military power when dealing with international problems outside Europe.[31] Only 46 percent believe the European Union should strengthen its military power in order to play a larger role in the world. Furthermore, 87 percent of Europeans agree with the statement, "Economic power is more important in world affairs than military power."[32] The Europeans want to be a strong force in the world, but a *civilian* force.

The ESDP has a great deal of potential as a tool to generate support for the European project; however, attempting this from a position of civilian power is a great handicap. In both the past and the present, states have equated successful security policy with military victories. However, the ESDP does not seek to win military victories for Europe, but rather seeks to mitigate human suffering and to promote the EU's recipe for peace; i.e., the EU's *mission civilisatrice*. As the EDA Long-Term Vision Report explained, "The presence of multinational forces, backed by, and indeed symbolizing, the collective political commitment of the Union, may well prevent hostilities from breaking out. . . . The objective is not 'victory' as traditionally understood, but moderation, balance of interests and peaceful resolution of conflicts—in short, stability."[33] The EU has built up its image as that of a "peace power" or a "civilian power with teeth" because that is what people want. To quote José Manuel Barroso, European Commission president: "I've tried to show that Europe's old raison d'être—consolidating peace—must be reinforced by a new sense of purpose. I've tried to show that Europe's new vocation is to be open, global and engaged, delivering twenty-first-century solutions to twenty-first-century concerns."[34]

Creating a glorious new future for its people from the position of a peace power facing no military threats is a difficult segue to make. As a peace power, the EU faces many obstacles. Specifically, acting from such a position raises expectations with regard to mandate, effectiveness, and behavior. As stated above, the EU touts itself as being "open, global and engaged." It seeks to be a world power; therefore, it wants to show that it is engaged on every continent; however, such a policy could lead to failure because of overstretch. It also touts itself as being a more effective power on the world stage because of the variety of humanitarian, developmental, civilian, and military instruments at its disposal.

Such an assertion raises the stakes: failure to effect change in a crisis could puncture public support. Finally, as a peace power, the EU explicitly promises to fight worldwide injustice, putting itself in direct contrast to the United States. Were these promises found to be disingenuous, the EU would not only lose face, but Europeans would disengage themselves from it. Ultimately, placing itself on the pedestal of a peace power raises both the expectations and the stakes. If these expectations are not met, the psychological blow could be devastating.

In addition, continuing globalization will increase the pressure placed on the ESDP. Mass media and the Internet will magnify the need for EU intervention as well as its successes and failures. The world stage is exactly that—a stage. Television cameras, and now even mobile phones, can record any event in any part of the world, from terrorist attacks to executions, public demonstrations, bombings, raids, and natural disasters. The Internet can publish any and all of this by video. While this eye on the world may bring home to Europeans the power and good the EU can do, it may just as easily have a more negative effect on the ESDP by publicizing its failures. As Bastian Giegerich and William Wallace observed, "It is indeed remarkable how little publicity these [EU] deployments have received, except when casualties have focused media attention."[35]

### Mandate

The Laeken Declaration says explicitly that the EU is "to play a stabilizing role worldwide and to point the way ahead for many countries and peoples."[36] Both the Laeken Declaration and the European Security Strategy give the European Union a broad mandate to involve itself in the world, whether it be providing humanitarian assistance, fighting organized crime, or peacekeeping. As President José Manuel Barroso of the European Commission described the situation, "[T]here is a rising demand for a European role in external crises. And the EU is responding. . . . [I]t is playing a central role in conflict prevention and resolution from Darfur to Palestine, from the Congo to Lebanon. . . . [T]his work is raising Europe's credibility as a stabilizing force, and raising expectations for even greater commitment."[37]

Although commendable and popular among the people of Europe, this broad mandate could come back to haunt them, as it has stretched the EU's resources to capacity. The majority of the missions taken on by the ESDP are ongoing. A major issue, especially with regard to the Congo mission, was whether missions should have an "end date" or an "end state." In other words, whether the EU should leave by a certain date or only when the political goal has been achieved.[38] With such a broad mandate, it becomes difficult to "declare victory" and to end the mission. As one PSC diplomat said, "It is more fun to launch a mission than to end one. It is the money situation that ends missions, but more is often miraculously found."[39] If Barroso is correct, and expectations are raised for even greater EU commitment, the EU could be embarrassed if it found that it lacked the resources to commit.

Already, these contradictions have caused embarrassment. As one senior EU diplomat noted, "How can we advocate the strengthening of Monuc [the UN mission in the DRC] and underscore its current inability to cope with the situation and at the same time refrain from sending our own troops?"[40] In 2006, France strongly advocated sending a muscular UN force to assist the Lebanese army in dismantling Hezbollah's armed militias south of the Litani River. Finding itself overstretched and nervous about the commitment, instead of promising a contingent of 3,500 troops, it offered only 200. *The (London) Times* derided this *"marche en arrière,"* saying, "For France to have retreated from a key role to the realm of 'symbolic' gestures 'symbolizes' only one thing: a French loss of nerve."[41] Fortunately, Italy saved the day (and saved face for the European Union) by providing a substantial force and heading the mission, but the force is still short of troops.

News reports and visuals of people suffering create public pressure for the EU to act, yet any attempt to limit the number of missions the EU takes on contradicts the image of the European Union as being a caring and powerful entity. One op-ed piece in *Die Welt* titled "Overtaxed Europeans" concluded,

> Currently, however, the EU cannot even pay for its existing aid projects for Iraq, the Palestinian [National] Authority, Afghanistan or Kosovo. The states in the western Balkans pushing to come into Europe will also feel the shortage despite the pompous announcements of the EU foreign ministers at the weekend that they would keep the door open for further enlargement. Additional commitments as in Congo would definitely be too much for the EU. Thus, the Europeans can only fail in a half-hearted attempt to emulate the United States and to play the role of world police.[42]

## Effectiveness

As the European Security Strategy explains, modern-day security problems cannot be dealt with through purely military means, but require a mixture of instruments. For example,

> Proliferation may be contained through export controls and attacked
> through political, economic and other pressures while the underlying
> political causes are also tackled. Dealing with terrorism may require
> a mixture of intelligence, police, judicial, military and other means.
> In failed states, military instruments may be needed to restore order,
> humanitarian means to tackle the immediate crisis. Regional con-
> flicts need political solutions, but military assets and effective polic-
> ing may be needed in the post-conflict phase. Economic instruments
> serve reconstruction, and civilian crisis management helps restore
> civil government.[43]

The ESS concludes, "The European Union is particularly well equipped
to respond to such multi-faceted situations." Viewing the EU as armed
with these special talents, Benita Ferrero-Waldner, European commissioner for external relations, argued that EU involvement is the key to
getting the Middle East peace process back on track.[44]

As explained in Chapter 6, the ESDP structures require that decisions to intervene in a crisis area be taken by consensus. In this way, the
PSC can be sure to find a mission with universal support, which is necessary if the member states are to support and finance it. Moreover, in
this way the member states can choose missions that fit the limited
instruments available to the EU.

However, the EU may come off as impotent if it either cannot positively influence the area in which it is working or cannot take on an area
that has caught the public's interest. For example, James Lyon, Serbia
project director for the International Crisis Group, an NGO, wrote an
op-ed piece in *The European Voice* titled "EU's Bosnia Police Mission
[EUPM] Is 'Laughing Stock.'" He wrote, "[D]espite the enormous
investment, the EUPM has largely failed to meet its goals. No matter
what criteria are used to assess EUPM performance, the indicators are
depressing." He blamed EU politicians for putting publicity before the
project itself: "Keen to score an early success for its nascent European
Security and Defence Policy, the Union underestimated both the size
and complexity of the task in Bosnia. The EUPM took over poorly prepared, lacking inspiration and expertise on how to devise an effective
strategy for 'Europeanising' the police."[45]

Although the EU has held up the Congo mission "as a shining
example of a successful peacekeeping mission," it also came under criticism for keeping many of its troops safe in neighboring Gabon rather
than placing them in the troubled eastern part of the country. Moreover,
"[T]here is also concern that the EU is pulling out although the situation
is still unstable with tensions between President Kabila and his election

rival, the ex-rebel Jean-Pierre Bemba, running high."[46] In response to this critique, one senior EU official explained that MONUC was strong in the east, so the EU was not needed there. Kinshasa was seen as the key. In the end, limited forces meant limited options; when one only has 2,000 people and not 20,000, where should they go?[47]

Despite such criticisms, the EU missions to date have been generally successful. However, it is only a matter of time until one fails. Considering the lack of resources; that the EU may be pressed to take on missions that do not fit its instruments; that its troops are already overstretched; and that these troops will probably have to answer to national, European, and international (i.e., organizations such as the UN) command structures, the EU could become involved in another Srebrenica. At Srebrenica, pressured to enter the fray, Dutch peacekeepers were unable to protect the civilians in the safe zone. Some academics and military analysts blamed the lack of troops, the poorly constructed military objectives, and the poor command structure. Solana explained that the absence of a strong and unified European Union was partly to blame.[48] This disaster happened in 1995, before the Internet was ubiquitous in European households. Even so, this catastrophe was such an embarrassment that ten years later, after a report came out, the government of the Netherlands resigned.[49] Considering that the EU is seriously considering making peace operations its vocation, it is very likely that it will be involved in such a scenario.

As the EU engages itself in more difficult and complex situations, the chances are slim that it will be able to get in and out quickly. More likely, it will need to keep its peacekeeping troops in these areas, possibly for years on end. The public could become bored or frustrated with the lack of progress and become disenchanted.

Manipulation of European public support to pressure EU governments to remove troops in Afghanistan is already at work. In an interview with the German magazine *Der Spiegel*, Wolfgang Schneiderhan, Germany's highest-ranking officer and inspector general of the German armed forces, discussed the risks of Germany's mission in Afghanistan. A majority of Germans want to withdraw from the mission because of German casualties and possible German complicity in civilian deaths there. Schneiderhan blames the terrorists who "are misusing public opinion for their purposes and are thereby gaining the upper hand." At the same time, Germany has been criticized for keeping its soldiers safe in the less volatile north while other allies, such as Canada and the United States, risk their lives in the more dangerous south. Schneiderhan answers, "if you're saying that the Germans should finally go south to improve their image, then we could end up paying a high price. The level of danger in the north is already high enough for me to fear the worst every time the telephone rings at an unusual hour. We shouldn't be trying to do everything at once." While the German people believe the government is doing too much in Afghanistan, other allies claim it is not doing enough. In any case, according to Schneiderhan, the terrorists are closely following public opinion as a way to sabotage support for the mission.[50]

Part of the problem is that Europe is perceived as part of the West in the rest of the world, and not as a distinct and positive force. Much of the EU's basis for its potential on the world stage is the perception that the EU is "an alternative to American unilateralism thanks to its stress on multilateralism, the rule of law, and its distaste of power politics." In other words, the EU is more effective because it is recognized as a "force for good." While this recognition is strong in Europe, "in other parts of the world, the EU and US are perceived as twins rather than alternatives." Considering their colonial past and their ties with the United States, Europeans may not always be a welcome presence. Even in Bosnia, opinion has turned against the EU as their presence is increasingly seen as "quasi-colonial."[51] Without a strong welcome on the ground, the European people may withdraw their support for EU interventions, and, consequently, for the ESDP.

## Behavior

Taking on the role of a peace power raises expectations. As a peace power, the ESDP will come under greater scrutiny, because the EU holds itself to a high standard. When nations or organizations cannot meet the standards they exact upon themselves, their image becomes tarnished. Already, the EU's image is tarnished with European complicity in CIA secret prisons, with weak human rights standards, and even accusations of the Commission's bullying developing countries. Moreover, European troops overseas do not always behave according to EU standards. Were such behavior to be associated with an EU mission, the EU brand would lose its appeal.

The idea of peace power is used in direct contrast to that of the United States superpower. Whereas the United States is militaristic, Europe is not. However, any evidence to the contrary could make EU claims seem disingenuous. For example, EU and national leaders, including Solana himself, have been accused of lying to the public with regard to CIA rendition flights (in which the United States flew terrorism suspects to Europe to prison camps where most faced torture). The

European Parliament has accused Austria, Italy, Portugal, Poland, and the United Kingdom of complicity in this matter. Javier Solana has been accused of withholding vital information. To make matters worse, it was not the Europeans who uncovered this travesty, but the *Washington Post* and Human Rights Watch.[52]

Furthermore, Human Rights Watch strongly and publicly criticized the European Union for its human rights record, not just with regard to the CIA flights, but also with regard to its policies toward China, Russia, and many countries in Africa. In its report in 2006, it claimed the EU "continued to punch well below its weight" on human rights. Moreover, "The EU position on Russia in 2005 made the US defense of human rights seem vigorous," the report added, with the UK, France, and Germany engaged in an "unseemly competition" to court Russian president Vladimir Putin.[53] Considering how much and how often the European Union distinguishes itself from the United States with regard to human rights, such complicity could be psychologically devastating to the public because their expectations have been raised so high.

Even the European Commission has come under criticism, accused of using EU aid to bully developing countries. The World Social Forum addressed this issue at its meeting in January 2007 in Nairobi. In a comment published by *euobserver.com*, Florent Sebban reported, "[I]f you delve beneath the spin, the reality is that the commission can be the kind of friend who twists the arms and pulls the ears of developing countries until they accept exactly what the Brussels bureaucracy wants."[54] Specifically, Eurostep, a network of European NGOs, presented a series of case studies demonstrating that the Commission has promoted the narrow interests of Western firms over the interest of Africa's poorest citizens.

The EU has very high standards for its military men and women overseas. As one EU politician put it, EU troops are the EU's calling card. Nevertheless, soldiers have been known to misbehave—even European soldiers. In 2006, German soldiers overseas were criticized for having photographs taken of themselves with their penises inside the skulls of the dead.[55] The French have been criticized for contributing to genocide in Rwanda.[56] Even the British, who pride themselves on cultural sensitivity, had video footage and photos published on the Internet showing them abusing Iraqi prisoners.[57] Since the EU is touting itself as a peace power, these crimes against humanity compromise its carefully cultivated image. There is no reason to think that European soldiers are more saintly than others.

Even an EU soldier properly behaving under the rules of engagement could compromise the image of the European Union as a peace power. A major issue for the European Union is force protection; politicians want as few casualties as possible. Therefore, the military tries to devise strong enough rules of engagement so that troops can protect themselves if the need arises. The EU force working in the DRC had robust rules of engagement, allowing "members of the force to defend themselves, even against drunk and drugged children soldiers."[58] However, the image of the EU peacekeepers firing on children could damage the EU's reputation forever.

### Defending Against the Most Serious Threat: Failure

In his 1966 book *The Troubled Partnership*, Henry Kissinger tried to explain to the people of the United States the importance of the European sense of identity:

> The margin of survival of the European countries has been more precarious than that of the United States. Each country—with the possible exception of Great Britain—has known national catastrophe as America has not. European reasoning is thus likely to be more complicated and less contingent than ours. Our European Allies think of themselves not simply as components of security schemes but as expressions of a historical experience. Policies that neglect their sense of identity may destroy the psychological basis of any common effort.[59]

Identity is key to understanding the ESDP. It is the psychological basis of the common effort.

Failure of the European project is the most serious threat to Europe today. Although this volume outlines serious obstacles to the EU's use of the ESDP to shore up its identity as a peace power, all states or organizations face the same issues of mandate, effectiveness, and behavior when they choose to get involved in events overseas. Vietnam tarnished the United States' image, yet the image of a strong democratic power still survives. Although a failed mission could damage the EU's credibility, abandoning the ESDP would be the greatest failure of all.

Using the ESDP to solidify European identity is risky, but the EU has few arrows left in its quiver. The EU has integrated in almost all other areas. Moreover, the Europeans are capable and determined; they have managed to create the ESDP on a shoestring budget and to capture the imagination of the world.

The United States can improve both the European integration process and transatlantic relations by not forcing a choice of loyalty; the

EU or NATO. Some European allies feel pressed by this question; others are annoyed and take it to mean that the United States is no longer supportive of the European project. As evidenced by the 2007 EU-US summit, Washington has already softened its line and agreed to improve transatlantic cooperation in crisis management. By seeing the EU as a partner in crisis management, the United States would, in effect, sanction the ESDP and remove any hesitation felt by the Atlanticists to proceed. In doing so, the United States could significantly increase the EU's chances of success.

The EU must steel itself for the long road ahead. The ESDP faces many obstacles. However, the very act of collectively overcoming these obstacles will strengthen European identity and resolve, and therefore mean success for the ESDP.

## Notes

1. European Defense Agency, "An Initial Long-Term Vision for European Defence Capability and Capacity Needs," 3 October 2006.

2. Javier Solana, summary of his remarks to the press on the results of the referenda in France and Brussels, 30 May 2005, S201/05, at http://ue.eu.int /ueDocs/cms_Data/-docs/pressdata/EN/declarations/84999.pdf.

3. Theo Sommer, untitled chapter in *EU Security and Defence Policy,* ed. Gnesotto, 253.

4. Kofi Annan, "A More Secure World: The Future Role of the United Nations," speech at a Munich conference on security, 13 February 2005, at http://www.security-conference.de/konferenzen/rede.php?menu_2005 =&menu_konferenzen=&sprache=en&id=156&.

5. As reported in Mark Beunderman, "Solana Rejects Chirac Criticism of the EU Lebanon Role," *euobserver.com,* 1 September 2006.

6. Ban Ki-moon, remarks at a joint press briefing with Javier Solana, doc. S022/07, Brussels, Belgium, 24 January 2007.

7. Representative from the Permanent Mission of the Netherlands to the EU, interview by author, Brussels, Belgium, 8 November 2005.

8. European Commission, "Reinforcing the Transatlantic Relationship: Focusing on Strategy and Delivering Results," communication from the Commission to the Council of the European Union and the European Parliament, COM(2001)154 final, Brussels, Belgium, 20 March 2001, 2, 5.

9. General Secretariat officials II and III of the Council of the European Union, interview by author, Brussels, Belgium, 8 December 2005.

10. US State Department official III, interview by author, Brussels, Belgium, 30 April 2007.

11. Pew Research Center for the People and the Press, "Allies, Trade and International Institutions," part 4 of article "Opinion Leaders Turn Cautious, Public Looks Homeward: America's Place in the World," 17 November 2005, at http://people-press.org/reports/-desplay.php3?pageID=1020.

12. The German Marshall Fund, "Transatlantic Trends: Topline Report 2007," 5–6, 8.

13. Ivan Krastev and Mark Leonard, "New World Order: The Balance of Soft Power and the Rise of Herbivorous Powers," European Council on Foreign Relations, 24 October 2007, 3.

14. The German Marshall Fund surveyed nine European countries: the United Kingdom, France, Germany, the Netherlands, Italy, Poland, Portugal, Slovakia, and Spain. The German Marshall Fund, Transatlantic Trends 2007, at http://www.transatlantictrends.org/trends/doc/TT07Topline_FINAL.pdf.

15. The figure 81 percent is derived from a 2002 poll of seven European countries surveyed: the United Kingdom, France, Germany, the Netherlands, Italy, Poland, and Portugal. I use this figure because there is no 2002 figure for the Nine (that is, including Slovakia and Spain). The 2007 figure for the seven European countries' desirability for a strong EU in world affairs is 79 percent. The German Marshall Fund, "Transatlantic Trends: Topline Report 2006," 5.

16. In 2002, the score among the seven was 70; in 2003, it was 71; in 2004, 70; in 2005, 66. Among the nine countries surveyed, the earliest reported score was in 2004 (70), followed by 2005 (67). For both the groups of seven and nine, the 2007 score was 68 and 69 respectively. The German Marshall Fund, "Transatlantic Trends: Topline Report 2007," 8.

17. *Eurobarometer* 66 (2006): 177.

18. *Eurobarometer* 56.2 (November 2001) and *Eurobarometer* 66 (2006), at http://ec.europa.eu/public_opinion/cf/index_en.cfm. *Eurobarometer* did not conduct a poll on this question between 2001 and 2004.

19. As quoted in "Finland Wants to Bring Europe Closer to Its Citizens," WEU Assembly press release, Paris, France, 19 June 2006.

20. *Eurobarometer* 55.1 (May 2001), at http://ec.europa.eu/public_opinion /cf/index_en.cfm.

21. *Eurobarometer* 56.2 (November 2001), at http://ec.europa.eu/public _opinion/cf/index_en.cfm.

22. *Eurobarometer* 61 (April 2004), at http://ec.europa.eu/public_opinion /cf/index_en.cfm.

23. *Eurobarometer* 56.2 (November 2001) and *Eurobarometer* 66 (2006), at http://ec.europa.eu/public_opinion/cf/index_en.cfm. *Eurobarometer* did not poll on this question between 2001 and 2004.

24. Ibid. *Eurobarometer* did not poll on this question between 2001 and 2004.

25. "Parliamentarians Should Lead Public Opinion," Speech given by Franz Kernic at the WEU Assembly seminar on the role of parliaments in shaping public opinion on European security and defense, WEU Assembly press release, 28 April 2006.

26. Rapporteur, "Public Opinion and the Althea Mission," speech at the WEU Assembly, Paris, France, 4 April 2006. The rapporteur noted the lack of public awareness of ESDP while on his visit to Sarajevo. Emphasis added.

27. "Althea: A Symbol of the ESDP Success," WEU Assembly press release, Paris, France, 20 June 2006.

28. "Parliamentarians Should Lead Public Opinion."

29. Ibid.

30. Ibid.

31. The German Marshall Fund, "Transatlantic Trends: Topline Report 2006," 4, 10.

32. Ibid., 59.

33. European Defense Agency, "An Initial Long-Term Vision," 13.

34. José Manuel Barroso, "Seeing Through the Hallucinations: Britain and Europe in the 21st Century," Hugo Young lecture, SPEECH/06/602, London, UK, 16 October 2006, 9. Barroso is president of the European Commission.

35. Giegerich and Wallace, "Not Such a Soft Power," 164.

36. Laeken Declaration on the Future of the European Union, Laeken European Council, 15 December 2001.

37. Barroso, "Seeing Through the Hallucinations."

38. Senior EU official I, interview by author, Brussels, Belgium, 2 May 2007. This official preferred not to have his department named.

39. Representative from the Permanent Representation of the Netherlands to the EU, interview by author, Brussels, Belgium, 8 November 2005.

40. As quoted in "Congo: UN Reinforcement Debate Reveals EU's Contradictions," *SouthScan,* 17 September 2004, 1.

41. "Marche en arrière: Nervous France Has Second Thoughts on Lebanon," *Times* (London), 18 August 2006.

42. Hannelore Crolly, "Overtaxed Europeans," *Die Welt* (Berlin), 13 March 2006, English translation by BBC Worldwide Monitoring.

43. European Security Strategy, "A Secure Europe in a Better World," Brussels, Belgium, 12 December 2003, 7.

44. Benita Ferrero-Waldner, "Statement on the Situation in the Middle East," statement to the European Parliament plenary, Strasbourg, France, 6 September 2006, 1.

45. James Lyon, "EU's Bosnia Police Mission Is 'Laughing Stock,'" *European Voice*, 15 September 2005, 16.

46. Honor Mahony, "General Eyes 'European Army' After Congo Mission," *euobserver.com,* 1 December 2006.

47. Senior EU official I, interview by author.

48. As quoted in Elitsa Vucheva, "International Community Failed in Srebrenica, Solana Says," *euobserver.com,* 11 July 2005.

49. "Dutch Court Hears Srebrenica Case," *BBC News*, 12 May 2005.

50. "Our Sacrifices Do Not Leave Me Cold," *Spiegel Online,* 23 July 2007.

51. Krastev and Leonard, "New World Order," 3.

52. Renata Goldirova, "MEP's Roast EU States and Solana for 'Lies' on CIA," *euobserver.com,* 23 January 2007.

53. Mark Beunderman, "Leading NGO Mauls EU on Human Rights Record," *euobserver.com,* 19 January 2006.

54. Florent Sebban, "Comment: EU Aid Masks a Big Bully Tactics in Developing World," *euobserver.com,* 19 January 2007.

55. "German Troops in Still Photos Row," *BBC News,* 25 October 2006.

56. "France Declassify Secret Rwanda Reports for Probe," Reuters, 2 November 2006.

57. "Photos Led to Abuse Convictions," *BBC News,* 23 February 2005.

58. Nicholas Fiorenza, "EU Force Seeks New Mission After Congo," *Defense News,* 8 September 2003, 42.

59. Kissinger, *The Troubled Partnership,* 24.

# Public Opinion on the Common Defense and Security Policy

---

*Proposal:* The European Union member states should have one common defense and security policy, yes or no? (percentage of "yes" answers)

| Country | 1990 | 1995 | 2000 | 2005 |
|---|---|---|---|---|
| Austria | n.a. | 53.9 | 65.0 | 61.0 |
| Belgium | 58.6 | 69.9 | 84.0 | 89.0 |
| Cyprus | n.a. | n.a. | n.a. | 94.0 |
| Czech Republic | n.a. | n.a. | n.a. | 86.0 |
| Denmark | 43.2 | 41.6 | 56.0 | 67.0 |
| Estonia | n.a. | n.a. | n.a. | 87.0 |
| Finland | n.a. | 10.3 | 47.0 | 63.0 |
| France | 44.5 | 60.3 | 79.0 | 81.0 |
| Germany | 52.7 | 76.0 | 79.0 | 85.0 |
| Greece | 35.3 | 33.9 | 83.0 | 80.0 |
| Hungary | n.a. | n.a. | n.a. | 83.0 |
| Ireland | 25.2 | 35.1 | 57.0 | 58.0 |
| Italy | 62.6 | 69.4 | 82.0 | 78.0 |
| Latvia | n.a. | n.a. | n.a. | 85.0 |
| Lithuania | n.a. | n.a. | n.a. | 76.0 |
| Luxembourg | 76.4 | 81.6 | 80.0 | 87.0 |
| Malta | n.a. | n.a. | n.a. | 61.0 |
| Netherlands | 70.0 | 79.9 | 78.0 | 81.0 |
| Poland | n.a. | n.a. | n.a. | 86.0 |
| Portugal | 31.5 | 66.5 | 71.0 | 71.0 |
| Slovakia | n.a. | n.a. | n.a. | 85.0 |
| Slovenia | n.a. | n.a. | n.a. | 90.0 |
| Sweden | n.a. | 18.9 | 57.0 | 58.0 |
| Spain | 43.3 | 56.6 | 76.0 | 70.0 |
| United Kingdom | 43.9 | 47.7 | 51.0 | 59.0 |

*Sources:* 1990: *Eurobarometer* 33; 1995: *Eurobarometer* 43.1; 2000: *Eurobarometer* 54; 2005: *Eurobarometer* 63.

*Note:* n.a. indicates those countries that were not part of the EU at the time.

# Acronyms

| | |
|---|---|
| ALAT | Asia and Latin America |
| ALTHEA | EU Military Operation in Bosnia and Herzegovina |
| ASPC | Euro-Atlantic Partnership Council |
| BiH | Bosnia and Herzegovina |
| CAP | Common Agricultural Policy |
| CDI | Center for Defense Information |
| C$^4$ISR | command, control, communications, computers, intelligence, surveillance, and reconnaissance |
| CFSP | Common Foreign and Security Policy |
| CIS | Community of Independent States |
| CIVCOM | Committee for Civilian Aspects of Crisis Management |
| COREPER | Permanent Representatives Committee |
| CSCE | Conference on Security and Cooperation in Europe |
| CSDP | Common Security and Defense Policy |
| DRC | Democratic Republic of Congo |
| EAPC | Euro-Atlantic Partnership Council |
| EC | European Community |
| ECAP | European capabilities action plan |
| ECHO | European Community Humanitarian Office |
| ECOWAS | Economic Community of West African States |
| ECSC | European Coal and Steel Community |
| EDA | European Defense Agency |
| EDC | European Defense Community |
| EDF | European Development Fund |
| EEC | European Economic Community |
| EMU | European Monetary Union |
| EPC | European Political Cooperation |

| | |
|---|---|
| ERRF | European Rapid Reaction Force |
| ESDI | European Security and Defense Identity |
| ESDP | European Security and Defense Policy |
| ESN | European Service Network |
| ESS | European Security Strategy |
| EUBAM | European Union Border Assistance Mission |
| EUCOM | US European Command |
| EUMC | European Union Military Committee |
| EUMS | European Union Military Staff |
| EUPAT | European Union Police Advisory Team |
| EUPM | European Union Police Mission |
| EUSR | European Union Special Representative |
| FRG | Federal Republic of Germany |
| GAERC | General Affairs and External Relations Council |
| GATT | General Agreement on Tariffs and Trade |
| IEPG | Independent European Program Group |
| ISS | Institute for Security Studies (European Union) |
| MEDA | Euro-Mediterranean Partnership |
| NAC | North Atlantic Council |
| NATO | North Atlantic Treaty Organization |
| NRF | NATO Response Force |
| NSS | National Security Strategy (US) |
| OSCE | Organization for Security and Cooperation in Europe |
| PfP | Partnership for Peace |
| PPEWU/PPU | Policy Planning and Early Warning Unit/ Policy Planning Unit |
| PSC | Political and Security Committee |
| QMV | qualified majority voting |
| RELEX | Directorate General for External Relations |
| SEA | Single European Act |
| SG/HR | Secretary General/High Representative (CFSP) |
| SHAPE | Supreme Headquarters Allied Powers Europe (NATO) |
| SIPRI | Stockholm International Peace Research Institute |
| SITCEN | European Union Joint Situation Centre |
| UN | United Nations |
| UNSC | United Nations Security Council |
| WEU | Western European Union |
| WMD | weapons of mass destruction |

# Bibliography

Aalberts, Tanja E. "The Future of Sovereignty in Multilevel Governance Europe: A Constructivist Reading." *Journal of Common Market Studies* 42, no. 1 (2004): 23–46.

Abellan, Miquel Medina. "Database of ESDP Missions." *CFSP Forum* 4, no. 6 (2007): 17–22.

Adler, Emanuel. "Imagined (Security) Communities: Cognitive Regions in International Relations." *Millennium: Journal of International Studies* 26, no. 2 (1997): 249–277.

Aggestam, Lisbeth. "Role Conceptions and the Politics of Identity and Foreign Policy." ARENA working papers, University of Oslo, 1999.

Agüera, Martin. "Reform of the Bundeswehr: Defense Policy Choices for the Next German Administration." *Comparative Strategy* 21, no. 3 (2002): 179–202.

Alexander, M., and T. Garden. "The Arithmetic of Defense Policy." *International Affairs* 77 (2001): 509–529.

Anderson, Benedict. *Imagined Communities: Reflections on the Origin and Spread of Nationalism*. Revised edition. London: Verso, 2003.

Anderson, Stephanie B. "The Amsterdam CFSP Components: A Lowest Common Denominator Agreement?" *Current Politics and Economics of Europe* 10, no. 1 (2000): 105–127.

———. "The Changing Nature of Diplomacy: The European Union, the CFSP and Korea." *European Foreign Affairs Review* 6, no. 4 (2001): 465–482.

———. "EU, NATO, and CSCE Responses to the Yugoslav Crisis: Testing Europe's New Security Architecture." *European Security* 4, no. 2 (1995): 328–353.

Anderson, Stephanie B., and Thomas R. Seitz. "European Security Policy Demystified: Nation-building and Identity in the EU." *Armed Forces and Society* 33 (2006): 24–42.

Andréani, Gilles, Christoph Bertram, and Charles Grant. "Europe's Military Revolution." *Defense Insides,* 14 February 2001, at http://www.cer.org.uk /pdf/p22xmilitary_revolution.pdf.

Art, Robert. "Correspondence: Striking a Balance." *International Security* 30, no. 3 (2005): 177–185.

199

———. "To What Ends Military Power?" *International Security* 4, no. 4 (Spring 1980): 4–35.

Ashley, Richard K. "The Poverty of Neorealism." *International Organization* 38, no. 2 (1984): 225–286.

Asmus, Ronald D. *Future US Defense Policy Toward Europe: The New Politics and Grand Strategy of Europe-American Relations.* Santa Monica, CA: RAND Corporation, 1993.

Asmus, Ronald D., Richard L. Kugler, and F. Stephen Larrabee. "Building a New NATO." *Foreign Affairs* 72, no. 4 (1993): 28–40.

Axelrod, Robert, and Robert O. Keohane. "Achieving Cooperation Under Anarchy: Strategies and Institutions." *World Politics* 38, no. 1 (1985): 226–254.

Ayache, Georges, and Pascal Lorot. *La conquête de l'est: Les atouts de la France dans le nouvel ordre mondial.* Paris: Calmann-Lévy, 1991.

Aysha, Emad El-Din. "September 11 and the Middle East Failure of US 'Soft Power': Globalisation Contra Americanisation in the 'New' US Century." *International Relations* 19, no. 2 (2005): 193–210.

Bailey, D., and L. de Propis. "A Bridge to Phare? EU Pre-Accession Aid and Capacity-Building in the Candidate Countries." *Journal of Common Market Studies* 42, no. 1 (2004): 77–98.

Banchoff, Thomas F., and Mitchell P. Smith. *Legitimacy and the European Union: The Contested Polity.* London: Routledge, 1999.

Bátora, Jozef. "Does the European Union Transform the Institution of Diplomacy?" *Journal of European Public Policy* 12, no. 1 (2005): 44–66.

Becher, Klaus. "Has-been, Wannabe, or Leader: Europe's Role in the World After the 2003 European Security Strategy." *European Security* 13, no. 4 (2004).

Berenskoetter, Felix. "Mapping the Mind Gap: A Comparison of US and European Security Strategies." *Security Dialogue* 36, no. 1 (2005): 71–92.

Bicchi, Federica. *European Foreign Policy Making Towards the Mediterranean.* New York: Palgrave, 2007.

———. "'Our Size Fits All': Normative Power Europe and the Mediterranean." *Journal of European Public Policy* 13, no. 2 (2006): 286–303.

———. "Want Funding? Don't Mention Islam: EU Democracy Promotion in the Mediterranean." *CFSP Forum* 4, no. 2 (2006): 10–12.

Bilgin, Pinar. "A Return to 'Civilisational Geopolitics' in the Mediterranean? Changing Geopolitical Images of the European Union and Turkey in the Post–Cold War Era." *Geopolitics* 9, no. 2 (2004): 269–291.

Billig, Michael. *Banal Nationalism.* Thousand Oaks, CA: Sage Publications, 1995.

Binnendijk, Hans, and Richard Kugler. "Transforming European Forces." *Survival* 44, no. 3 (2002): 117–132.

Bloom, William. *Personal Identity, National Identity, and International Relations.* New York: Cambridge University Press, 1990.

Boulding, Kenneth E. "The Nature and Causes of National and Military Self-Images in Relation to War and Peace." In *The Political Geography of Conflict and Peace*, edited by Nurit Kliot and Stanley Waterman, pp. 142–152. London: Belhaven Press, 1991.

Bracken, Paul, and Stuart E. Johnson. "Beyond NATO: Complementary Militaries." *Orbis* 37, no. 2 (Spring 1993): 205–222.

Bretherton, Charlotte, and John Vogler. *The European Union as a Global Actor.* New York: Routledge, 1999.

Brewer, Marilynn B. "Multiple Identities and Identity Transition: Implications for Hong Kong." *International Journal of Intercultural Relations* 23, no. 2 (1999): 187–197.

Brooks, Stephen G., and William Wohlforth. "Hard Times for Soft Balancing." *International Security* 30, no. 1 (2005): 72–108.

Buchan, Alastair. *Europe's Futures, Europe's Choices.* London: Chatto and Windus, 1969.

Buchan, David. "The Constraints of the European Community." *The Political Quarterly* 62, no. 2 (1991): 181–192.

Bull, Hedley. *The Anarchical Society: A Study of Order in World Politics.* London: Macmillan Education, 1977.

———. "Civilian Power Europe: A Contradiction in Terms?" *Journal of Common Market Studies* 21, no. 2 (1982): 149–164.

Burrows, Bernard, Geoffrey Denton, and Geoffrey Edwards, eds. *Federal Solutions to European Issues.* New York: St. Martin's Press, 1978.

Burrows, Bernard, and Geoffrey Edwards. *The Defence of Western Europe.* London: Butterworth Scientific, 1982.

Buzan, Barry, et al. *The European Security Order Recast.* London: Pinter Publishers, 1990.

Cahen, Alfred. *The Western European Union and NATO.* London: Brassey's UK, 1989.

———. "Western European Union: Birth, Development and Re-activation." *Army Quarterly and Defense Journal* 117 (October 1987): 391–399.

Calhoun, Craig, ed. *Social Theory and the Politics of Identity.* Cambridge, MA: Blackwell, 1994.

Calleo, David P. *Beyond American Hegemony: The Future of the Western Alliance.* New York: Basic Books, 1987.

Campbell, David. *Writing Security: United States Foreign Policy and the Politics of Identity.* Minneapolis: University of Minnesota Press, 1998.

Carey, Sean, and Jonathan Burton. "Research Note: The Influence of the Press in Shaping Public Opinion Towards the European Union in Britain." *Political Studies* 52, no. 3 (2004): 623–640.

Carlsnaes, Walter, Helena Sjursen, and Brian White. *Contemporary European Foreign Policy.* London: Sage Publications, 2004.

Carlsnaes, Walter, and Steve Smith, eds. *European Foreign Policy: The EC and Changing Perspectives in Europe.* London: Sage Publications, 1994.

Cederman, Lars-Erik, ed. *Constructing Europe's Identity: The External Dimension.* Boulder, CO: Lynne Rienner, 2001.

Cerny, Philip G. "European Defence and the New Détente: The Collapse of the Cold War System." *West European Politics* 13, no. 1 (1990): 139–151.

Chalmers, Malcolm. "Beyond the Alliance System." *World Policy Journal* 7, no. 2 (1990): 216–250.

Checkel, Jeffrey T. "Norms, Institutions, and National Identity in Contemporary Europe." *International Studies Quarterly* 43, no. 1 (1999): 83–114.

———. "Social Constructivisms in Global and European Politics: A Review Essay." *Review of International Studies* 30, no. 2 (2004): 229–244.

———. "Why Comply? Social Learning and European Identity Change." *International Organization* 55, no. 3 (2001): 553–588.

Chévènement, Jean-Pierre. "La France et la sécurité de l'Europe." *Politique Étrangère* 56, no. 3 (1991).

Christiansen, Thomas, Knud Erik Jørgensen, and Antje Wiener, eds. *The Social Construction of Europe.* London: Sage, 2001.

Cimbalo, Jeffrey L. "Saving NATO from Europe." *Foreign Affairs* 83 (2004): 111–120.

Claude, Inis L. *Power and International Relations.* New York: Random House, 1962.

Cogan, Charles G. *The Third Option: The Emancipation of European Defense, 1989– 2000.* Westport, CT: Praeger Publishers, 2001.

Coker, Christopher. *The Future of the Atlantic Alliance.* London: Macmillan Press, 1984.

Cooper, Robert. *The Postmodern State and the World Order.* London: Demos and the Foreign Policy Centre, 2000.

Corbett, Richard. "The Intergovernmental Conference on Political Union." *Journal of Common Market Studies* 30, no. 3 (September 1992): 271–298.

Cornish, Paul, and Geoffrey Edwards. "Beyond the EU/NATO Dichotomy: The Beginnings of a European Strategic Culture." *International Affairs* 77, no. 3 (2001): 587–603.

Cox, Michael. "Commentary: Martians and Venusians in the New World Order." *International Affairs* 79, no. 3 (2003): 523–532.

———. "From the Truman Doctrine to the Second Superpower Détente: The Rise and Fall of the Cold War." *Journal of Peace Research* 27, no. 1 (February 1990): 25–41.

Danspeckgruber, Wolfgang F. *Emerging Dimensions of European Security Policy.* Boulder, CO: Westview Press, 1991.

Debouzy, Olivier. "Anglo-French Nuclear Cooperation: Perspectives and Problems." *Whitehall Paper Series.* London: Royal United Institute for Defence Studies, 1991.

DeCillia, Rudolf, Martin Reisigl, and Rugh Wodak. "The Discursive Construction of National Identities." *Discourse and Society* 10, no. 2 (1999): 149–173.

Deighton, Anne. "The European Security and Defence Policy." *Journal of Common Market Studies* 40, no. 4 (2002): 719–741.

Delanty, Gerard. *Inventing Europe: Idea, Identity, Reality.* New York: St. Martin's Press, 1995.

Delcourt, Barbara. "The Normative Underpinnings of the Use of Force: Doctrinal Foundations and Ambiguities and a CFSP/CESDP Discourse." ARENA working papers, University of Oslo, 2005.

Delors, Jacques. "European Integration and Security." *Survival* 33, no. 2 (1991): 99–109.

———. "European Unification and European Security." In *European Security After the Cold War* (Part 1). Adelphi Paper No. 284, 3–14. London: International Institute for Strategic Studies, 1994.

Dembinski, Matthias. "Europe and the UNIFIL II Mission: Stumbling into the Conflict Zone of the Middle East." *CFSP Forum* 5, no. 1 (2007): 1–4.

Dembinski, Matthias, and Lothar Brock. "The EU: A Reliable Partner for Peace of the UN?" *CFSP Forum* 2, no. 1 (2004): 14–16.

de Schouteete, Philippe. *La coopération politique européenne*. Brussels: Labor, 1980.

Deutsch, Karl W., et al. *Political Community and the North Atlantic Area*. Princeton, NJ: Princeton University Press, 1957.

Deutsch, Karl W., and William J. Foltz. *Nation-building*. New York: Atherton, 1966.

DeVreese, Claes, and Hajo G. Boomgaarden. "Media Effects on Public Opinion About the Enlargement of the European Union." *Journal of Common Market Studies* 44, no. 2 (2006): 419–436.

Diez, Thomas. "Constructing the Self and Changing Others: Reconsidering 'Normative Power Europe,'" *Millennium* 33, no. 3 (2005): 613–636.

———. "Speaking 'Europe': The Politics of Integration Discourse." *Journal of European Public Policy* 6, no. 4 (1999): 598–613.

DiMaggio, Paul J., and Walter W. Powell. "The Iron Cage Revisited: Institutional Isomorphism and Collective Rationality in Organizational Fields." In *The New Institutionalism in Organizational Analysis,* edited by Walter W. Powell and Paul J. DiMaggio. Chicago: University of Chicago Press, 1991.

Duchêne, François. "Europe and Changing Superpower Relations." *The Round Table* 61 (October 1971): 577–584.

———. "Europe's Role in World Peace." In *Europe Tomorrow*, edited by Richard Mayne, pp. 32–47. London: Fontana, 1972.

Duff, Andrew, et al. *Maastricht and Beyond: Building the European Union*. London: Routledge, 1994.

Duffield, John S. "International Regimes and Alliance Behavior: Explaining NATO Conventional Force Levels." *International Organization* 46, no. 4 (1992): 819–855.

Duke, Simon. "The European Security Strategy in a Comparative Framework: Does It Make for Secure Alliances in a Better World?" *European Foreign Affairs Review* 9, no. 4 (2004): 459–481.

———. "The Rhetoric-Resources Gap in EU Crisis Management." *EIPASCOPE* 3 (2002): 1–7.

Dunay, Pál. "Euphoria and Realism in Post–Cold War European Security." *Journal of Peace Research* 30, no. 3 (1993): 347–355.

Edwards, Geoffrey R., and Elfriede Regelsberger, eds. *Europe's Global Links*. London: Pinter Publishers, 1990.

Ehrhart, Hans-Georg. "What Model for CFSP?" *Chaillot Papers* 55. EU Institute for Security Studies. October 2002.

Eichenberg, Richard C. "Having It Both Ways: European Defense Integration and the Commitment to NATO." *Public Opinion Quarterly* 67, no. 4 (2003): 627–659.

———. *Public Opinion and National Security in Western Europe*. Ithaca, NY: Cornell University Press, 1989.

Eichenberg, Richard C., and Russell J. Dalton. "Europeans and the European Community: The Dynamics of Public Support for European Integration." *International Organization* 47, no. 4 (1993): 507–534.

Eilstrup-Sangiovanni, Mette. "Why a Common Security and Defense Policy Is Bad for Europe." *Survival* 45, no. 4 (2003–2004): 193–206.

Eriksen, Erik Oddvar. "The EU—A Cosmopolitan Polity?" *Journal of European Public Policy* 13, no. 2 (2006): 252–269.

Etzioni, Amitai. *Political Unification.* New York: Holt, Rinehart and Winston, 1965.

Etzold, Thomas H., and John Lewis Gaddis, eds. *Containment: Documents on American Policy and Strategy, 1945–1950.* New York: Columbia University Press, 1978.

European Council. "A Secure Europe in a Better World—European Security Strategy." Brussels: European Institute for Security Studies, 2003.

Fedorov, Yuri, François Heisbourg, Dana H. Allin, and Roberto Menotti. "European Security Strategy: Is It for Real?" European Security Forum Working Paper No. 14. October 2003.

Feld, Werner J. *The Future of European Security and Defense Policy.* Boulder, CO: Lynne Rienner Publishers, 1993.

Feldstein, Martin. "EMU and International Conflict." *Foreign Affairs* 76, no. 6 (1997): 60–73.

Ferguson, Yale H. *The Elusive Quest.* Columbia: University of South Carolina Press, 1988.

Ferguson, Yale H., and Richard W. Mansbach. "Political Space and Westphalian States and a World of 'Polities': Beyond Inside/Outside." *Global Governance* 2, no. 2 (1996): 261–287.

Ferreira-Pereira, Laura C. "The Militarily Non-Allied States in the Foreign and Security Policy at the European Union: Solidarity 'ma non troppo.'" *Journal of Contemporary European Studies* 13, no. 1 (2005): 21–37.

Flockhart, Trine. "Critical Junctures and Social Identity Theory: Explaining the Gap Between Danish Mass and Elite Attitudes to Europeanization." *Journal of Common Market Studies* 43 (2005): 251–271.

Flockhart, Trine, and Norrie MacQueen, eds. "European Security After Iraq." *Perspectives in European Politics and Society* 5, no. 3 (2004): 385–542. Special Issue.

Flynn, Gregory, and Hans Rattinger, eds. *The Public and Atlantic Defense.* Totowa, NJ: Rowman and Allanheld, 1985.

Fontaine, André. *L'Un sans l'autre.* Paris: Fayard, 1991.

Foradori, Paolo, and Paolo Rosa. "Italy and the Politics of European Defence: Playing by the Logic of Multilevel Networks." *Modern Italy* 9, no. 2 (2004): 217–231.

Foster, Edward. "The Franco-German Corps: A 'Theological' Debate?" *RUSI Journal* 137 (August 1992): 63–67.

Franklin, Mark, Michael March, and Lauren McLaren. "Uncorking the Bottle: Popular Opposition to European Unification in the Wake of Maastricht." *Journal of Common Market Studies* 32, no. 4 (1994): 455–472.

Freedman, Lawrence, ed. *Europe Transformed: Documents on the End of the Cold War.* New York: St. Martin's Press, 1990. (Uncorrected proofs.)

Fursdon, Edward. *The European Defence Community: A History.* London: Macmillan Press, 1980.

Gaddis, John Lewis. "International Relations Theory and the End of the Cold War." *International Security* 17, no. 3 (1992–1993): 5–58.

Galtung, Johan. *The European Community: A Superpower in the Making.* London: George Allen, 1981.

Gambles, Ian. *European Security Integration in the 1990s*. Paris: Institute for Security Studies, 1991.

Gates, William R., and Katsuaki L. Terasawa. "Commitment, Threat Perceptions, and Expenditures in a Defense Alliance." *International Studies Quarterly* 36, no. 2 (1992): 101–118.

Gebhard, Paul R. S. "The United States and European Security." Adelphi Paper No. 286. London: Brassey's, 1994.

Gegout, Catherine. "The EU and Security in the Democratic Republic of Congo in 2006: Unfinished Business." *CFSP Forum* 4, no. 6 (2007): 5–9.

Gellner, Ernest. *Nations and Nationalism.* Ithaca, NY: Cornell University Press, 1983.

Genscher, Hans-Dietrich. "Security for the New Germany in the New Europe: The View from Bonn and Foreign Minister Hans-Dietrich Genscher." *World Affairs* 152, no. 4 (1990): 229–232. Policy statement to the Bundestag.

Gheciu, Alexandra. "Security Institutions as Agents of Socialization? NATO and the 'New Europe.'" *International Organization* 59, no. 4 (2005): 973–1012.

Giddens, Anthony. *The Constitution of Society: Outline of the Theory of Structuration.* Berkeley: University of California Press, 1984.

———. *The Nation-State and Violence.* Cambridge: Polity Press, 1985.

———. *Social Theory and Modern Sociology.* Cambridge: Polity Press, 1987.

Giegerich, Bastian, and William Wallace. "Not Such a Soft Power: The External Deployment of European Forces." *Survival* 46, no. 2 (2004): 163–182.

Ginsberg, Roy. "Conceptualizing the European Union as an International Actor." *Journal of Common Market Studies* 37, no. 3 (1999): 429–454.

———. *The European Union International Politics: Baptism by Fire.* New York: Rowman and Littlefield, 2001.

———. *Foreign Policy Actions of the European Community: The Politics of Scale.* Boulder, CO: Lynne Rienner Publishers, 1989.

Giraud, André. "Construction européenne et défense." *Politique Étrangère* 56, no. 3 (1991): 513.

Glarbo, Kenneth. "Wide-awake Diplomacy: Reconstructing the Common Foreign and Security Policy of the European Union." *Journal of European Public Policy* 6, no. 4 (1999): 634–651.

Glaser, Charles L. "Why NATO Is Still Best: Future Security Arrangements for Europe." *International Security* 18, no. 1 (Summer 1993): 5–50.

Gnesotto, Nicole. *EU Security and Defence Policy: The First Five Years (1999–2004).* Paris: EU Institute for Security Studies, 2004.

———. "European Union After Minsk and Maastricht." *International Affairs* 68, no. 2 (1992): 223–231.

Gomez, Ricardo. *Negotiating the Euro-Mediterranean Partnership: Strategic Action in EU Foreign Policy?* Aldershot: Ashgate, 2003.

Gordon, Philip H. "Bush, Missile Defence, and the Atlantic Alliance." *Survival* 43, no. 1 (2001): 17–36.

———. "Europe's *Un*Common Foreign Policy." *International Security* 22 (Winter 1997–1998): 74–100.

———. "Their Own Army? Making European Defense Work." *Foreign Affairs* 79, no. 4 (2000): 12–17.

Gourlay, Catriona. "European Union Procedures and Resources for Crisis Management." *International Peacekeeping* 11, no. 3 (2004): 404–422.

Gower, Jackie. "Russia and the European Union." In *Russia and Europe: Conflict or Cooperation?* edited by Mark Webber, pp. 66–98. New York: St. Martin's Press, 2000.

Grabbe, Heather. "Europeanization Goes East: Power and Uncertainty in the EU Accession Process." In *The Politics of Europeanization*, edited by K. Featherstone and C. Radaelli. Oxford, UK: Oxford University Press, 2003.

Græger, Nina. "Norway Between NATO, the EU, and the US: A Case Study of Post–Cold War Security and Defense Discourse." *Cambridge Review of International Affairs* 18, no. 1 (2005): 86–103.

Greenwood, Ted, and Stuart Johnson. "NATO Force Planning Without the Soviet Threat." *Parameters* 22, no. 1 (1992): 27–37.

Gross, Eva. "The EU in Afghanistan: What Role for EU Conflict Prevention and Crisis Management Policies?" *CFSP Forum* 4, no. 4 (2006): 11–14.

Grosser, Alfred. *The Western Alliance.* New York: Continuum Publishing, 1980.

Guzzini, Stefano. "A Reconstruction of Constructivism in International Relations." *European Journal of International Relations* 6, no. 2 (2000): 147–182.

Haas, Ernst B. "The Balance of Power: Prescription, Concept or Propaganda?" *World Politics* 5, no. 4 (1953): 442–477.

———. *Beyond the Nation-State.* Stanford, CA: Stanford University Press, 1964.

———. "Nationalism: An Instrumental Social Construction." *Millennium: Journal of International Studies* 22, no. 3 (1993): 505–545.

———. *The Obsolescence of Regional Integration Theory.* Berkeley: University of California Press, 1975.

———. *The Uniting of Europe.* Stanford, CA: Stanford University Press, 1958.

Haas, Richard N. *The Reluctant Sheriff: The United States After the Cold War.* New York: Council on Foreign Relations, 1997.

Habermas, Jürgen. *The Inclusion of the Other.* Cambridge, MA: MIT Press, 1998.

Haftendorn, Helga. "The Security Puzzle: Theory-building and Discipline-building in International Security." *International Studies Quarterly* 35, no. 1 (1991): 3–17.

Haglund, David G. *Alliance Within the Alliance? Franco-German Military Cooperation and the European Pillar of Defense.* Boulder, CO: Westview Press, 1991.

———. *From Euphoria to Hysteria: Western European Security After the Cold War.* Boulder, CO: Westview Press, 1993.

Haine, Jean-Yves. *Berlin PLUS.* Institute for Security Studies, 2004.

Halliday, Fred. *The Making of the Second Cold War.* London: Verso, 1983.

Haltiner, Karl. "The Definite End of the Mass Army in Western Europe?" *Armed Forces and Society* 25, no. 1 (1998): 7–37.

Hanrieder, Wolfram. *Germany, America, Europe: Forty Years of German Foreign Policy.* New Haven, CT: Yale University Press, 1989.

Hansen, Lene, and Ole Wæver, eds. *European Integration and National Identity: The Challenge of the Nordic States.* London: Routledge, 2002.

Harnisch, Sebastian, and Hanns Maull, eds. *Germany as a Civilian Power? The Foreign Policy of the Berlin Republic.* Manchester, UK: Manchester University Press, 2001.

Heisbourg, François. "The European-US Alliance: Valedictory Reflections on Continental Drift in the Post–Cold War Era." *International Affairs* 68, no. 4 (1992): 665–678.

———. "Europe's Strategic Ambitions: The Limits of Ambiguity." *Survival* 42, no. 2 (2000): 5–15.

Hettne, Björn. "Security and Peace in Post–Cold War Europe." *Journal of Peace Research* 28, no. 3 (1991): 279–294.

Hill, Christopher. "The Capability-Expectations Gap, or Conceptualizing Europe's International Role." *Journal of Common Market Studies* 31, no. 3 (September 1993): 305–328.

———. "Closing the Capabilities-Expectations Gap." In *A Common Foreign Policy for Europe,* edited by John Peterson and Helen Sjursen, pp. 18–38. London: Routledge, 1998.

———. "European Foreign Policy: Power Bloc, Civilian Power—or Flop?" In *The Evolution of an International Actor: Western Europe's New Assertiveness,* edited by Reinhardt Rummel, pp. 31–55. Boulder, CO: Westview Press, 1990.

———. "The EU's Capacity for Conflict Prevention." *European Foreign Affairs Review* 6, no. 3 (2001): 315–333.

Hinsley, F. H. *Sovereignty.* Cambridge: Cambridge University Press, 1986.

Hodson, Dermont, and Imelda Maher. "The Open Method as a New Mode of Governance: The Case of Soft Economic Policy Co-ordination." *Journal of Common Market Studies* 39, no. 4 (2001): 719–746.

Hoffmann, Stanley. "Discord in Community: The North Atlantic Area as a Partial System." In *The Atlantic Community: Progress and Prospects,* edited by Francis Wilcox and Henry Field Haviland. New York: Praeger, 1963.

———. "French Dilemmas and Strategies in the New Europe." In *The Cold War and After,* edited by Robert Keohane, Joseph Nye, and Stanley Hoffmann. Cambridge, MA: Harvard University Press, 1993.

———. *Janus and Minerva: Essays in the Theory and Practice of International Politics.* Boulder, CO: Westview Press, 1987.

———. "Obstinate or Obsolete? The Fate of the Nation-State and the Case of Western Europe." *Daedalus* 95, no. 3 (Summer 1966): 862–915.

———. "Reflections on the Nation-State in Western Europe Today." *Journal of Common Market Studies* 21, no. 112 (1982): 21–37.

Holbraad, Carsten. *Danish Neutrality.* Oxford: Clarendon Press, 1991.

Holland, Martin. *The European Union and the Third World.* Houndmills, Basingstoke: Palgrave, 2002.

———. *The Future of European Poltical Cooperation.* Basingstoke, England: Macmillan, 1991.

Holland, Martin, ed. *Common Foreign and Security Policy: The Record and the Reform.* London: Pinter, 1997.

Holmes, John W. *The United States and Europe After the Cold War: A New Alliance?* Columbia: University of South Carolina Press, 1997.

Hooghe, Liesbet, and Gary Marks. "Does Identity or Economic Rationality Drive Public Opinion on European Integration?" *PS: Political Science and Politics* 37, no. 3 (2004): 415–420.

Hopf, Ted. "The Promise of Constructivism in International Relations Theory." *International Security* 23, no. 1 (1998): 171–200.

Hopmann, P. Terrence. "French Perspectives on the International Relations After the Cold War." *Mershon International Studies Review* 38, no. 1 (1994): 69–93.

Howe, Paul. "A Community of Europeans: The Requisite Underpinnings." *Journal of Common Market Studies* 33, no. 1 (1995): 27–46.

Howorth, Jolyon. "Britain, France and the European Defence Initiative." *Survival* 42, no. 2 (2000): 33–55.

———. "European Defence and the Changing Politics of the European Union: Hanging Together or Hanging Separately?" *Journal of Common Market Studies* 39, no. 4 (2001): 765–789.

———. "France, Britain and the Euro-Atlantic Crisis." *Survival* 45, no. 4 (2003): 173–192.

———. *Security and Defence Policy in the European Union*. London: Palgrave, 2007.

Howorth, Jolyon, and John T. S. Keeler. *Defending Europe: The EU, NATO, and the Quest for European Autonomy*. New York: Palgrave Macmillan, 2003.

Hunter, Robert. *The European Security and Defense Policy: NATO's Companion or Competitor?* Santa Monica, CA: RAND Corporation, 2002.

———. *Security in Europe*. 2nd ed. Bloomington: Indiana University Press, 1972.

Hurd, Douglas. "Developing the Common Foreign and Security Policy." *International Affairs* 70, no. 3 (1994): 421–428.

Hutchinson, John, and Anthony D. Smith, eds. *Nationalism*. Oxford: Oxford University Press, 1994.

Hyde-Price, Adrian. "European Security, Strategic Culture, and the Use of Force." *European Security* 13, no. 4 (2004): 323–343.

———. "'Normative' Power Europe: A Realist Critique." *Journal of European Public Policy* 13, no. 2 (2006): 217–234.

Ickstadt, Heinz. "Uniting a Divided Nation: Americanism and Anti-Americanism in Post-War Germany." *European Journal of American Culture* 23, no. 2 (2004): 157–170.

Ifestos, Panayiotis. *European Political Cooperation*. Aldershot, UK: Gower Publishing, 1987.

Jansen, Thomas, ed. *Reflections on European Identity*. European Commission Forward Studies Unit, Working Paper, 1999.

Jervis, Robert. "Security Regimes." *International Organization* 36, no. 2 (Spring 1982): 357–378.

Joffe, Josef. "Collective Security and the Future of Europe: Failed Dreams and Dead Ends." *Survival* 34, no. 1 (Spring 1992): 36–50.

———. "Europe's American Pacifier." *Foreign Policy* 54 (Spring 1984): 64–82.

Jones, Seth. *The Rise of European Security Cooperation*. Cambridge: Cambridge University Press, 2007.

Jopp, Mathias, Reinhardt Rummel, and Peter Schmidt, eds. *Integration and Security in Western Europe*. Oxford: Pinter Press, 1991.

Jordan, Robert, ed. *Europe and the Superpowers*. London: Pinter Publishers, 1971.

Jørgensen, Knud Erik. "The Social Construction of the Acquis Communautaire:

A Cornerstone of the European Edifice." European Integration Online Papers (EIoP) 3, 1999, at http://eiop.or.at/eiop/texte/1999-005.htm.

Kagan, Robert. *Of Paradise and Power: America and Europe in the New World Order.* New York: Alfred A. Knopf, 2003.

———. "Power and Weakness." *Policy Review* 113 (2002): 5–23.

Kaiser, Karl, and John Roper, eds. *British-German Defence Co-operation.* London: Jane's Publishing Company, 1988.

Kaldor, Mary. "Avoiding a New Division of Europe." *World Policy Journal* 8, no. 1 (1990–1991): 181–193.

Kaldor, Mary, ed. *Europe from Below.* London: Verso, 1991.

Katzenstein, Peter J., ed. *The Culture of National Security.* New York: Columbia University Press, 1996.

Keane, Rory. "European Security and Defense Policy: From Cologne to Sarajevo." *Global Society* 19, no. 1 (2005): 89–103.

Kegley Jr., Charles W. "The Neoidealist Moment in International Studies? Realist Myths and the New International Realities." *International Studies Quarterly* 37, no. 2 (1993): 131–147.

Kelley, Judith G. *Ethnic Politics in Europe: The Power of Norms and Incentives.* Princeton, NJ: Princeton University Press, 2004.

———. "New Wine in Old Wineskins: Promoting Political Reforms Through the New European Neighbourhood Policy." *Journal of Common Market Studies* 44, no. 1 (2006): 29–55.

Keohane, Robert O. *After Hegemony: Cooperation and Discord in the World Political Economy.* Princeton, NJ: Princeton University Press, 1984.

———. *International Institutions and State Power.* Boulder, CO: Westview Press, 1989.

———. "Ironies of Sovereignty: The European Union and the United States." *Journal of Common Market Studies* 40, no. 4 (2002): 743–765.

Keohane, Robert O., ed. *Neorealism and Its Critics.* New York: Columbia University Press, 1986.

Keohane, Robert, and Stanley Hoffmann. *The New European Community.* Boulder, CO: Westview Press, 1991.

Keohane, Robert, and Joseph Nye. *Power and Interdependence: World Politics in Transition.* Boston: Little, Brown, 1977.

Keohane, Robert, Joseph Nye, and Stanley Hoffmann. *After the Cold War: International Institutions and State Strategies in Europe, 1989–1991.* Cambridge, MA: Harvard University Press, 1993.

Kielinger, Thomas. "Waking Up in the New Europe—with a Headache." *International Affairs* 66, no. 2 (1990): 249–263.

Kirchner, Emil J. "Security Threats and Institutional Response: The European Context." *Asia Europe Journal* 3, no. 2 (2005): 179–197.

Kirste, Knut, and Hanns W. Maull. "Zivilmacht und Rollentheorie." *Zeitschrift für Internationale Beziehungen* 3, no. 2 (1996): 283–312.

Kissinger, Henry A. *Diplomacy.* New York: Touchstone, 1995.

———. *The Troubled Partnership: A Re-appraisal of the Atlantic Alliance.* New York: Doubleday Anchor Books, 1966.

Knowles, Vanda, and Silke Thomson-Pottebohm. "The UK, Germany and ESDP: Developments at the Convention and the IGC." *German Politics* 13, no. 4 (2004): 581–604.

Kochenov, Dimitry. "Behind the Copenhagen Facade: The Meaning and Structure of the Copenhagen Political Criteria of Democracy and the Rule of Law." *European Integration On-line Papers* 8 (2004).

Koslowski, Rey, and Friedrich V. Kratochwil. "Understanding Change in International Politics: The Soviet Empire's Demise and the International System." *International Organization* 48, no. 2 (1994): 215–247.

Kostakapoulou, Theodora. "Why a 'Community of Europeans' Could Be a Community of Exclusion: A Reply to Howe." *Journal of Common Market Studies* 35, no. 2 (1997): 301–308.

Kramer, Heinz. "The European Community's Response to the 'New Eastern Europe.'" *Journal of Common Market Studies* 31, no. 2 (1993): 213–244.

Krasner, Stephen. *International Regimes*. Ithaca, NY: Cornell University Press, 1983.

Kubalkova, Vendulka, Nicholas Onuf, and Paul Kowert, eds. *International Relations in a Constructed World*. New York: M. E. Sharpe, 1998.

Kugler, Richard L. *The Future of NATO and US Policy in Europe*. Santa Monica, CA: RAND Corporation, 1992.

———. *The Future US Military Presence in Europe: Forces and Requirements for the Post–Cold War Era*. Santa Monica, CA: RAND Corporation, 1992.

———. *NATO's Future Role in Europe*. Santa Monica, CA: RAND Corporation, 1990.

Kupchan, Charles A. *The End of the American Era: U.S. Foreign Policy and the Geopolitics of the Twenty-first Century*. New York: Alfred A. Knopf, 2002.

———. "In Defence of European Defence: An American Perspective." *Survival* 42, no. 2 (2000): 16–32.

Kupchan, Charles A., and Clifford A. Kupchan. "Concerts, Collective Security, and the Future of Europe." *International Security* 16, no. 1 (1991): 114–161.

Laffan, Brigid. "The Politics of Identity and Political Order in Europe." *Journal of Common Market Studies* 34, no. 1 (1996): 81–102.

Lak, Maarten W. J. "Interaction Between European Political Cooperation and the European Community (External): Existing Rules and Challenges." *Common Market Law Review* 26, no. 2 (1989): 281–299.

Lapid, Yosef, and Friedrich Kratochwil, eds. *The Return of Culture and Identity in IR Theory*. Boulder, CO: Lynne Rienner, 1996.

Larrabee, F. Stephen. *The Two German States and European Security*. New York: St. Martin's Press, 1989.

Laursen, Finn, and Sophie Vanhoonacker, eds. *The Intergovernmental Conference on Political Union: Institutional Reforms, New Policies and International Identity of the European Community*. Maastricht, the Netherlands: European Institute of Public Administration, 1992.

Lebow, Richard Ned. "The Long Peace, the End of the Cold War, and the End of Realism." *International Organization* 48, no. 2 (1994): 249–277.

Lellouche, Pierre. "France in Search of Security." *Foreign Affairs* 72, no. 2 (1993): 122–131.

———. *Le Nouveau monde: De l'ordre de Yalta au désordre des nations*. Paris: Grasset, 1992.

Leonard, Mark. *Why Europe Will Run the 21st Century*. New York: Public Affairs, 2005.

Leontidou, Lila. "The Boundaries of Europe: Deconstructing Three Regional Narratives." *Identities: Global Studies on Culture and Power* 11, no. 4 (2004): 593–617.

Lerch, Marika and Schwellnus, Guido. "Normative by Nature? The Role of Coherence in Justifying the EU's External Human Rights Policy." *Journal of European Public Policy* 13, no. 2 (2006): 304–321.

Levine, Robert A., ed. *Transition and Turmoil in the Atlantic Alliance.* New York: Crane Russak, 1992.

Lindberg, Leon N. "The European Community as a Political System: Notes Towards the Construction of a Model." *Journal of Common Market Studies* 5 (1967): 344–387.

———. *The Political Dynamics of European Economic Integration.* Stanford, CA: Stanford University Press, 1963.

Lindberg, Leon N., and Stuart A. Scheingold, eds. *Regional Integration: Theory and Research.* Cambridge, MA: Harvard University Press, 1971.

Lindley-French, Julian. "In the Shade of Locarno? Why European Defence Is Failing." *International Affairs* 78, no. 4 (2002): 789–811.

Lintner, Valerio, and Sonia Mazey. *The European Community: Economic and Political Aspects.* London: McGraw Hill, 1991.

Lodge, Juliet, ed. *The European Community and the Challenge of the Future.* New York: St. Martin's Press, 1989.

Loedel, Peter H., and Mary M. McKenzie. *Common Foreign and Security Policy: The Record and Reforms.* Westport, CT: Praeger, 1998.

Lynn-Jones, Sean M. *The Cold War and After: Prospects for Peace.* Cambridge, MA: MIT Press, 1991.

Mace, Catriona. "Operation Concordia: Developing a 'European' Approach to Crisis Management." *International Peacekeeping* 11, no. 3 (2003): 474–491.

Mally, Gerhard. *The European Community in Perspective.* Lexington, MA: Lexington Books, 1973.

Mandelbaum, Michael. *The Fate of Nations.* Cambridge: Cambridge University Press, 1988.

Manners, Ian. "Normative Power Europe: A Contradiction in Terms?" *Journal of Common Market Studies* 40, no. 2 (2002): 235–258.

———. "Normative Power Europe Reconsidered: Beyond the Crossroads." *Journal of European Public Policy* 13, no. 2 (2006): 182–199.

Manners, Ian, and Richard G. Whitman. "The 'Difference Engine': Constructing and Representing the International Identity of the European Union." *Journal of European Public Policy* 10, no. 3 (2003): 380–404.

Maresceau, Marc. "Pre-Accession." In *The Enlargement of the European Union,* edited by Marc Cremona. Oxford, UK: Oxford University Press, 2003.

Marquis, Jefferson. "The Other Warriors: American Social Science and Nation-building in Vietnam." *Diplomatic History* 24, no. 1 (2000): 79–105.

Martin, Denis-Constant. "The Choices of Identity." *Social Identities* 1, no. 1 (1995): 5–20.

Maull, Hanns. "Die 'Zivilmacht Europa' bleibt Projekt: Zur Debatte um Kagan, Asmus/Pollack und das Strategiedokument NSS 2002." *Blätter für deutsche und internationale Politik*, 12 (2002): 1467–1478.

———. "Germany and Japan: The New Civilian Powers." *Foreign Affairs* 69, no. 5 (1990): 91–106.

———. "Germany and the Use of Force: Still a 'Civilian Power.'" *Survival* 42, no. 2 (2000): 56–80.

———. "Germany's Foreign Policy, Post-Kosovo: Still a Civilian Power?" In *Germany as a Civilian Power? The Foreign Policy of the Berlin Republic,* edited by S. Harnisch and Hanns Maull. Manchester, UK: Manchester University Press, 2001.

Mauro, Paolo. *Let's Draw Europe Together: Discovering the European Union.* Luxembourg: Office for Official Publications of the European Communities, 1997.

Mazzucelli, Colette. "The French Rejection of the European Constitutional Treaty: Two-Level Games Revisited." In *The Rise and Fall of the EU's Constitutional Treaty*, edited by Finn Laursen. Leiden, the Netherlands: Nijhoff/Brill, 2008.

McKenzie, Mary M., and Peter H. Loedel, eds. *The Promise and Reality of European Security Cooperation.* Westport, CT: Praeger, 1998.

Mearsheimer, John J. "Back to the Future: Instability in Europe After the Cold War." *International Security* 15, no. 1 (1990): 5–56.

———. "The Case for a Ukrainian Nuclear Deterrent." *Foreign Affairs* 72, no. 3 (1993): 50–66.

———. "The False Promise of International Institutions." *International Security* 19, no. 3 (Winter 1994–1995): 5–49.

Menon, Anand, Anthony Forster, and William Wallace. "A Common European Defence?" *Survival* 34, no. 3 (1992): 98–118.

Meyer, Christoph O. "Convergence Towards a European Strategic Culture? A Constructivist Framework for Explaining Changing Norms." *European Journal of International Relations* 11, no. 4 (2005): 523–549.

———. "Theorising European Strategic Culture Between Convergence and the Persistence of National Diversity." CEPS Working Document No. 204 (2004).

Mileham, Patrick. "But Will They Fight and Will They Die?" *International Affairs* 77, no. 3 (2001): 621–629.

Minc, Alain. *La Grande illusion.* Paris: Bernard Grasset, 1989.

Mitrany, David. *The Functional Theory of Politics.* London: Martin Robertson, 1975.

———. *A Working Peace System.* Chicago: Quadrangle Books, 1966.

Mitzen, Jennifer. "Anchoring Europe's Civilizing Identity: Habits, Capabilities and Ontological Security." *Journal of European Public Policy* 13, no. 2 (2006): 270–285.

Moïsi, Dominique, and Jacques Rupnik. *Le Nouveau continent: Plaidoyer pour une Europe renaissante.* Paris: Calmann-Lévy, 1991.

Monnet, Jean. *Memoirs.* Garden City, NY: Doubleday and Co., 1978.

Moravcsik, Andrew. *The Choice for Europe: Social Purpose and State Power from Messina to Maastricht.* Ithaca, NY: Cornell University Press, 1998.

———. "The Future of European Integration Studies: Social Science or Social Theory?" *Millennium: Journal of International Studies* 28, no. 2 (1999): 371–391.

———. "In the Defence of the 'Democratic Deficit': Reassessing Legitimacy in the European Union." *Journal of Common Market Studies* 40, no. 4 (2002): 603–624.

————. "Is Something Rotten in the State of Denmark? Constructivism and European Integration." *Journal of European Public Policy* 6, no. 4 (1999): 669–681. Special issue.

————. "Preferences and Power in the European Community: A Liberal Intergovernmentalist Approach." *Journal of Common Market Studies* 31, no. 4 (December 1993): 473–524.

Morgenthau, Hans. *Politics Among Nations*. 5th ed. New York: Knopf, 1978.

Münch, Richard. "Between Nation-State, Regionalism and World Society: The European Integration Process." *Journal of Common Market Studies* 34, no. 3 (1996): 379–401.

Neumann, Iver B. "Identity and Security." *Journal of Peace Research* 29, no. 2 (1992): 221–226.

Neville-Jones, Pauline. "The Genscher/Colombo Proposals on European Union." *Common Market Law Review* 20, no. 4 (1983): 657–699.

Nicolaidis, Kalypso. "We, the Peoples of Europe. . . ." *Foreign Affairs* 83, no. 6 (2004): 97–111.

Nicolaidis, Kalypso, and Robert Howse. "'This Is My EUtopia . . .': Narrative as Power." *Journal of Common Market Studies* 40, no. 4 (2002): 767–792.

Novosseloff, Alexandra. *EU-UN Partnership in Crisis Management: Developments and Prospects*. New York: International Peace Academy, 2004.

Nuttall, Simon J. *European Political Co-operation*. Oxford: Clarendon Press, 1992.

Nye, Joseph S. *Bound to Lead: The Changing Nature of American Power*. New York: Basic Books, 1990.

————. *Peace in Parts*. Lanham, MD: University Press of America, 1987.

————. *Soft Power: The Means to Success in World Politics*. New York: Public Affairs, 2004.

Obradovic, Daniela. "Policy Legitimacy and the European Union." *Journal of Common Market Studies* 34, no. 2 (1996): 191–221.

Ottaway, Marina. "Nation-building." *Foreign Policy* 132 (2002): 16–24.

Overhaus, Marco. "In Search of a Post-Hegemonic Order: Germany, NATO and the European Security and Defense Policy." *German Politics* 13, no. 4 (2004): 551–568.

Pagden, Anthony, ed. *The Idea of Europe: From Antiquity to the European Union*. Cambridge: Cambridge University Press, 2002.

Palmer, Glenn. "Alliance Politics and Issue-Areas: Determinants of Defense Spending." *American Journal of Political Science* 34, no. 1 (1990): 190–211.

Palmer, John. *Europe Without America*. Oxford: Oxford University Press, 1988.

Pape, Robert. "Soft Balancing Against the United States." *International Security* 30, no. 1 (2005): 7–45.

Parmentier, Guillaume. "Redressing NATO's Imbalances." *Survival* 42, no. 2 (2000): 96–112.

Patten, Chris. "A Security Strategy for Europe." *Oxford Journal of Good Governance* 1, no. 1 (2004): 13–16.

Paul, T. V. "Soft Balancing in the Age of U.S. Primacy." *International Security* 30, no. 1 (2005): 46–71.

Pentland, Charles. *International Theory and European Integration*. New York: The Free Press, 1973.

Perkovich, George. "The Plutonium Genie." *Foreign Affairs* 72, no. 3 (Summer 1993): 153–165.

Petiteville, Franck. "Exporting 'Values'? EU External Co-operation as 'Soft Diplomacy.'" In *Understanding the European Union's External Relations*, edited by M. Knodt and S. Princen. New York: Routledge, 2003.

Piening, Christopher. *Global Europe: The European Union in World Affairs.* Boulder, CO: Lynne Rienner, 1997.

Pierson, Jean-Luc. *La Yugoslavie disintégrée.* Bruxelles: GRIP, 1992.

Pijpers, Alfred E. *The European Community at Crossroads.* Dordrecht, the Netherlands: Martinus Nijhoff Publishers, 1992.

———. *The Vicissitudes of European Political Cooperation.* Gravenhage, the Netherlands: By the author, 1990.

Pijpers, Alfred, Elfriede Regelsberger, and Wolfgang Wessels, eds. *European Political Cooperation in the 1980s: A Common Foreign Policy for Western Europe.* Dordrecht, the Netherlands: Martinus Nijhoff Publishers, 1988.

Pocock, Gordon. "Nation, Community, Devolution and Sovereignty." *Political Quarterly* 61, no. 3 (1990): 319–327.

Popper, Karl. *Conjectures and Refutations.* London: Routledge and Kegan Paul, 1972.

Prate, Alain. *Quelle Europe?* Paris: Julliard, 1991.

Prentoulis, Nikos. "All the Technology of Collective Identity: Normative Reconstructions of the Concept of EU Citizenship." *European Law Journal* 7, no. 2 (2001): 196–218.

Prizel, Ilya. *National Identity and Foreign Policy.* Cambridge: Cambridge University Press, 1998.

Puchala, Donald J. "Of Blind Men, Elephants, and International Integration." *Journal of Common Market Studies* 10, no. 3 (1972): 267–284.

Pugh, Michael C., ed. *European Security: Towards 2000.* Manchester, UK: Manchester University Press, 1992.

Pye, Lucien W. *Politics, Personality and Nation-building: Burma's Search for Identity.* New Haven, CT: Yale University Press, 1962.

Regelsberger, Elfriede, ed. *Die Gemeinsame Außen- und Sicherheitspolitik der Europäische Union.* Bonn: Europa Union Verlag, 1993.

Regelsberger, Elfriede, Philippe de Schoutheete, and Wolfgang Wessels, eds. *Foreign Policy of the European Union: From the EPC to CFSP and Beyond.* Boulder, CO: Lynne Rienner, 1997.

Reid, T. R. *The United States of Europe: The New Superpower and the End of American Supremacy.* New York: Penguin, 2004.

Remacle, Eric. *La Politique étrangère européenne: De Maastricht à la Yugoslavie.* Bruxelles: GRIP, 1992.

Rhodes, Carolyn. *The European Union in the World Community.* Boulder, CO: Lynne Rienner, 1998.

Richardson, Jeremy, ed. *European Union: Power and Policy Making.* London: Routledge, 1996.

Ricoeur, Paul. *Oneself as Another.* Chicago: University of Chicago Press, 1995.

Rieker, Pernille. "Europeanization of Nordic Security: The European Union and the Changing Security Identities of the Nordic States." *Cooperation and Conflict* 39, no. 4 (2004): 369–392.

Ringmar, Erik. *Identity, Interest, and Action: A Cultural Explanation of*

*Sweden's Intervention in the Thirty Years' War.* Cambridge: Cambridge University Press, 1996.

Risse-Kappen, Thomas. "Ideas Do Not Float Freely: Transnational Coalitions, Domestic Structures, and the End of the Cold War." *International Organization* 48, no. 2 (1994): 185–214.

Rummel, Reinhardt, ed. With the assistance of Collette Mazzucelli. *The Evolution of an International Actor.* Boulder, CO: Westview Press, 1990.

———. *Toward Political Union: Planning a Common Foreign and Security in the European Community.* Boulder, CO: Westview Press, 1992.

———. "West European Cooperation in Foreign and Security Policy." *Annals of the American Academy of Political and Social Science* 531 (1994): 112–123.

Russell, Robert W. "*L'Engrenage,* Collegial Style, and the Crisis Syndrome: Lessons from Monetary Policy in the European Community." *Journal of Common Market Studies* 13, no. 1 (1975): 61–86.

Rynning, Sten. "The European Union: Towards a Strategic Culture." *Security Dialogue* 34, no. 4 (2003): 479–496.

———. "Why Not NATO? Military Planning in the European Union." *Journal of Strategic Studies* 26, no. 1 (2003): 53–72.

Salmon, Trevor C. "Testing Times for European Political Cooperation: The Gulf and Yugoslavia, 1990–1992." *International Affairs* 68, no. 2 (1992): 233–253.

———. "'United in Its Diversity' (or Disunited in Adversity): That Is the Question for the European Union and the European Security and Defense Policy." *Perspectives on European Politics and Society* 5, no. 3 (2004): 447–468.

———. *Unneutral Ireland: An Ambivalent and Unique Security Policy.* Oxford: Oxford University Press, 1989.

Salmon, Trevor C., and Alistair Shepherd. *Toward a European Army.* Boulder, CO: Lynne Rienner, 2003.

Sandler, Todd. "The Economic Theory of Alliances: A Survey." *Journal of Conflict Resolution* 37, no. 3 (1993): 446–483.

Santos, Carla. *Human Rights Clauses: Unraveling the Pattern of Implementation.* PhD dissertation, European University Institute, Florence, 2006.

Sauerwein, Brigitte. "European Security: The Institutional Challenge." *International Defense Review* 26, no. 1 (1993): 31–34.

Schake, Kori, Amaya Bloch-Laine, and Charles Grant. "Building a European Defence Capability." *Survival* 41, no. 1 (1999): 20–40.

Scheipers, Sybille, and Daniela Sicurelli. "Normative Power Europe: A Credible Utopia?" *Journal of Common Market Studies* 45, no. 2 (2007): 435–457.

Schelling, Thomas C. *Arms and Influence.* New Haven, CT: Yale University Press, 1966.

Schimmelfennig, Frank. *The EU, NATO and the Integration of Europe: Rules and Rhetoric.* Cambridge: Cambridge University Press, 2003.

———. *Rules and Rhetoric: The Eastern Enlargement of NATO and the European Union.* Cambridge, UK: Cambridge University Press, 2003.

Schimmelfennig, Frank, and Ulrich Sedelmeier, eds. *The Europeanization of Central and Eastern Europe.* Ithaca, NY: Cornell University Press, 2005.

Senghaas, Dieter. *Europa 2000: Ein Friedensplan.* Frankfurt am Main, Germany: Suhrkamp, 1990.

Shapiro, Ian, and Alexander Wendt. "The Difference That Realism Makes:

Social Science and the Politics of Consent." *Politics and Society* 20, no. 2 (1992): 197–223.

Sharp, Jane O., ed. *Europe After an American Withdrawal*. Oxford: Oxford University Press, 1990.

Sherwood, Elizabeth D. *Allies in Crisis: Meeting Global Challenges to Western Security*. New Haven, CT: Yale University Press, 1990.

Simon, Jeffrey. "Does Eastern Europe Belong in NATO?" *Orbis* 37, no. 1 (Winter 1993): 21–36.

Simon, Jeffrey, ed. *European Security Policy After the Revolutions of 1989*. Washington, DC: National Defense University Press, 1991.

Sivonen, Pekka. "European Security: New, Old and Borrowed." *Journal of Peace Research* 27, no. 4 (1990): 385–397.

Sjursen, Helene. "The EU as a 'Normative' Power: How Can This Be?" *Journal of European Public Policy* 13, no. 2 (2006): 235–251.

———. "What Kind of Power?" *Journal of European Public Policy* 13, no. 2 (2006): 169–181.

Sloan, Stanley R. *NATO, the European Union, and the Atlantic Community: The Transatlantic Bargain Reconsidered*. Lanham, MD: Rowman & Littlefield Publishers, 2002.

Smith, Anthony D. *National Identity*. Reno: University of Nevada Press, 1991.

———. "National Identity and the Idea of European Unity." *International Affairs* 68, no. 1 (1992): 55–76.

Smith, Karen E. "The End of Civilian Power EU: A Welcome Demise or Cause for Concern?" *International Spectator* 35, no. 2 (2000): 11–28.

Smith, Michael. "Comment: Crossroads or Cul-de-Sac? Reassessing European Foreign Policy." *Journal of European Public Policy* 13, no. 2 (2006): 322–327.

———. "'The Devil You Know': The United States and a Changing European Community." *International Affairs* 68, no. 1 (1992): 103–120.

———. *Europe's Foreign and Security Policy*. Cambridge: Cambridge University Press, 2004.

———. "The Framing of European Foreign and Security Policy: Towards a Postmodern Policy Framework?" *Journal of European Public Policy* 10, no. 4 (2003): 556–575.

———. "From the 'Year of Europe' to a Year of Carter: Continuing Patterns and Problems in Euro-American Relations." *Journal of Common Market Studies* 17 (1978): 26–44.

Snyder, G. H. *Deterrence and Defense*. Princeton, NJ: Princeton University Press, 1961.

Sokolsky, Richard. "Imagining European Missile Defence." *Survival* 43, no. 3 (2001): 111–128.

Spinner-Halev, Jeff, and Elizabeth Theiss-Morse. "National Identity and Self Esteem." *Perspectives on Politics* 1, no. 3 (2003): 515–532.

Stavridis, Stelios. "Confederal Consociation and Foreign Policy: The Case of the CFSP of the EU." *European Integration* 22, no. 4 (2000): 381–408.

Stein, George J. *Benelux Security Cooperation: A New European Defense Community?* Boulder, CO: Westview Press, 1990.

Steinberg, James B. *The Transformation of the European Defense Industry*. Santa Monica, CA: RAND Corporation, 1993.

Strang, David. "Anomaly and Commonplace in European Political Expansion:

Realist and Institutional Accounts." *International Organization* 45, no. 2 (1991): 143–162.

Stuart, Douglas T., and Stephen F. Szabo, eds. *Discord and Collaboration in a New Europe: Essays in Honor of Arnold Wolfers*. Washington, DC: Johns Hopkins University Foreign Policy Institute, 1994.

Taylor, Paul. "The European Community and the State: Assumptions, Theories and Propositions." *Review of International Studies* 17, no. 2 (1991): 109–125.

———. *The Limits of European Integration*. London: Croom Helm, 1983.

Taylor, Trevor. "West European Security and Defence Cooperation: Maastricht and Beyond." *International Affairs* 70, no. 1 (1994): 1–16.

Tocci, Nathalie. "Has the EU Promoted Democracy in Palestine and Does It Still?" *CFSP Forum* 4, no. 2 (2006): 7–10.

Tonra, Ben. "Constructing the Common Foreign and Security Policy: The Utility of the Cognitive Approach." *Journal of Common Market Studies* 41, no. 4 (2003): 731–756.

Trondal, Jarle. "Is There Any Social Constructivist-Institutionalist Divide? Unpacking Social Mechanisms Affecting Representational Roles Among EU Decision-Makers." *Journal of European Public Policy* 8, no. 1 (2001): 1–23.

Tsakaloyannis, Panos, ed. *The Reactivation of the Western European Union: The Effects on the EC and Its Institutions*. Maastricht: European Institute of Public Administration, 1985.

Twitchett, Kenneth, ed. *Europe and the World: The External Relations of the Common Market*. London: Europa, 1976.

Ullman, Richard H. *Securing Europe*. Princeton, NJ: Princeton University Press, 1991.

Valentin, François. "Quelle défense pour quelle Europe?" *Politique Étrangère* 56, no. 3 (1991): 533.

van Eekelen, Willem. "European Security in a European Union." *Studia Diplomatica* 44 (1991): 41–57.

van Ham, Peter. "The Rise of the Brand State." *Foreign Affairs* 80 (2001): 2–6.

van Heuven, Marten. *Europe at the End of 1992: Coping with a Sense of Failure*. Santa Monica, CA: RAND Corporation, 1993.

Wæver, Ole. "Identity, Integration and Security: Solving the Sovereignty Puzzle in E.U. Studies." *Journal of International Affairs* 48, no. 2 (1995): 389–432.

Wagner, Wolfgang. "The Democratic Control of Military Power Europe." *Journal of European Public Policy* 13, no. 2 (2006): 200–216.

———. "The Democratic Legitimacy of European Security and Defense Policy." *Occasional Paper* 57. Paris: Institute for Security Studies, 2005.

———. "Why the EU's Common Foreign and Security Policy Will Remain Intergovernmental: A Rationalist Institutional Choice Analysis of European Crisis Management Policy." *Journal of European Public Policy* 10, no. 4 (2003): 576–595.

Wallace, William. "European Defence Co-operation: The Reopening Debate." *Survival* 26, no. 6 (1984): 251–261.

———. "Rescue of Retreat? The Nation State in Western Europe, 1945–93." *Political Studies* 42, no. 1 (1994): 52–76. Special issue.

———. *The Transformation of Western Europe*. London: Pinter Press, 1990.

Waltz, Kenneth. *Theory of International Politics*. Reading, MA: Addison-Wesley, 1979.

Warkotsch, Alexander. "The Rhetoric-Reality Gap in the EU's Democracy Promotion in Central Asia." *CFSP Forum* 4, no. 6 (2006): 14–16.

Weiler, Joseph. "The Reformation of European Constitutionalism." *Journal of Common Market Studies* 35, no. 1 (1997): 97–131.

Weisser, Ulrich. *NATO ohne Feindbild: Konturen einer Europäischen Sicherheitspolitik*. Bonn: Bouvier, 1992.

———. "Sicherheitspolitik in Westeuropa." In *Jahrbuch der Europäischen Integration 1990–91*. Bonn: Europa Union Verlag GMBH, 1991.

Wendt, Alexander. "Collective Identity Formation and the International State." *American Political Science Review* 88, no. 2 (1994): 384–396.

———. *Social Theory of International Politics*. Cambridge: Cambridge University Press, 1999.

Wessel, Ramses A. "The State of Affairs in EU Security and Defense Policy: The Breakthrough in the Treaty of Nice." *Journal of Conflict and Security Law* 8, no. 2 (2003): 265–288.

Westerlund, John S., and Volker F. Fritze. "The Franco-German Brigade." *Defense and Diplomacy* 7 (June 1989): 24–28.

Western European Union. *The Reactivation of WEU Statements and Communiqués 1984–1987*. Batley, West Yorkshire, UK: Newsomeprinters, Ltd., for the Western European Union, 1988.

Wettig, Gerhard. "Security in Europe: A Challenging Task." *Aussenpolitik* 1 (1992): 5.

Wilcox, Francis, and Henry Field Haviland, eds. *The Atlantic Community: Progress and Prospects*. New York: Praeger, 1963.

Williams, Andrew J., ed. *Reorganizing Eastern Europe: European Institutions and the Refashioning of Europe's Security Architecture*. Aldershot, UK: Dartmouth Publishing Company, 1994.

Willis, F. Roy. *France, Germany, and the New Europe, 1945–1963*. Stanford, CA: Stanford University Press, 1965.

Wise, Mark. "War, Peace and the European Community." In *The Political Geography of Conflict and Peace*, edited by Nurit Kliot and Stanley Waterman, pp. 110–125. London: Belhaven Press, 1991.

Wivel, Anders. "The Security Challenges of Small EU Member States: Interest Identity and the Development of the EU as a Security Actor." *Journal of Common Market Studies* 43, no. 2 (2005): 393–412.

Wodak, Ruth, Rudolf de Cillia, Martin Reisigl, and Karen Liebhart. *The Discursive Construction of National Identity*. Edinburgh: Edinburgh University Press, 1999.

Wright, Sue. *Community and Communication: The Role of Language in Nation-State Building and European Integration*. Tonawanda, NY: Multilingual Matters, 2000.

Yergin, Daniel. *Shattered Peace: The Origins of the Cold War*. New York: Penguin Books, 1990.

Yost, David S. "The NATO Capabilities Gap and the European Union." *Survival* 42, no. 4 (2000): 97–128.

Youngs, Richard. "European Approaches to Democracy Assistance: Learning the Right Lessons?" *Third World Quarterly* 24, no. 1 (2003): 127–138.

———. "Normative Dynamics and Strategic Interests in the EU's External Identity." *Journal of Common Market Studies* 42, no. 2 (2004): 415–435.

Zehfuss, Maja. *Constructivism in International Relations: The Politics of Reality.* Cambridge: Cambridge University Press, 2002.
Zielonka, Jan. "Europe's Security: A Great Confusion." *International Affairs* 67, no. 1 (January 1991): 127–137.

# Index

# About the Book

In the absence of external security threats—and especially given that most EU member states are also members of NATO—what explains the European Union's commitment to a distinct, common security policy? What justifies channeling funds from cash-strapped European governments to finance that policy?

Ranging from the early post–Cold War years to the present, Stephanie Anderson explores the arguably surprising motivation behind the EU's security and defense policy, how the ESDP has developed, how it has transformed the EU, and how it might further the European integration project.

**Stephanie B. Anderson** is assistant professor of political science at the University of Wyoming.